RUSSIA, CHINA AND EURASIA: SOCIAL, HISTORICAL AND CULTURAL ISSUES

RUSSIA, CHINA AND EURASIA: SOCIAL, HISTORICAL AND CULTURAL ISSUES, VOLUME 1

RUSSIA, CHINA AND EURASIA: SOCIAL, HISTORICAL AND CULTURAL ISSUES

Russia, China and Eurasia: Social, Historical and Cultural Issues, Volume 1
Davon R. Moore (Editor)
2010. ISBN: 978-1-61668-016-9

RUSSIA, CHINA AND EURASIA: SOCIAL, HISTORICAL AND CULTURAL ISSUES

RUSSIA, CHINA AND EURASIA: SOCIAL, HISTORICAL AND CULTURAL ISSUES, VOLUME 1

DAVON R. MOORE
EDITOR

Nova Science Publishers, Inc.
New York

For permission to use material from this book please contact us:
Telephone 631-231-7269; Fax 631-231-8175
Web Site: http://www.novapublishers.com

LIBRARY OF CONGRESS CATALOGING-IN-PUBLICATION DATA

Available Upon Request

ISBN : 978-1-61668-016-9

Published by Nova Science Publishers, Inc. + New York

CONTENTS

PREFACE

This book explores the current political and economical climates of Pakistan and the People's Republic of China. It explores China's foreign aid activities in Africa, Latin America, and Southeast Asia. In the past several years, China has bolstered its diplomatic presence and garnered international goodwill through its financing of infrastructure and natural resource development projects, assistance in the carrying out of such projects, and large economic investments in many developing countries. Examined here is China's economic impact in three regions; Africa, Latin America and Southeast Asia. Also explored in this book is Pakistan, whose stability, democracy and prosperity are considered vital to U.S. interests.

Chapter 1 - In the past several years, the People's Republic of China (PRC) has bolstered its diplomatic presence and garnered international goodwill through its financing of infrastructure and natural resource development projects, assistance in the carrying out of such projects, and large economic investments in many developing countries. This report examines China's economic impact in three regions — Africa, Latin America (Western Hemisphere), and Southeast Asia — with an emphasis on bilateral foreign assistance.

China's foreign aid is difficult to quantify. The PRC government does not release or explain Chinese foreign aid statistics and much of PRC foreign aid does not appear to be accounted for in the scholarly literature on foreign aid. Some Chinese foreign assistance partially resembles *official development assistance* (ODA) as defined by the Organization for Economic Cooperation and Development (OECD), but in other aspects shares characteristics of foreign investment. In terms of development grants, the primary form of assistance provided by major OECD countries, China is a relatively small source of global aid. However, when China's concessional loans and state-sponsored or subsidized overseas investments are included, the PRC becomes a major source of foreign aid.

This report is based on research done by the New York University Robert F. Wagner Graduate School of Public Service in 2007-2008. The Wagner School study, while not comprehensive, suggests a dramatic increase in PRC foreign aid and related activity. According to the research, which is largely based upon news reports of Chinese foreign economic activity, PRC foreign assistance and government-supported economic projects in Africa, Latin America, and Southeast Asia grew from less than $1 billion in 2002 to $27.5 billion in 2006 and $25 billion in 2007. Aid and related investment to Africa showed the most significant increase. These totals, however, should be interpreted with caution. Some aggregate values may be inflated: Some PRC loans or aid pledges may not have been fulfilled and some aid pledges that include multiple projects or that span several years may have been counted more than once. Some PRC investment activities may more closely resemble FDI than aid. In other ways, totals may be undervalued, such as when economic projects or data have not been reported or when the values of Chinese materials and labor have not been included.

Overall, China's foreign assistance during the past several years has been driven primarily by Beijing's desire to secure and transport natural resources and secondarily for diplomatic reasons. According to the NYU Wagner School study, during the 2002-2007 period, Africa received the greatest amount of loans and development assistance, followed by Latin America and Southeast Asia. The study suggests that China's foreign aid activities in Africa and Latin America serve the PRC's immediate economic interests, while those in Southeast Asia relate to longer term diplomatic or strategic objectives. In Africa and Southeast Asia, Chinese infrastructure and public works projects constitute the most common form of aid, while in Latin America, where some countries are more developed, PRC-sponsored natural resource development activities are more prominent.

China is fast becoming a top trading partner to Africa and Southeast Asia, and it is second to the United States as a market for Latin American commodities and goods. Although the PRC's aid projects are a highly visible reminder of China's growing "soft power," other countries and regions, such as the European Union, the United States, and Japan, continue to dominate foreign direct investment in Africa, Latin America, and Southeast Asia. This report will not be updated.

Chapter 2 - A stable, democratic, prosperous Pakistan is considered vital to U.S. interests. U.S. concerns regarding Pakistan include regional and global terrorism; Afghan stability; democratization and human rights protection; the ongoing Kashmir problem and Pakistan-India tensions; and economic development. A U.S.-Pakistan relationship marked by periods of both cooperation and discord was transformed by the September 2001 terrorist attacks on the United States and the ensuing enlistment of Pakistan as a key ally in U.S.-led counterterrorism efforts. Top U.S. officials have praised Pakistan for its ongoing cooperation, although long-held doubts exist about Islamabad's commitment to some core U.S. interests. Pakistan is identified as a base for terrorist groups and their supporters operating in Kashmir, India, and Afghanistan. Pakistan's army has conducted unprecedented and largely ineffectual counterterrorism operations in the country's western tribal areas, where Al Qaeda operatives and pro-Taliban militants are said to enjoy "safe haven." U.S. officials increasingly are concerned that the cross-border infiltration of Islamist militants from Pakistan into Afghanistan is a key obstacle to defeating the Taliban insurgency.

The United States strongly encourages maintenance of a bilateral cease-fire and continued, substantive dialogue between Pakistan and neighboring India, which have fought three wars since 1947. A perceived Pakistan-India nuclear arms race has been the focus of U.S. nonproliferation efforts in South Asia. Attention to this issue intensified following nuclear tests by both countries in 1998. The United States has been troubled by evidence of transfers of Pakistani nuclear technologies and materials to third parties, including North Korea, Iran, and Libya. Such evidence became stark in 2004, and related illicit smuggling networks may still be operative.

Pakistan's macroeconomic indicators turned positive after 2001, with some meaningful poverty reduction seen in this still poor country. However, economic conditions deteriorated sharply in 2008. Democracy has fared poorly in Pakistan, with the country enduring direct military rule for more than half of its existence. In 1999, the elected government was ousted in a coup led by Army Chief General Pervez Musharraf, who later assumed the title of president. Musharraf retained the position as army chief until his November 2007 retirement. Late 2007 instability included Musharraf's six-week-long imposition of emergency rule and the assassination of former Prime Minister and leading opposition figure Benazir Bhutto. However, February 2008 parliamentary elections were relatively credible and seated a coalition led by Bhutto's widower, Asif Zardari, and opposed to Musharraf's continued rule. The coalition's August vow to launch impeachment proceedings spurred

Musharraf to resign the presidency and exit Pakistan's political stage. Zardari subsequently was elected as the new President. The Bush Administration determined that a democratically elected government was restored in Islamabad, thus permanently removing coup-related aid sanctions.

The Obama Administration states an intention to continue pursuing close and mutually beneficial relations with Islamabad. As part of its "new strategy" for Afghanistan, the Administration seeks development of a "more coherent" Pakistan policy to include conditioning U.S. military aid to Islamabad on that government's progress in combating militancy and also tripling nonmilitary aid to improve the lives of the Pakistani people. A Special Representative was appointed to coordinate U.S. government efforts with both Pakistan and Afghanistan. Pakistan is among the world's leading recipients of U.S. aid, obtaining more than $5.3 billion in overt assistance since 2001, including about $3.1 billion in development and humanitarian aid. Pakistan also has received about $6.7 billion in military reimbursements for its support of counterterrorism efforts.

In: Russia, China and Eurasia: Social, Historical... ISBN: 978-1-61668-016-9
Editor: Davon R. Moore

Chapter 1

CHINA'S FOREIGN AID ACTIVITIES IN AFRICA, LATIN AMERICA AND SOUTHEAST ASIA

Thomas Lum, Hannah Fischer, Julissa Gomez-Grangerand and Anne Leland

SUMMARY

In the past several years, the People's Republic of China (PRC) has bolstered its diplomatic presence and garnered international goodwill through its financing of infrastructure and natural resource development projects, assistance in the carrying out of such projects, and large economic investments in many developing countries. This report examines China's economic impact in three regions — Africa, Latin America (Western Hemisphere), and Southeast Asia — with an emphasis on bilateral foreign assistance.

China's foreign aid is difficult to quantify. The PRC government does not release or explain Chinese foreign aid statistics and much of PRC foreign aid does not appear to be accounted for in the scholarly literature on foreign aid. Some Chinese foreign assistance partially resembles *official development assistance* (ODA) as defined by the Organization for Economic Cooperation and Development (OECD), but in other aspects shares characteristics of foreign investment. In terms of development grants, the primary form of assistance provided by major OECD countries, China is a relatively small source of global aid. However, when China's concessional loans and state-sponsored or subsidized overseas investments are included, the PRC becomes a major source of foreign aid.

This report is based on research done by the New York University Robert F. Wagner Graduate School of Public Service in 2007-2008. The Wagner School study, while not comprehensive, suggests a dramatic increase in PRC foreign aid and related activity. According to the research, which is largely based upon news reports of Chinese foreign economic activity, PRC foreign assistance and government-supported economic projects in Africa, Latin America, and Southeast Asia grew from less than $1 billion in 2002 to $27.5 billion in 2006 and $25 billion in 2007. Aid and related investment to Africa showed the most significant increase. These totals, however, should be interpreted with caution. Some aggregate values may be inflated: Some PRC loans or aid pledges may not have been fulfilled and some aid pledges that include multiple projects or that span several years may have been counted more than once. Some PRC investment activities may more closely resemble FDI than aid. In other ways, totals may be undervalued, such as when economic projects or data have not been reported or when the values of Chinese materials and labor have not been included.

Overall, China's foreign assistance during the past several years has been driven primarily by Beijing's desire to secure and transport natural resources and secondarily for diplomatic reasons. According to the NYU Wagner School study, during the 2002-2007 period, Africa received the greatest amount of loans and development assistance, followed by Latin America and Southeast Asia. The study suggests that China's foreign aid activities in Africa and Latin America serve the PRC's immediate economic interests, while those in Southeast Asia relate to longer term diplomatic or strategic objectives. In Africa and Southeast Asia, Chinese infrastructure and public works projects constitute the most common form of aid, while in Latin America, where some countries are more developed, PRC-sponsored natural resource development activities are more prominent.

China is fast becoming a top trading partner to Africa and Southeast Asia, and it is second to the United States as a market for Latin American commodities and goods. Although the PRC's aid projects are a highly visible reminder of China's growing "soft power," other countries and regions, such as the European Union, the United States, and Japan, continue to dominate foreign direct investment in Africa, Latin America, and Southeast Asia. This report will not be updated.

INTRODUCTION

This report examines China's aid-related activities in Africa, Latin America, and Southeast Asia.[1] In the past several years, China's growing "soft power" — primarily diplomatic and economic influence in the developing world — has become a concern among many U.S. foreign policy leaders, including Members of Congress.[2] One of the most important ways in which the People's Republic of China (PRC) has bolstered its economic presence and garnered international goodwill has been through its offers of financing or concessional loans for infrastructure projects, large economic investments, and the signing of trade agreements. Many observers have praised Chinese aid and investment as filling unmet development needs, particularly in countries that have been relatively neglected by major aid donors. Others have criticized China for failing to promote democracy, equitable and sustainable development, and environmental preservation in these countries. Some U.S. policy-makers and others have expressed frustration that because of China's policy of providing foreign assistance without conditions, they are losing the ability to influence the behaviors of aid recipients regarding human rights and economic reforms. Some reports indicate, however, that PRC foreign aid, investment, and trade activities may begin to contract as the global economic crisis unfolds.

MEASURING CHINA'S FOREIGN AID

PRC foreign assistance is difficult to quantify. Still a developing country itself, China appears to administer foreign aid in an ad hoc fashion, without a centralized system, foreign aid agency and mission, or regularized funding schedule.[3] Nor does Beijing publicly release foreign aid-related data. Some analysts surmise that the Chinese leadership is reluctant to be perceived as a major aid donor, since the PRC itself continues to be a recipient of foreign assistance and because the government fears that its citizens may object to lavish spending on economic projects abroad.

Estimates of China's foreign assistance, which consists mainly of concessional or low-interest loans and government-backed or subsidized investments in infrastructure and natural resources, vary widely due to the different definitions of aid. A relatively small portion of Chinese aid includes what typically is characterized as "official development assistance" (ODA) by the world's major aid donors, such as development grants, humanitarian assistance, social welfare programs, and food aid. China also provides relatively little military and security-related assistance. Few of China's foreign aid activities fit the Organization for Economic Co-operation and Development's (OECD) definition of ODA — "flows of official financing to developing countries provided by official agencies which have a clear development or anti-poverty purpose and are at least partially concessional in nature," with a grant element of at least 25%.[4]

China's aid projects to a large extent serve its own development needs, facilitating the export of raw materials to China, and requiring that 50% of project materials and services are to be sourced in the PRC. By contrast, the foreign aid programs of the United States, European countries, and most other major aid donors are not directly or strongly linked to their own economies. Furthermore, they often include objectives or conditions related to political development and democratic reform. Among OECD countries, Japan's history of ODA, with its relatively large loan component (from 60% in the mid-1990s to roughly 25% a decade later),[5] emphasis on infrastructure projects, and links to its own economy, may come closest to providing a model for China's foreign assistance.[6]

China reportedly has taken some tentative steps toward making its foreign aid process more centralized and transparent, coordinating its programs with other aid providers, and offering more development-oriented assistance, while continuing to eschew the label of major ODA donor. The PRC has begun sending abroad "youth volunteers," similar to U.S. Peace Corps volunteers, engaged in teaching and training in such subjects as Chinese language and medicine, computer skills, agricultural technologies, and sports.[7]

Many forms of Chinese foreign assistance that are included in this report share only some characteristics with traditional development assistance as provided by major aid donors, and have often been overlooked in the literature on global foreign aid. Although they often do not fit the OECD's narrow definition of development assistance, many of China's economic activities in developing countries are supported by the PRC government and provide benefits to recipient countries that otherwise may not be available. Furthermore, many PRC economic investments abroad can be counted as aid rather than foreign direct investment (FDI) because they are secured by official bilateral agreements, do not impose real financial risks upon the PRC companies involved, or do not result in Chinese ownership of foreign assets. See **Table 1**.

Many estimates of China's foreign assistance in PRC official publications and in the existing scholarly literature do not appear to capture much of PRC aid activity. The *China Statistical Yearbook 2003-06* reportedly released an annual aid figure of $970 million. According to other sources, annual PRC foreign assistance ranges from $1.5 billion to $2 billion.[8] These figures would place China's aid levels comparable to those of Australia, Belgium, or Denmark.[9] However, many analysts, applying more flexible definitions of foreign aid, consider actual PRC aid numbers to be far higher. Some of the discrepancy may be caused by regarding many Chinese economic activities abroad as foreign investment rather than aid. In 2006 and 2007, according to various sources referring to PRC official statistics, China's annual FDI outflows totaled roughly $21 billion annually.[10] Counting some of these outflows as aid would raise PRC foreign assistance estimates; however, doing so also would lower calculations of China's outward investment levels, which are small compared to those of the United States ($216 billion in 2006).

The NYU Wagner School study on China's foreign aid tabulated PRC foreign assistance and related activities — pledges of aid or loans and government-sponsored investment projects — that had been reported in 62 African, Latin American, and Southeast Asian countries between 2001 and 2008. In 2007, the last full year for which Chinese aid-related activities were examined in the study, the Wagner School research team found projects worth up to $25 billion in aggregate. Of this amount, $16.6 billion, or 66%, was provided in the form of loans (concessional loans or credit lines), $7.2 billion, or 29%, represented state-sponsored investment, and the remaining 5% included grants, debt cancellation or debt relief, and in-kind aid.[11]

Although the NYU Wagner School study strongly indicates that China has been providing significant and growing amounts of economic assistance to developing countries — if not ODA as defined by the OECD — the totals should be interpreted with caution. Some values may be inflated: Many loans represent offers or pledges that may not have been fulfilled; some projects have been cancelled; some aid endeavors involving several activities or taking several years to complete may have been counted more than once; and some PRC investments that were counted as aid may actually be FDI. In other ways, however, totals may be undervalued, such as when projects or data have not been reported or when Chinese materials and labor have not been included.

Table 1. Similarities and Differences between OECD-Defined "Official Development Assistance" (ODA) and "Chinese Aid"

	Government to Government	Financing through Development Agency	Strong Links to Donor Country Economy	Concessional or Favorable Lending Terms	Receives Payment of Debt in Kind	Grant Element of at Least 25%	Private or Corporate Financing
OECD Aid Donor	yes[a]	yes	no	yes	no	yes	no
China	yes	no[b]	yes[c]	yes	yes[d]	no	no

Sources: Penny Davies, "China and the End of Poverty in Africa," August 2007; "Building Bridges: China's Growing Role as Infrastructure Financier for Sub-Saharan Africa," The World Bank, No. 5 (2008).

a. Grants may be awarded to NGOs based in either the donor country or recipient country.

b. PRC aid is provided largely in the form of concessional loans administered by the China Eximbank.

c. Aid projects facilitate the export of natural resources and commodities to China and utilize PRC companies, materials, and labor.

d. In some cases, aid recipients make payments on loans from China with oil or minerals.

In terms of official development assistance as defined by the OECD, United States ODA is the largest among OECD member countries, followed by Japan, the United Kingdom, France, and Germany. The United States' foreign operations budget (bilateral development, economic, security, and military assistance, multilateral assistance, and food aid) was estimated at $24 billion in FY2008.[12]

China's Foreign Aid Impact

In addition to their actual monetary value, Chinese assistance and related economic activities often garner appreciation disproportionate to their size, for several reasons:

- They often are made available relatively quickly and easily — without the political, economic, social, and environmental conditions and safeguards and bureaucratic procedures that major OECD aid donors, multilateral financial institutions, and multinational corporations typically impose.[13]
- China often promotes economic projects in countries, areas, and sectors that developed country governments and multinational corporations have avoided because they have determined them to be unfriendly, too arduous, or infeasible.
- Many PRC funded or built public works in foreign countries, such as national cultural centers, stadiums, and highways, are highly visible and provide tangible, short-term benefits.
- Such aid and investment activities are often announced at bilateral summit meetings with great fanfare, powerfully symbolizing the friendship between China and other developing countries.

MAJOR FINDINGS OF THE NYU WAGNER SCHOOL STUDY

The NYU Wagner School research may serve as a basis for conducting further research and thinking about U.S. policy responses to China's growing foreign aid and investment. The study's findings are not meant to be exhaustive, but may suggest the broad contours and trajectory of Chinese aid and related activities in Africa, Latin America, and Southeast Asia:

- China's foreign aid is driven primarily by the need for natural resources and secondarily by diplomatic objectives, such as the objectives of isolating Taiwan and garnering support in international organizations such as the United Nations. Beijing also aims to open up foreign markets for Chinese goods and help PRC companies invest, set up manufacturing plants, and develop markets overseas.
- Unlike major aid donors, China lacks a centralized aid agency affiliated with its foreign affairs ministry. PRC assistance consists primarily of concessional loans administered by the Ministry of Commerce through its Department of Aid to Foreign Countries. To lesser extents, the Export-Import Bank of China (Eximbank) the Ministry of Finance, and the Ministry of Foreign Affairs also play roles.

- Reported Chinese aid activities to the three regions grew from $1.5 billion in 2003 to $27.5 billion in 2006 and $25 billion in 2007. Africa received the largest year-on-year increases and showed the clearest growth trend. See **Figure 1** and **Table 2.**

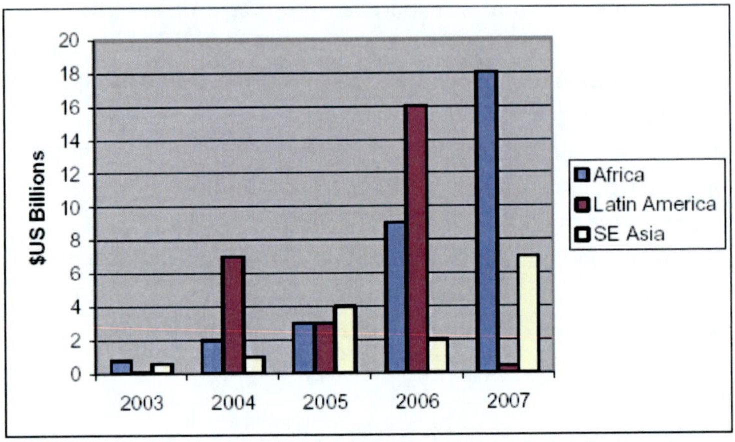

Source: NYU Wagner School, *Understanding Chinese Foreign Aid: A Look at China's Development Assistance to Africa, Southeast Asia, and Latin America,* April 25, 2008.

Notes: Annual totals represent announced loans and other reported aid and economic projects using PRC financing.

Figure 1. Reported PRC Aid by Year and Region, 2003-2007

Table 2. Reported PRC Aid by Year, 2002-2007 (Million US$)

Year	Total Aid
2002	51
2003	1,482
2004	10,485
2005	10,106
2006	10,106
2007	25,098

Source: NYU Wagner School, *Understanding Chinese Foreign Aid: A Look at China's Development Assistance to Africa, Southeast Asia, and Latin America,* April 25, 2008.

Notes: Annual totals represent announced loans and other reported aid and economic projects using PRC financing.

- In terms of financing, the NYU Wagner research team found that most aid to the three regions is provided in the form of state-sponsored investment. During the 2002-2007 period, PRC government-backed investments made up 53% of reported aid activity, concessional loans constituted 42%, and grants and debt cancellations accounted for the remaining 5%. See **Figure 2** and **Table 3.**

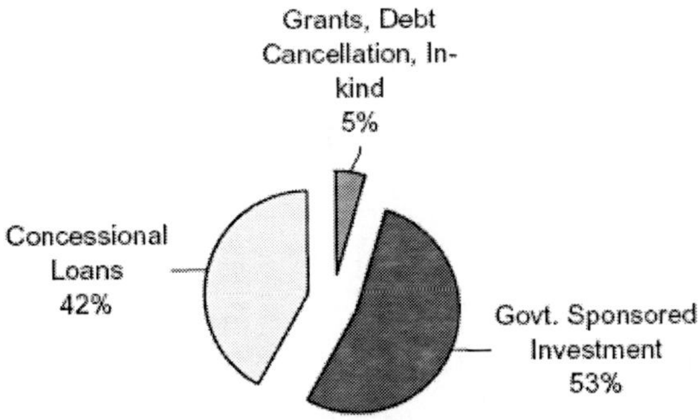

Source: NYU Wagner School, *Understanding Chinese Foreign Aid: A Look at China's Development Assistance to Africa, Southeast Asia, and Latin America,* April 25, 2008.

Notes: Annual totals represent announced loans and other reported aid and economic projects using PRC financing.

Figure 2. Reported PRC Foreign Aid by Funding Source

Table 3. Reported PRC Aid by Funding Source and Region, 2002-2007 (Million US$)

	Africa	Latin America	Southeast Asia
Govt.-Sponsored Investment	8,042	24,389	7,429
Concessional Loan	22,379	1,950	7,114
Grant	1,851	421	231
Debt Cancellation	850	0	60
In-kind Aid	21	1	0

Source: NYU Wagner School, *Understanding Chinese Foreign Aid: A Look at China's Development Assistance to Africa, Southeast Asia, and Latin America*, April 25, 2008.

Notes: Annual totals represent announced loans and other reported aid and economic projects using PRC financing.

- Of the loans, infrastructure projects, and other aid provided by China to the three regions between 2002 and 2007, 44% was allocated to Africa, 36% to Latin America, and 20% to Southeast Asia. See **Table 4**.
- During the same period (2002-2007), 44.5% of aid and investment was directed at the natural resources and agricultural sectors while 43% supported infrastructure development. See **Table 5**.

Table 4. Reported PRC Aid by Year and Region, 2002-2007 (Million US$)

	Africa	Latin America	Southeast Asia
2002	10	4	36
2003	838	1	644
2004	2,292	7,000	1,193
2005	2,953	2,931	4,221
2006	9,088	16,425	2,004
2007	17,962	401	6,735

Source: NYU Wagner School, *Understanding Chinese Foreign Aid: A Look at China's Development Assistance to Africa, Southeast Asia, and Latin America*, April 25, 2008.

Notes: Annual totals represent announced loans and other reported aid and economic projects using PRC financing.

Table 5. Reported PRC Aid by Type and Region, 2002-2007 (Million US$)

	Africa	Latin America	Southeast Asia
Natural Resources Extraction/Production	9,432	18,585	4,788
Infrastructure/Public Works	17,865	7,535	6,438
Not Specified/Other	5,024	608	2,276
Humanitarian	802	32	159
Military	4	0	170
Technical Assistance	10	1	3

Source: NYU Wagner School, *Understanding Chinese Foreign Aid: A Look at China's Development Assistance to Africa, Southeast Asia, and Latin America*, April 25, 2008.

Notes: Annual totals represent announced loans and other reported aid and economic projects using PRC financing.

REGIONAL HIGHLIGHTS

Africa

In the past several years, China's aid to Africa has grown dramatically. During the 1970s and 1980s, China provided assistance in the form of infrastructure projects, public works, technical and public health assistance, and scholarships to study in China. Its motivations were largely diplomatic: to forge friendships among "non-aligned" nations and to compete with Taiwan (the Republic of China) for recognition. Only four of 48 sub-Saharan African countries (Burkina Faso, Sao Tome, Gambia, and Swaziland) still maintain official relations with Taiwan. In 2007, China reportedly offered Malawi aid and investment worth $6 billion in major economic sectors. In January 2008, Malawi switched diplomatic relations to the PRC. However, in 2008, China reportedly offered Malawi only $287 million in aid. [14] While traditional types of aid activities remain staples of Chinese assistance in the region, many of them now complement much grander development projects that serve China's direct economic interests.[15]

According to some of the more conservative definitions and estimates, China's foreign aid on the continent ranges from roughly $1.4 billion annually to $2.7 billion, with outstanding concessional loans of $8 billion-$9 billion.[16] More inclusive totals from the World Bank and PRC government refer to "infrastructure financing" ($7 billion) and "economic cooperation" ($9.5 billion) in Africa in 2006.[17] In 2007, the China Development Bank reportedly set up a $5 billion China-Africa Development Fund to finance infrastructure, industrial, and agricultural projects.[18] The NYU Wagner School research team found PRC aid and state-sponsored investment projects in Africa reported during the 2002-2007 period that amounted to several billion dollars annually ($6.6 billion on average). These aid activities included financing (concessional loans), grants, debt cancellations, and economic investments. However, as explained above, these totals may be inflated or represent the high end of a possible range of estimates.

The following data from OECD countries provide an indication of ODA levels to Africa. They are not meant to be directly compared to estimates of Chinese assistance to the region, which are based upon different definitions of aid. U.S. assistance to Sub-Saharan Africa, the second-largest regional recipient of U.S. foreign assistance after the Near East and the largest recipient of U.S. development assistance, totaled an estimated $5.2 billion in 2008 and

$4.7 billion in 2007.[19] The United States, the United Kingdom, and France are the largest bilateral donors of ODA to Africa, providing $5.8 billion, $5.4 billion, and $5.1 billion, respectively, in assistance in 2006.[20]

Estimates of PRC direct investment in Africa range from under $500 million to roughly $1 billion annually. Historically, Europe (UK, France, and Germany), Japan, and the United States have been the principal sources of FDI on the continent. Some studies indicate that India has more cumulative investment in Africa ($1.8 billion in 2004) than China ($1.3 billion in 2005) and is a major source of infrastructure financing.[21] According to some estimates, in 2005, Chinese FDI flows to Africa totaled $392 million or 3% of total PRC outward investment.[22] Other studies report that China had $2.6 billion in cumulative FDI and over $0.5 billion in annual investment in Africa in 2006. Higher estimates include figures of nearly $1 billion in PRC annual direct investment in Africa during 2000-2006.[23] By contrast, in 2006, the United States reportedly invested $1.5 billion in Africa out of a total of $36 billion in global FDI received by Africa that year.[24] OECD countries reportedly pledged $5 billion in ODA for infrastructure projects in Sub-Saharan Africa in 2006.[25]

China has exerted growing influence as a trading partner. As part of its integrated approach, China's diplomatic outreach to the region is accompanied by aid, investment, and trade. China is Africa's third largest trading partner after the European Union and the United States.[26] PRCAfrica trade reportedly was worth $106.6 billion in 2008 compared to U.S.-Africa trade of $142 billion.[27]

China's aid to Africa is driven largely by its objective of securing access to oil and minerals for its growing economy. African oil reportedly accounts for 80% of China's trade in the region and about one-third of its oil imports.[28] Nearly 70% of PRC infrastructure financing on the continent reportedly is concentrated in Angola, Nigeria, Ethiopia, and Sudan, all of which have oil fields.[29] Angola, Congo, and Sudan have major oil fields and pay for much of their assistance or loans from China with oil. Sudan reportedly sends 60% of its crude oil to China.[30] However, Europe and the United States remain the largest buyers of African petroleum (33% and 36% of Africa's oil exports, respectively).[31] Estimates of China's share of the African oil market range from 10%- 16%, although the PRC reportedly plays a larger role in the continent's minerals markets.[32] See **Table 6**.

Table 6. Selected African Countries with Large Reported Aid and Investment Projects, 2002-2007

Country	Main Exports to China	Pledged Aid, Loans, Credit Lines, and Investments	Major Types of Financing (as Reported)	Major Types of Projects Financed (as Reported)
Angola [a b c]	oil	$7.4 billion	loans, interest-free loans, credit lines	infrastructure (railways)
Congo (DRC) [a b c]	oil, minerals	$5 billion	loans	infrastructure, mining
Sudan [a b c]	oil	$4.2 billion	investment, loans, grants	oil refining; infrastructure, hydro power, humanitarian
Gabon [d]	oil, minerals	$3 billion	investment, grants	iron ore mining, infrastructure, port facilities, hydro power
Mozambique	wood, ores	$2.4 billion	debt cancellation, concessional loans, grants	dam construction, infrastructure, national stadium
Equatorial Guineab [c]	oil	$2 billion	concessional loans, credit lines	not specified
Ethiopia	oil drilling rights	$2 billion (includes 2008 aid of $150 million) $1.6 billion	loans, grants, investment	infrastructure, telecommunications, public buildings, hydropower, light industry
Nigeria [a b]	oil	$1.6 billion	debtcancellation, investment, grants	offshore oil development, infrastructure railways), medical training

Source: NYU Wagner School, *Understanding Chinese Foreign Aid: A Look at China's Development Assistance to Africa, Southeast Asia, and Latin America,* April 25, 2008.

a. major African trading partner of China

b. loan payments in oil

c. major African oil supplier of China

d. loan payments in minerals

Table 7. Selected Major PRC Financing and Aid-Related Economic Projects in Africa

Amount	Funding (Year)	Project Type(s)	Country
$5 billion	loan (2007)	Transportation infrastructure	Congo
$4 billion	investment (2007)	oil production	Sudan

Table 7. (Continued)

Amount	Funding (Year)	Project Type(s)	Country
$3 billion	investment (2006)	port, railway, hydropower, mining (iron)	Gabon
$2.5 billion	loan (credit line) (2007)	unspecified	Angola
$2.3 billion	loan (2006)	hydropower (dam)	Mozambique
$2 billion	loan (credit line) (2006)	unspecified	Equatorial Guinea
$2 billion	loan (credit line) (2004)	unspecified	Angola

Source: NYU Wagner School, *Understanding Chinese Foreign Aid: A Look at China's Development Assistance to Africa, Southeast Asia, and Latin America*, April 25, 2008.

China's aid to Africa is dominated by concessional loans and export credits provided through the Ministry of Commerce and Eximbank. PRC loans to Africa, which reportedly grew by 35% annually between 2001 and 2005, have been used chiefly to finance infrastructure projects in over 35 African countries (mainly hydropower and transportation).[33] See **Table 7.** The NYU Wagner School research team compiled a list of PRC aid and related investment projects or offers in Africa reported during the 2002-2007 period. The combined values amounted to $33 billion.[34] In dollar terms, 54% was related to infrastructure and other public works projects, 28.5% to the extraction or production of natural resources, and 2.5% to humanitarian activities, technical assistance, and military assistance (15% was unspecified). In many cases, especially when the recipient country has poor credit, loans are to be repaid in kind (oil or commodities). The China Eximbank reported in 2007 that its outstanding loans to the continent totaled $8 billion-$9 billion.[35] According to the Wagner School study, examples of PRC development and humanitarian aid in the region include the construction of schools and hospitals, medical training and equipment, agricultural technical assistance, food aid, and disaster assistance.

Latin America

China's growing engagement with Latin America and the Caribbean (the Western Hemisphere) lacks the deep historical ties of its relations with Southeast Asia and legacy of its Cold War friendships in Africa. China's growing interest in the region appears to be principally linked to its objective of gaining broader access to natural resources and agricultural commodities, such as oil, ores, and soybeans. Beijing also aims to fully isolate Taiwan — 12 Latin American and Caribbean nations still maintain diplomatic relations with Taiwan — and bolster China's diplomatic presence in the region. China's recent aid to Costa Rica reportedly was directly linked to the Central American country's establishment of diplomatic relations with the PRC (and termination of relations with Taiwan) in 2007. Other goals include opening up alternative markets and opportunities for Chinese goods and investment. According to many analysts, however, Beijing acknowledges that the United States remains the dominant economic and political influence in the Western Hemisphere.[36]

The PRC is not a major foreign investor in the region. The European Union (EU) is the largest source of FDI in Latin America, with $620 billion invested in the region in 2006, followed by the United States with $350 billion. According to PRC official data, Latin America had received $22 billion in cumulative PRC investment at the end of 2006, about 25% of PRC total overseas investment. However, the vast majority of PRC FDI in the region reportedly goes to off-shore financial havens such as the Cayman Islands and the Virgin Islands, to be reinvested in China (thereby taking advantage of tax breaks for "foreign companies"). When these destinations are excluded, only about $1.9 billion remains.[37] According to some sources, in 2006, PRC direct investment flows to the Western Hemisphere totaled roughly $100 million, less than its outbound investment to Africa ($500 million).[38] Conversely, Latin American companies have made sizable investments in China with $20 billion in cumulative FDI.[39]

China's trade with Latin America grew ten-fold between 2000 and 2007 and reached $142 billion in 2008. China's total trade with the region is only about one-fifth that of the United States ($664 billion in 2008), but growing at a faster rate.[40] The United States reportedly imports 12 times more oil from Venezuela than does China.[41] Nonetheless, China has become an important trading partner to major countries in the region, and is second only to the United States as an importer of commodities and goods from Latin America. China's largest trading partners in the region are Brazil, Mexico, Chile, Argentina, and Peru.[42]

The NYU Wagner School research team compiled a list of PRC aid and related investment projects or offers in the Western Hemisphere reported during the 2002-2007 period. The combined values amounted to $26.7 billion.[43] Over two-thirds of these projects were in natural resource sectors, while 28% were related to infrastructure and public works, 1% involved humanitarian activities and technical assistance, and 2% of aid was unspecified. In the past several years, Chinese humanitarian assistance has included infrastructure repair in Costa Rica, hospitals in Cuba, funding to the Bolivian Red Cross for mudslide victims, and help to people affected by an earthquake in Peru and flood in Uruguay. In 2008, China joined the Inter American Development Bank and committed $350 million for public and private sector projects.[44] The emphasis on natural resources implies a strongly commercial nature to China's aid in Latin America, less oriented toward infrastructure development than China's foreign assistance to Africa and Southeast Asia. See **Table 8** and **Table 9**.

In terms of official development assistance as measured by the OECD, which often refers to different types of aid than that typically provided by China, the EU, the United States, and Japan are the largest providers in the region. U.S. foreign assistance to the Western Hemisphere, including regional assistance, was an estimated $1.46 billion in 2008 and $1.55 billion in 2007.[45]

Table 8. Selected Latin American Countries with Large Reported Aid and Investment Projects, 2002-2007

Country	Main Exports to China	Pledged Aid, Loans, Credit Lines, and Investments	Major Types of Financing (as Reported)	Major Types of ProjectsFinanced (as Reported)
Venezuela	oil	$16.4 billion	investment	oil, gas exploration and production; transportation; telecom; light industry
Brazil	iron ore, agricultural commoditie, oil	$8.2 billion	investment, loans	infrastructure (ports, aviation, rail)
Chile	minerals, ores	$0.5 billion	investment	natural resources (copper)
Columbia	iron, oil	$0.4 billion	investment	steel,, oil exploration,, mining
Costa Rica	electrical machinery	$0.4 billion	grants, loans	humanitarian, infrastructure

Source: NYU Wagner School, *Understanding Chinese Foreign Aid: A Look at China's Development Assistance to Africa, Southeast Asia, and Latin America,* April 25, 2008.

Table 9. Selected Major PRC Financing and Aid-Related Economic Projects in Latin America

Amount	Funding (Year)	Project Type(s)	Country
$9 billion	investment (2006)	infrastructure (railways), telecom, mining, agriculture	Venezuela
$7 billion	investment (2004)	infrastructure (port, railways, aviation), steel	Brazil
$5 billion	investment (2006)	energy	Venezuela

Source: NYU Wagner School, *Understanding Chinese Foreign Aid: A Look at China's Development Assistance to Africa, Southeast Asia, and Latin America,* April 25, 2008.

Southeast Asia

China has become an important source of infrastructure financing in Southeast Asia. While China is not counted as a major regional provider of ODA as defined by the OECD, some reports and observations suggest that the PRC is one of the largest sources of economic assistance in Southeast Asia. Although access to natural resources plays a prominent role in China's engagement in the region, strategic interests are likely to influence China's activities in Southeast Asia to a greater extent than they do in Africa and Latin America. Many of China's aid activities in the region appear to provide relatively greater long-term diplomatic benefits and comparatively few short-term economic ones.

China has a large economic presence in Southeast Asia, owing in part to its proximity and historical ties to the region. Southeast Asia's largest sources of FDI in 2006 (net inflow) were the EU ($13.3 billion), Japan, ($10.8 billion), the United States ($3.8 billion), South Korea ($1 billion), and China ($900 million).[46] The EU, the United States, Japan, and China are the largest trading entities in the region. In 2008, China's trade with the Association of Southeast Asian Nations (ASEAN) countries, at $230 billion, was larger than its trade with Africa ($106 billion) and Latin America ($142 billion).[47]

China and the least developed countries of mainland Southeast Asia are becoming increasingly economically integrated, although each of these countries also has sought to hedge against the PRC's rising influence. China is considered the "primary supplier of economic and military assistance" to Burma (Myanmar), Cambodia, and Laos and provides them with an "implicit security guarantee," according to some analysts.[48] In recent years, PRC government entities have financed many infrastructure, energy-related (especially hydro power), agricultural, and other high profile development projects in these countries, which also rely upon Chinese construction materials, equipment, technical expertise, and labor. There are some indications that Chinese aid in this part of the region is diversifying, including support for counter-trafficking in persons and counter-narcotics efforts, programs involving Chinese youth volunteers (Laos), elections (Cambodia), and historical preservation (Cambodia). The PRC also has financed railway construction, hydro power development, and ship building facilities in Vietnam.[49]

In the past few years, China has become a major financer and investor in infrastructure, energy, agriculture, and mining in the Philippines. According to one source, in 2006, China was the third largest source of bilateral development assistance to the Philippines after Japan and the United Kingdom.[50] The Philippines reportedly is the largest recipient of PRC loans in Southeast Asia, which totaled $2 billion in 2007, of which about half has been disbursed.[51] One of the largest PRC-funded projects in the country is the $1 billion North Rail line.[52]

The NYU Wagner School research team compiled a list of PRC aid and related investment projects or offers in Southeast Asia reported during the 2002-2007 period. The combined values amounted to $14.8 billion.[53] Of this amount, 43% was channeled toward infrastructure and public works projects, 32% to natural resource extraction or development, 3% to military, humanitarian, and technical assistance activities, and 22% to purposes not specified. See **Table 10** and **Table 11**.

In terms of official development assistance as measured by the OECD, which often refers to different types of aid than that typically provided by China, Japan remains the largest bilateral aid donor in Southeast Asia, providing $2 billion in 2006.[54] The United States funded an estimated $517 million in aid programs in Southeast Asian countries in 2008.[55] Since 2001, Indonesia and the Philippines have received the largest increases in U.S. foreign assistance in the region, chiefly for counter-terrorism programs. Vietnam has also received large increases in U.S. ODA, including significant funding for HIV/AIDS programs.

Table 10. Selected Southeast Asian Countries with Large Reported Aid and Investment Projects, 2002-2007

Country	Main Exports to China	Pledged Aid, Loans, Credit Lines, and Investments	Major Types of Financing (as Reported)	Major Types of Projects Financed (as Reported)
Philippines	ores, copper	$5.4 billion	loans, grants	infrastructure (railways), mining, non-lethal military
Vietnam	oil, rubber, wood, ores	$3.4 billion	loans, investment	Infrastructure (power), shipyards, mining
Burma	wood, ores	$3.1 billion	investment, loans	hydropower, nickel ore

Source: NYU Wagner School, *Understanding Chinese Foreign Aid: A Look at China's Development Assistance to Africa, Southeast Asia, and Latin America*, April 25, 2008.

Table 11. Selected Major PRC Financing and Aid-Related Economic Projects in Southeast Asia

Amount	Funding (Year)	Project Type(s)	Country
$2.4 billion	Investment (2005)	steel plant	Thailand
$2 billion	Loan (2007)	infrastructure	Philippines
$2 billion	Investment (2006- 2007)	infrastructure, hydropower, oil pipeline	Burma
$1.6 billion	Investment (2007)	mining	Vietnam
$1 billion	Loan (2005)	power plant	Vietnam

Source: NYU Wagner School, *Understanding Chinese Foreign Aid: A Look at China's Development Assistance to Africa, Southeast Asia, and Latin America*, April 25, 2008.

Appendix. Recent PRC Foreign Assistance and Investment Projects (2008)

Table A-1. Selected PRC Aid and Investment Projects in 2008 (Announced or Begun): Africa

Country	Type of Assistance or Investment	Funding Source	Description	Value in $US (b = billion m = million)
Angola	Development	Govt-Sponsored Investment	housing and related infrastructure	$3.5 b
Congo	Infrastructure/ Public Works	Concessional Loan	optical cable network	$35 m
Congo	Infrastructure/ Public Works; Natural Resources	Govt-Sponsored Investment; Concessional Loan	transportation, mining sector	$9 b
Ethiopia	Infrastructure/ Public Works	Grant/Donation	construction of African Union Hall	$150 m
Ethiopia	Infrastructure/ Public Works	In-kind	vehicles and office equipment	not specified
Ethiopia	Infrastructure; Development	Govt-Sponsored Investment	industrial park	$713 m
Gabon	Infrastructure/ Public Works	Concessional Loan	hydroelectric dam	$83 m
Kenya	Infrastructure/ Public Works	Concessional Loan	road construction	$120 m
Liberia	Infrastructure/ Public Works	Grant; In-kind	hospital and medical supplies	$10 m
Madagascar	Humanitarian; Development	Grant	medical aid team	not specified
Niger	Natural Resources	Govt-Sponsored Investment	oil drilling,, refinery	$5 b
Nigeria	Infrastructure/ Public Works	Govt-Sponsored Investment	road construction	$1 b
Nigeria	Infrastructure/ Public Works	Govt-Sponsored Investment	power plant	$2.4 b
Rwanda	Infrastructure/ PublicWorks	Grant	hospitals	$1.5 m
Sierra Leone	Infrastructure/ Public Works	Concessional Loan	telecommunications network	$20 m
Sudan	Humanitarian	Grant; In-kind	de-mining training, mine sweeping equipment	not specified
Sudan	Humanitarian	Grant; In-kind	housing shelters, health equipment	$11 m
Uganda	Military	Grant; In-kind	military training, trucks and equipment	not specified

Uganda	Development	Grant	upgrade health centers	$15 m
Uganda	Infrastructure/ Public	Grant/Donation	government office	$20 m
Zambia	Infrastructure/ Public Works	Govt-Sponsored Investment; Concessional Loan	power station expansion	$400 m
Zambia	Infrastructure/ Public Works	Grant/Donation	sports stadium	$65 m

Source: various international news reports

Table A-2. Selected PRC Aid and Investment Projects in 2008 (Announced or Begun): Latin America

Country	Type of Assistance or Investment	Funding Source	Description	Value in $US (b = billion m = million)
Brazil	Infrastructure/Public Works	Govt-Sponsored Investment	power plant	$850 m
Brazil	Natural Resources	Concessional Loan	oil exploration	$10 b
Chile	Infrastructure/Public	Concessional Loan	ports, shipping,	$100 m
	Works; Natural Resources	(joint credit lines)	mining	
Costa Rica	Infrastructure/Public Works; Natural Resources	Grant/Donation	stadium, oil refinery	$130 m
Cuba	Humanitarian	Concessional Loan	hurricane relief – repair of hospitals	$70 m
Grenada	Infrastructure/Public Works	Concessional Loan	tourist marina	$83 m
Venezuela	Infrastructure/Public Works;	Concessional Loan	infrastructure, electricity, health, and education	$4 b (to be paid back in oil)

Source: various international news reports

Table A-3. Selected PRC Aid and Investment Projects in 2008 (Announced or Begun): Southeast Asia

Country	Type of Assistance or Investment	Funding Source	Description	Value in $US (b = billion m = million)
Cambodia	Infrastructure/ Public Works	Grant; Concessional Loan	road construction	$ 215 m

Table A-3 (Continued)

Country	Type of Assistance or Investment	Funding Source	Description	Value in $US (b = billion m = million)
Laos/ Thailand	Infrastructure/ Public Works	Govt-Sponsored Investment	construction of China-Laos-Thailand railroad	$3 b
Myanmar (Burma)	Natural Resources	Govt-Sponsored Investment	nickel mining	not specified (profit sharing arrangement)
Myanmar (Burma)	Natural Resources	Govt-Sponsored Investment	2 oil and gas pipelines	$350 m
Indonesia	Infrastructure/Publi c Works	Concessional Loan	power plants	$615 m

Source: various international news reports

End Notes

1 This report is based on research done by the New York University Robert F. Wagner Graduate School of Public Service, *Understanding Chinese Foreign Aid: A Look at China's Development Assistance to Africa, Southeast Asia, and Latin America*, April 25, 2008. For questions or further information, please contact Thomas Lum of the Congressional Research Service who served as project manager for this study.

2 For a discussion of China's soft power, see CRS Report RL34620, *Comparing Global Influence: China's and U.S. Diplomacy, Foreign Aid, Trade, and Investment in the Developing World*, section by Thomas Lum.

3 Carol Lancaster, "The Chinese Aid System," Center for Global Development, June 2007 http://www.cgdev.org.

4 OECD Glossary of Statistical Terms, http://stats.oecd.org/glossary/index.htm.

5 Japan's Official Development Assistance White Paper 2007; "Japan Urged to Improve Quality of Foreign Aid," *Inter Press Service News Agency*, August 18, 2005; "Japan and Asia: Developing Ties," *OECD Observer*, 2008; Japan Ministry of Foreign Affairs.

6 Edward J. Lincoln, "Japan: Using Power Narrowly," Council on Foreign Relations, Winter 2003.

7 China reportedly has youth volunteers in 50 countries, mostly in Africa and Southeast Asia, and has begun to send volunteers to Latin America. The Chinese government has pledged to send 300 volunteers to Africa by 2009. "China to Send Youth Volunteers to Africa this Year," *The Ethiopian Herald*, February 17, 2007.

8 Lancaster, op. cit.; See also Phillip C. Saunders, "China's Global Activism: Strategy, Drivers, and Tools," Institute for National Strategic Studies, National Defense University, 2006.

9 Organization for Economic Co-operation and Development (OECD) data. See http://www.globalissues.org/.

10 CRS Report RL34620, *Comparing Global Influence: China's and U.S. Diplomacy, Foreign Aid, Trade, and Investment in the Developing World*, op. cit., section by Dick Nanto; "Chinese Investment Pouring into Thailand's Neighbors," *The Nation (Thailand)*, December 4, 2007.

11 Because of the lack of official data, either from China or recipient countries, the NYU Wagner School research team relied largely upon the international press and scholarly research.

Sources included allAfrica.com, the Economist Intelligence Unit (EIU), International Relations and Security Network, the PRC Ministry of Commerce, ReliefWeb (United Nations), Reuters, Xinhua, and other news agencies.

[12] CRS Report RL34552, *State, Foreign Operations, and Related Programs: FY2009 Appropriations*, by Susan B. Epstein and Kennon H. Nakamura.

[13] China's conditions on aid are often international rather than domestic —— requiring aid recipients to support the "one- China" principle regarding Taiwan and China's agenda in the United Nations.

[14] Pilirani Semu-Banda, "NGO Keeping an Eye on Malawi's New Best Friend, China," Inter Press Service News Agency, May 26, 2008, http://allafrica.com/; Mabvuto Banda, "Malawi Leader Says China to Give $287 Mln in Aid," *Reuters News*, April 4, 2008.

[15] For further discussion of Chinese influence in Africa, see Congressional Research Service, "China's Foreign Policy and 'Soft Power' in South America, Asia, and Africa: A Study Prepared for the Committee on Foreign Relations, United States Senate," April 2008, section by Nicolas Cook.

[16] Deborah Brautigam, "China's Africa Aid," The German Marshall Fund of the United States, April 2008; Penny Davies, "China and the End of Poverty in Africa," August 2007; China Exim Bank.

[17] Nick Tattersall, "Chinese Firm to Build $1 Bln Road in Nigeria Oil Hub," *Reuters News*, July 13, 2008; China National Bureau of Statistics.

[18] Tom Miller, "U.S. $5 b Fund to Make First Forays into Africa," *South China Morning Post*, January 8, 2009.

[19] Congressional Budget Justification for Foreign Operations, FY2008.

[20] Organization for Economic Co-operation and Development, *OECD and Africa*, March 2008.

[21] "U.S.-African Trade Profile," U.S. Department of Commerce, International Trade Administration (2008); Harry G. Broadman, "China and India Go to Africa," *Free Republic*, March 16, 2008.

[22] Leonard K. Cheng and Zihui Ma, "China's Outward FDI: Past and Future," July 2007; Jian-Ye Wang, "What Drives China's Growing Role in Africa," IMF Working Paper, October 2007; Mauro De Lorenzo, "China and Africa: A New Scramble?" *American Enterprise Institute*, April 6, 2007.

[23] Jian-Ye Wang, "What Drives China's Growing Role in Africa," op. cit.

[24] Hany Besada, Yang Wang, and John Whalley, "China's Growing Economic Presence in Africa," *Policy Brief*, The Centre for International Governance Innovation, No. 6 (October 2008); CRS Report RL34620, *Comparing Global Influence: China's and U.S. Diplomacy, Foreign Aid, Trade, and Investment in the Developing World*, op. cit., section by Dick Nanto (data excludes Egypt).

[25] "Building Bridges: China's Growing Role as Infrastructure Financier for Sub-Saharan Africa," The World Bank, No. 5 (2008); China National Bureau of Statistics.

[26] Jian-Ye Wang and Abdoulaye Bio-Tchane, "Africa's Burgeoning Ties with China," *Finance and Development*, International Monetary Fund, *http://www.imf.org/external/pubs/ft/fandd/2008/03/wang.htm.*

[27] World Trade Atlas.

[28] Building Bridges, op. cit.; "Africa Accounts For 30 Percent Of China's Oil Imports: Official," *People's Daily Online,* http://english.peopledaily.com.cn, October 19, 2006.

[29] "Building Bridges," op. cit.

[30] Stephanie Hanson, "China, Africa, and Oil," *Council on Foreign Relations Backgrounder*, June 6, 2008.

[31] Zong He, "Some Responses to the 'China Threat in Africa,'" *China Daily*, November 7, 2007.

[32] "Building Bridges," op. cit.

[33] "Building Bridges," op. cit.; Brautigam, "China's Africa Aid," op. cit.; World Bank, "Press Release: New Financiers are Narrowing Africa's Infrastructure Deficit," July 10, 2008.

[34] This aggregate number may include some double counting of aid that involved multiple projects or spanned several years. The figure is not based upon a precise definition of aid and does not represent an exact aid total.

[35] Davies, "China and the End of Poverty in Africa," op. cit.

[36] Peter Brookes, "Russia, China, Move In on Latin America," Heritage Foundation, November 27, 2008; Cynthia A. Watson, "U.S. Responses to China's Growing Interests in Latin America: Dawning Recognition of a Changing Hemisphere," in *Enter the Dragon? China's Presence in Latin America*, Woodrow Wilson International Center for Scholars, February 2007. For further discussion of Chinese influence in Latin America and the Caribbean, see Congressional Research Service, "China's Foreign Policy and 'Soft Power' in South America, Asia, and Africa," op. cit., section by Mark P. Sullivan.

[37] Daniel P. Erikson, "The New Challenge: China and the Western Hemisphere," Testimony before the House Committee on Foreign Affairs, Subcommittee on the Western Hemisphere, June 11, 2008.

[38] CRS Report RL34620, *Comparing Global Influence: China's and U.S. Diplomacy, Foreign Aid, Trade, and Investment in the Developing World*, op. cit., section by Dick Nanto.

[39] Erikson, "The New Challenge," op. cit.

[40] Frank Bajak, "Slowdown Doesn't Shrink China's LatAm Ambitions," *Associated Press*, November 17, 2008; World Trade Atlas.

[41] CRS Report RL34620, *Comparing Global Influence: China's and U.S. Diplomacy, Foreign Aid, Trade, and Investment in the Developing World*, op. cit., section by Dick Nanto.

[42] He Li, "China's Growing Interest in Latin America," *The Journal of Strategic Studies*, Vol. 30, No. 4-5 (August- October 2007); Global Trade Atlas.

[43] This aggregate number may include some double counting of aid that involved multiple projects or spanned several years. The figure is not based upon a precise definition of aid and does not represent an exact aid total.

[44] "China Makes IDB Aid Commitment to Bolivia, Guyana, Haiti, Honduras," *BBC Monitoring Americas*, October 23, 2008.

[45] Congressional Budget Justification for Foreign Operations, FY2008.

[46] ASEAN Foreign Direct Investment Database, August 2007.

[47] World Trade Atlas; "China, ASEAN become 4th-Largest Trade Partners," *Xinhua*, March 1, 2008. Data among different sources varies.

[48] Catherin E. Dalpino, "Consequences of a Growing China," *Statement before the Senate Committee on Foreign Relations Subcommittee on East Asian and Pacific Affairs*, June 7, 2005; Heritage Foundation, "Southeast Asia's Forgotten Tier: Burma, Cambodia and Laos," July 26, 2007; Marvin C. Ott, "Southeast Asian Security Challenges: America's Response? *Strategic Forum*, October 1, 2006; Joshua Kurlantzick, "China's Charm Offensive in Southeast Asia," *Current History*, Vo. 105, no. 692 (September 2006).

[49] For further information, see CRS Report RL34620, *Comparing Global Influence: China's and U.S. Diplomacy, Foreign Aid, Trade, and Investment in the Developing World*, op. cit., section by Bruce Vaughn, Thomas Lum, and Wayne Morrison.

[50] Michelle Remo, "RP Should Look to China for its Infra Funding Needs," *Philippine Daily Inquirer*, March 9, 2008.

[51] Katrice R. Jalbuena, "Ties with PRC, Now Most Important to RP, Also Involves Security Matters," *Manila Times*, June 29, 2008.

[52] Walter Lohman, "Off the Rails in the Philippines," Heritage Foundation, Web Memo no. 1856, March 14, 2008; Darwin G. Amojelar, "Chinese Loans to RP Rising," *The Manila Times*, December 3, 2007.

[53] This aggregate number may include some double counting of aid that involved multiple projects or spanned several years. The figure is not based upon a precise definition of aid and does not represent an exact aid total.

[54] Organization for Economic Cooperation and Development (OECD), *http://www.oecd.org/home/*.

[55] Congressional Budget Justification for Foreign Operations, FY2008; Japan's Official Development Assistance White Paper 2007.

In: Russia, China and Eurasia: Social, Historical... ISBN: 978-1-61668-016-9
Editor: Davon R. Moore

Chapter 2

PAKISTAN-U.S. RELATIONS

K. Alan Kronstadt

SUMMARY

A stable, democratic, prosperous Pakistan is considered vital to U.S. interests. U.S. concerns regarding Pakistan include regional and global terrorism; Afghan stability; democratization and human rights protection; the ongoing Kashmir problem and Pakistan-India tensions; and economic development. A U.S.-Pakistan relationship marked by periods of both cooperation and discord was transformed by the September 2001 terrorist attacks on the United States and the ensuing enlistment of Pakistan as a key ally in U.S.-led counterterrorism efforts. Top U.S. officials have praised Pakistan for its ongoing cooperation, although long-held doubts exist about Islamabad's commitment to some core U.S. interests. Pakistan is identified as a base for terrorist groups and their supporters operating in Kashmir, India, and Afghanistan. Pakistan's army has conducted unprecedented and largely ineffectual counterterrorism operations in the country's western tribal areas, where Al Qaeda operatives and pro-Taliban militants are said to enjoy "safe haven." U.S. officials increasingly are concerned that the cross-border infiltration of Islamist militants from Pakistan into Afghanistan is a key obstacle to defeating the Taliban insurgency.

The United States strongly encourages maintenance of a bilateral cease-fire and continued, substantive dialogue between Pakistan and neighboring

India, which have fought three wars since 1947. A perceived Pakistan-India nuclear arms race has been the focus of U.S. nonproliferation efforts in South Asia. Attention to this issue intensified following nuclear tests by both countries in 1998. The United States has been troubled by evidence of transfers of Pakistani nuclear technologies and materials to third parties, including North Korea, Iran, and Libya. Such evidence became stark in 2004, and related illicit smuggling networks may still be operative.

Pakistan's macroeconomic indicators turned positive after 2001, with some meaningful poverty reduction seen in this still poor country. However, economic conditions deteriorated sharply in 2008. Democracy has fared poorly in Pakistan, with the country enduring direct military rule for more than half of its existence. In 1999, the elected government was ousted in a coup led by Army Chief General Pervez Musharraf, who later assumed the title of president. Musharraf retained the position as army chief until his November 2007 retirement. Late 2007 instability included Musharraf's six-week-long imposition of emergency rule and the assassination of former Prime Minister and leading opposition figure Benazir Bhutto. However, February 2008 parliamentary elections were relatively credible and seated a coalition led by Bhutto's widower, Asif Zardari, and opposed to Musharraf's continued rule. The coalition's August vow to launch impeachment proceedings spurred Musharraf to resign the presidency and exit Pakistan's political stage. Zardari subsequently was elected as the new President. The Bush Administration determined that a democratically elected government was restored in Islamabad, thus permanently removing coup-related aid sanctions.

The Obama Administration states an intention to continue pursuing close and mutually beneficial relations with Islamabad. As part of its "new strategy" for Afghanistan, the Administration seeks development of a "more coherent" Pakistan policy to include conditioning U.S. military aid to Islamabad on that government's progress in combating militancy and also tripling nonmilitary aid to improve the lives of the Pakistani people. A Special Representative was appointed to coordinate U.S. government efforts with both Pakistan and Afghanistan. Pakistan is among the world's leading recipients of U.S. aid, obtaining more than $5.3 billion in overt assistance since 2001, including about $3.1 billion in development and humanitarian aid. Pakistan also has received about $6.7 billion in military reimbursements for its support of counterterrorism efforts.

INTRODUCTION

A stable, democratic, prosperous Pakistan actively working to counter Islamist militancy is considered vital to U.S. interests. Current top-tier U.S. concerns regarding Pakistan include regional and global terrorism; Afghan stability; domestic political stability and democratization; nuclear weapons proliferation and security; human rights protection; and economic development. Pakistan remains a vital U.S. ally in U.S.-led anti-terrorism efforts. Yet the outcomes of U.S. policies toward Pakistan since 9/11, while not devoid of meaningful successes, have seen a failure to neutralize anti-Western militants and reduce religious extremism in that country, and a failure to contribute sufficiently to the stabilization of neighboring Afghanistan. In the assessment of a former senior U.S. government official, "Pakistan is the most dangerous country in the world today. All of the nightmares of the twenty-first century come together in Pakistan: nuclear proliferation, drug smuggling, military dictatorship, and above all, international terrorism."[1] Terrorist bombings and other militant attacks have become a near-daily scourge in 2008.

Pakistan suffered a series of destabilizing developments in 2007, including a months- long political crisis and a November emergency proclamation which severely undermined the status of the military- dominated government of then-President and Army Chief Gen. Pervez Musharraf; a surge in domestic Islamist militancy following the July denouement of a standoff involving Islamabad's Red Mosque complex; and the December assassination of former Prime Minster and leading opposition figure Benazir Bhutto, who had returned to Pakistan from self-imposed exile only months earlier. These developments led many Washington-based critics to more forcefully question the Bush Administration's largely uncritical support for President Musharraf as a key U.S. ally. Following February 2008 parliamentary elections that seated a coalition of former opposition parties vehemently opposed to Musharraf's continued rule, the U.S. government became more measured in its public posturing and, when Musharraf came under imminent threat of impeachment in August, the Bush Administration called his fate a matter of internal Pakistani politics. Abandoned by many political allies and perhaps even by his military successor, Musharraf made the decision to resign the presidency and exit Pakistan's political stage on August 18. Within one week of the resignation, Islamabad's ruling parliamentary coalition fractured.

Pakistan in Brief

Population: 168 million; growth rate: 1.8% (2008 est.) Area: 803,940 sq. km. (slightly less than twice the size of California)

Capital: Islamabad

Heads of Government: President Asif Ali Zardari and Prime Minister Yousaf Raza Gillani (both of the Pakistan People's Party)

Ethnic Groups: Punjabi, Sindhi, Pashtun, Baloch, Muhajir (immigrants from India at the time of partition and their descendants)

Languages: Punjabi 58%, Sindhi 12%, Pashtu 8%, Urdu (official) 8%; English widely used

Religions: Muslim 96% (Sunni 81%, Shia 15%), Christian, Hindu, and other 4%

Life Expectancy at Birth: female 65 years; male 63 years (2008 est.)

Literacy: 50% (female 36%; male 63%; 2005 est.)

Gross Domestic Product (at PPP): $446 billion; per capita: $2,681; growth rate 6% (2008 est.)

Currency: Rupee (100 = $1.27)

Inflation: 23.3% (December 2008)

Defense Budget: $3.56 billion (2.8% of GDP; 2008)

U.S. Trade: exports to U.S. $3.6 billion; imports from U.S. $2.1 billion (2008 est.)

Sources: CIA, The World Factbook; Departments of Commerce and State; Government of Pakistan; Economist Intelligence Unit; Global Insight; The Military Balance

There exist widely-held suspicions among foreign governments and independent analysts alike that Islamabad's civilian government does not fully control the army, that the army does not fully control the intelligence agencies, and that the these intelligence agencies have lost their ability to rein in the very militant groups they helped to create. Moreover, anti-American sentiments are widespread in Pakistan, and a significant segment of the populace has viewed years of U.S. support for President Musharraf and the Pakistani military as an impediment to, rather than facilitator of, the process of democratization there. Underlying the anti-American sentiment is a pervasive, but perhaps malleable perception that the United States is fighting a war against Islam.[2] The Bush Administration continued to proclaim its ongoing support for Musharraf even after his imposition of emergency rule and the later sweeping rejection of his parliamentary allies by Pakistani voters. However, in 2008, the Administration showed signs of a shift in its longstanding Pakistan policies, in particular on the issue of democratization. As articulated by then- Deputy Secretary of State John Negroponte in March:

> The United States is committed to working with all of Pakistan's leaders on the full spectrum of bilateral issues, from fighting violent extremism to improving educational and economic opportunities.... The United States looks forward to engaging Pakistan's new government on how best to promote economic growth and reduce poverty. The United States will continue to help the Pakistani people build a secure, prosperous, and free society.[3]

Still, many Pakistanis are resentful of perceived U.S. interference and pressure. In the words of one senior Pakistani commentator and former army general,

> In trying to impose its will against the wishes of Pakistani people, the Bush administration further heightens anti-American sentiment; discredits the war on terror; and makes it more difficult for the new civilian government to stabilize. Air strikes by U.S. forces in the tribal belt, threats of more to follow, and Washington's fierce opposition to peace agreements also lead to widespread resentment and instability.[4]

Many in Pakistan have been hopeful that the incoming administration of President Barack Obama will be less overbearing in its dealings with Islamabad and will also do more to nurture Pakistan's nascent democratic institutions.[5]

In 2008, Islamabad's new civilian ruling dispensation was welcomed by U.S. leaders. In July, President George W. Bush hosted Prime Minister Yousaf Raza Gillani at the White House, where the two leaders issued a joint statement reaffirming the U.S.-Pakistan "Strategic Partnership."[6] In September, Benazir Bhutto's widower Asif Ali Zardari—a controversial figure long bedeviled by corruption charges who had taken the reins of her Pakistan People's Party (PPP) upon her demise—ascended to the Pakistani presidency with the congratulations of senior U.S. officials. Later that month, then-Deputy Secretary Negroponte hosted Foreign Minister Shah Mehmood Qureshi in Washington for the third round of the Pakistan-U.S. Strategic Dialogue, where the two sides "reaffirmed their commitments to a wide-ranging, substantive, and long-term strategic partnership."7

A "Friends of Pakistan" (FOP) group was launched in September 2008, when co-chairs President Zardari and the top diplomats of the United Arab Emirates, Britain, and the United States were joined by foreign ministers from Australia, Canada, France, Germany, Italy, Japan, and Turkey, and representatives of China, the European Union, and the United Nations. A resulting statement expressed agreement to work in strategic partnership with Pakistan to combat violent extremism; develop a comprehensive approach to economic and social development; coordinate an approach to stabilizing and developing border regions; address Pakistan's energy shortfall; and support democratic institutions.[8] The FOP met in Abu Dhabi in mid-November to discuss the parameters of its work. Participants noted Pakistan's formidable challenges and called for well-coordinated international action to address them. Such cooperation is planned for four broad areas: development, security, energy, and institution-building.[9]

KEY CURRENT ISSUES AND DEVELOPMENTS

Pakistan's worsening economic conditions, fluid political setting, and perilous security circumstances make the job of U.S. decision makers difficult. On the economic front, the newly elected civilian government in Islamabad faces crises that erode their options and elicit growing public resentment. On the political front, an unprecedented ruling coalition including the country's two leading mainstream parties proved fragile and collapsed almost immediately upon the resignation of President Musharraf, without having enacted any major policies. On the security front, Pakistan is the setting for multiple armed Islamist insurgencies, some of which span the border with Afghanistan and contribute to the destabilization of that country. Al Qaeda forces remain active on Pakistani territory.

On September 20, 2008, at least 53 people were killed and hundreds wounded when a suicide truck bomber attacked the American-owned Marriott hotel in Islamabad. Pakistani officials suspect Taliban militants based in western tribal areas of perpetrating the attack, which may have been targeting Pakistani political leaders who, by some accounts, were slated to be dining there later in the day.[10] The attack—called "Pakistan's 9/11" by some observers—spurred numerous commentaries arguing that the "war on terrorism" could no longer be perceived as an "American war" as it clearly requires Pakistanis to fight in their own self-defense.[11]

The Newly-Seated U.S. Administration

A new concentration on stabilizing Afghanistan

As part of its "new strategy for Afghanistan," the Administration of President Obama intends to substantially increase the number of U.S. troops there. A key aspect of the new approach is the development of a more coherent Pakistan policy to include conditioning U.S. military aid to Islamabad on that government's progress in combating militancy and also the tripling nonmilitary aid to improve the lives of the Pakistani people, with a particular focus on the FATA region. President Obama, Vice President Joseph Biden, and Secretary of State Hillary Clinton all supported the Enhanced Partnership With Pakistan Act as Senators (S. 3263) in the 110th Congress, and they are said to look forward to working with the 111th Congress on any new version of that legislation that may arise.[12] In this regard, the new Senate Foreign Relations Committee Chairman, Senator John Kerry, has said he will seek swift passage of a major new aid package that includes a demand for greater accountability from Pakistan's military, calling Pakistan "ground zero for the terrorist threat we face."[13]

As President-elect, Barack Obama asserted that Afghanistan cannot be "solved" without "solving Pakistan" and working more effectively with that country:

> [W]hat I want to do is to create the kind of effective, strategic partnership with Pakistan that allows us, in concert, to assure that terrorists are not setting up safe havens in some of these border regions between

> Pakistan and Afghanistan. So far President Zardari has sent the right signals. He's indicated that he recognizes this is not just a threat to the United States, but it is a threat to Pakistan as well. ... I think this democratically-elected government understands that threat and I hope that in the coming months that we're going to be able to establish the kind of close, effective, working relationship that makes both countries safer.[14]

Some observers warn that escalating the war against the Afghan Taliban with more foreign troops, and prodding Islamabad to ramp up its own militarized efforts, could worsen rather than ameliorate the situation.[15]

Pakistani President Asif Zardari has said his country looks forward to a "new beginning" in bilateral relations, but repeated his admonition that Pakistan "needs no lectures on our commitment [to fighting terrorism]. This is our war." He has asked the Obama Administration to strengthen Pakistan's democracy and economic development in the interest of fighting extremism.[16] Despite Pakistani hopes that President Obama will more energetically engage diplomatic efforts to resolve the Kashmir problem, the Administration has offered no public expressions of support for such a shift. Secretary of State Clinton has recognized the dangers of rising tensions in Kashmir while also deferring calls for greater U.S. involvement there, saying the U.S. role will continue to be as it was under the previous Administration: settlement facilitation, but no mediation.[17]

The Appointment of a U.S. Special Representative

Two days after taking office, President Obama announced the appointment of former Clinton Administration diplomat Richard Holbrooke to be Special Representative to Afghanistan and Pakistan. Holbrooke's central task will be to coordinate across the entire U.S. government to achieve U.S. strategic goals in the region. Secretary of State Clinton strongly recommended such an appointment on the grounds that Afghan-Pakistani relations were troubled and required special attention from Washington.[18] In accepting the job, Holbrooke called the Pakistan situation "infinitely complex" and noted the need to coordinate what he called a "clearly chaotic foreign assistance program."[19] Prior to the announcement, there was speculation that the new U.S. President would appoint a special envoy to the region with a wider brief, perhaps to include India and even Kashmir. Some earlier reporting listed Holbrooke's title as "Special Representative for Afghanistan, Pakistan, *and related issues*" [italics added], yet this latter phrase was omitted from his official title. Upon persistent questioning, a State Department spokesman insisted that Holbrooke's mandate is "strictly" limited to dealing with "the Pakistan-Afghanistan situation."[20]

Given Holbrooke's reputation as a "bulldozer" with strong and sometimes negative views about South Asia's circumstances, his appointment has caused consternation throughout the region.21 One senior analyst—seeing "dim and dismal" prospects for Holbrooke—predicts that efforts to get Islamabad to finally shut down militant sanctuaries on Pakistani territory will be the single hardest test of both the Special Representative. Other independent analysts warn that South Asian circumstances are not amenable to increased U.S. diplomatic engagement and/or pressure, and that U.S. involvement could even backfire by breeding resentments in regional capitals. These observers urge instead a measured approach focused on the creation of a coherent and comprehensive U.S. regional strategy.22

Deteriorating Economic Circumstances[23]

Soaring inflation, along with serious food and energy shortages, has elicited considerable economic anxiety in Pakistan. Such concerns weigh heavily on the new government. In June, the Finance Ministry released its annual Economic Survey, which reported dismal economic performance, growing fiscal and current account deficits, rising external debt, dwindling foreign exchange reserves, and a depreciating currency. The country's consumer prices are at their highest level since 1975, with an inflation rate above 25%. The rupee's value hit record lows, down more than 20% against the U.S. dollar in 2008, and net international reserves have declined by more than half in only one year to around $7 billion. Two major international investor rating indices recently cut Pakistan's sovereign debt rating to "negative." Moreover, serious power shortages have led to nationwide outages, triggering protests that turned violent at times and further harmed the economy.[24]

A senior International Monetary Fund (IMF) official saw Pakistan requiring "substantial external financing" to stabilize its economy. Estimates in the fall of 2008 had Pakistan urgently requiring at least $4 billion to avoid defaulting on its balance of payments. Islamabad first looked to intergovernmental organizations such as the World Bank and to traditional close state allies such as China and Saudi Arabia. Meeting with no clear assurances, it then shifted attention to the recently-created, informal "Friends of Pakistan" grouping of countries, which met in mid- November. Yet this "Plan B" also failed to generate the desired results.[25]

As a fallback position, Pakistani leaders approached the IMF to discuss infusions of desperately sought capital, although these would come with stringent fiscal belt-tightening conditions that may damage the government's domestic political standing. Pakistan could need as much as $15 billion in international capital infusions over the next two years.[26] On November 15, the IMF reached an agreement to provide a $7.6 billion loan to Pakistan aimed at resolving the country's serious balance of payments difficulties. An IMF official later expressed confidence that Islamabad possessed a sound strategy of action to include reducing unsustainably high fiscal deficits and tightening monetary policy to reduce inflation and boost foreign exchange reserves. In January, Beijing delivered a $500 million deposit to Islamabad meant to be used only as foreign reserves and not for budgetary purposes.[27] Despite Pakistan's many serious economic difficulties, Islamabad expects the national economy to grow by up to 4% in the current fiscal year, a respectable amount driven especially by a thriving textile export industry.[28]

Increasing Islamist Militancy

Islamist extremism and militancy has been a menace to Pakistani society throughout the post- 2001 period, becoming especially prevalent in 2007 and 2008. According to the U.S. Director of National Intelligence, the loss of human life related to Islamist militancy was greater in 2007 than in the previous six years combined. The U.S. National Counterterrorism Center's most recent annual report found the incidence of terrorism in Pakistan in 2007 up by 137% over the previous year, with 1,335 terrorism-related fatalities placing the country third in the world on such a scale, after Iraq and Afghanistan. In issuing assurances that his government understands the problem, the Pakistani President claimed that Pakistan suffered more than 2,000 lives lost in more than 600 "terrorism-related incidents" in 2008.[29]

Only two suicide bombings were reported in Pakistan in all of 2002; that number grew to 59 in 2008. According to Pakistan's intelligence agency, Pakistan has overtaken Iraq as site of the world's most suicide-bombing deaths. Pakistani police have proven unable to deal with suicide attacks, given a dearth of proper training and equipment. By nearly all accounts, Pakistani law enforcement personnel are outgunned and out-financed by militants.[30]

The myriad militant groups operating in Pakistan, many of which have in the past displayed mutual animosity, may be increasing their levels of coordination and planning. Moreover, a new generation of militants is comprised of battle-hardened jihadis with fewer allegiances to religious and tribal leaders and customs.[31] One Western press report called Pakistan's Federally Administered Tribal Areas (FATA) "the most ungoverned, combustible region in the world," and an unrelenting surge in Islamist-related violence in Pakistan has some observers fearing for the stability of the civilian government in Islamabad and even the potentially total collapse of the Pakistani state.[32]

In 2008, the influence of Islamist militants appears to have grown unchecked in large parts of Pakistan beyond the FATA, bringing insecurity even to the North West Frontier Province (NWFP) capital of Peshawar, which reportedly has been in serious danger of being overrun by pro-Taliban militants.[33] Other so-called "settled areas" of Pakistan beyond the tribal regions have come under attack from pro-Taliban militants.[34] Indeed, the "Talibanization" of western Pakistan appears to be ongoing and may threaten the territorial integrity of the Pakistani state.[35] Top Islamabad government officials identify terrorism and extremism as Pakistan's most urgent problems. They vow that combating terrorism, along with addressing poverty and unemployment, will be their top priority. Opinion surveys in Pakistan have found strong support for an Islamabad government emphasis on negotiated resolutions. They also show scant support for unilateral U.S. military action on Pakistani territory.[36] As Islamist-related violence in Pakistan increases in intensity, Pakistani animosity toward U.S. policies appears to grow, as well.[37]

According to the U.S. Director of National Intelligence in early 2008,

> Pakistan's law and order problems arising from tribal and religious militancy can be effectively addressed in the long term only if police and paramilitary forces can more reliably provide justice and border security. All of these administrative reforms require effective political leadership focused on improving the capabilities of Pakistani institutions for effective governance and development of economic opportunity.[38]

For many observers, successful counterinsurgency in the FATA must look beyond military efforts and focus on improving local governance and normalizing politics there. Religion, too, is a key factor, and some analysts urge U.S. diplomacy to better engage with the regions religious parties, which could have the benefit of depoliticizing the role of religion.[39]

Multiple armed Islamist uprisings

Pakistan is the site of numerous armed insurgencies of various scales that represent an increasingly severe threat to domestic and regional security. According to the U.S. intelligence community, "Radical elements in Pakistan have the potential to undermine the country's cohesiveness." A September 2008 report by leading U.S.-based experts on Pakistan said, "Militant groups freely meet, train, and raise funds throughout Pakistan."40

Al Qaeda Presence[41]

U.S. officials remain concerned that Al Qaeda terrorists operate with impunity on Pakistani territory, and the group appears to have increased its influence among the myriad Islamist militant groups operating along the Pakistan-Afghanistan border. Numerous press reports indicate Al Qaeda has reestablished terrorist training camps in that region. Al Qaeda founder Osama Bin Laden and his lieutenant, Egyptian Islamic radical leader Ayman al-Zawahri, are believed by many to be hiding somewhere in northwestern Pakistan. In late 2007, Defense Secretary Robert Gates said, "Al Qaeda right now seems to have turned its face toward Pakistan and attacks on the Pakistani government and Pakistan people."[42] In its very first official policy statement on Pakistan, the Obama White House called the resurgence of Al Qaeda and the Taliban in western Pakistan the greatest threat to U.S. security and it expressed an intention to increase nonmilitary aid to Islamabad while holding that government accountable for security in the border region.[43]

The number of Al Qaeda suspects estimated killed or captured in Pakistan—approximately 700— has remained essentially unchanged since 2004. Some Pakistani and Western security officials see Islamabad losing its war against religious militancy and Al Qaeda forces enjoying new areas in which to operate, due in part to the Pakistan army's poor counterinsurgency capabilities and to the central government's eroded legitimacy. At an April 2008 congressional hearing on Al Qaeda, a panel of nongovernmental experts agreed that the ongoing hunt for the group's top leaders was foundering.[44] In September 2008, Pakistan's top internal security official conceded that Al Qaeda operatives moved freely in his country.[45]

The Swat Valley

Pakistan has since late 2007 faced a "neo-Taliban" insurgency in the scenic Swat Valley just 100 miles northwest of the capital, where radical Islamic cleric Maulana Fazlullah and up to 5,000 of his armed followers seek to impose *Sharia* law. Fazlullah, also known as "Maulana Radio" for his fiery (and unlicensed) FM broadcasts, moved to create a parallel government like that established by pro-Taliban militant Baitullah Mehsud in South Waziristan. Some 2,500 Frontier Corps soldiers were deployed to the Swat Valley, and the army soon took charge of the counterinsurgency effort at the request of the provincial governor, massing about 15,000 regular troops. By the close of 2007, most militant elements in the area were reported to be in retreat, and the Pakistani government claimed victory.[46] Yet, in 2008, with militants still active in Swat, government officials apparently struck a peace deal. That deal appeared to have failed by midyear, with sporadic and sometimes heavy fighting in Swat continuing throughout the year.[47]

By all accounts, Islamist insurgents only expanded their influence in Swat in 2008, and many observers today assert that the state writ has completely vanished from the scenic valley. Over the course of last year, some 70 police officers were killed by insurgents, many of them beheaded, and fully half of the region's police officers reportedly have deserted in the face of brutal Taliban assaults.[48] Aggressively pursuing their radical social agenda, pro-Taliban militants issued an edict that girls' education cease as of January 15. In response, the government ordered all private schools closed in the region. Pakistan's army chief claimed in late January that his forces "had both the will and resolve to establish the writ of government" in Swat.[49]

Pro-Taliban militants in the tribal agencies

Fighting between government security forces and religious militants also flared anew in the FATA in 2008. Shortly after former Prime Minister Benazir Bhutto's December 2007 assassination the Pakistan army undertook a major operation against militants in the South Waziristan agency assumed loyal to Baitullah Mehsud. Fierce fighting continued in that area throughout the year. According to one report, nearly half of the estimated 450,000 residents of the Mehsud territories were driven from their homes by the fighting.[50] The NWFP governor has claimed Mehsud oversees an annual budget of up to $45 million devoted to perpetuating regional militancy. Most of this amount is thought to be raised through narcotics trafficking, although pro-Taliban militants also sustain themselves by demanding fees and taxes from profitable regional businesses such as marble quarries. The apparent impunity with which Mehsud is able to act has caused serious alarm in Washington, where officials worry that his power and influence are only growing.[51] As part of their terror tactics, Taliban militants have made targeted attacks on gatherings of pro-government tribal elders.

The Tehrik-i-Taliban Pakistan (TTP) emerged as a coherent grouping in late 2007 under Baitullah Mehsud's leadership. This "Pakistani Taliban" is said to have representatives from each of Pakistan's seven tribal agencies, as well as from many of the "settled" districts abutting the FATA. There appears to be no reliable evidence that the TTP receives funding from external states. The group's principal aims are threefold: (1) to unite disparate pro-Taliban groups active in the FATA and NWFP; (2) to assist the Afghan Taliban in its conflict across the Durand Line; and (3) to establish a Taliban-style Islamic state in Pakistan and perhaps beyond. As an umbrella group, the TTP is home to tribes and sub-tribes, some with long-held mutual antagonism. It thus suffers from factionalism. Mehsud himself is believed to command some 5,000 militants. In August 2008, the Islamabad government formally banned the TTP due to its involvement in a series of suicide attacks in Pakistan. The move allowed for the freezing of all TTP bank accounts and other assets (though these are not known to exist in any official context) and for the interdiction of printed and visual propaganda materials.[52]

Militancy in western Pakistan is not coherent, and Taliban forces there are riven by deep-seated tribal rivalries that may prevent the TTP from ever becoming a truly unified force. Some analysts believe that—by pursuing sometimes contradictory military strategies in the region—the United States and Pakistan have missed a chance to exploit such divisions. According to this argument, U.S.-launched missile strikes have a unifying effect on the militants and so undermine the Pakistani strategy of driving a wedge between various Islamist factions.[53]

Conflict in Western Pakistan and the Afghan Insurgency[54]

An ongoing Taliban insurgency in Afghanistan and its connection to developments in Pakistan are matters of serious concern to U.S. policy makers. It is widely held that success in Afghanistan cannot come without the close engagement and cooperation of Pakistan, and that the key to stabilizing Afghanistan is to improve the longstanding animosity between Islamabad and Kabul.[55] In September, the Chairman of the U.S. Joint Chiefs of Staff, Adm. Mike Mullen, said he viewed the two countries as "inextricably linked in a common insurgency" and had directed that maps of the Afghan "battle space" be redrawn to include the tribal areas of western Pakistan.[56] As President-elect, Barack Obama asserted that Afghanistan cannot be "solved" without "solving Pakistan" and working more effectively with that country.[57] Numerous other senior U.S. officials—both civilian and military—share the view that Pakistan and Afghanistan are best considered as a single "problem set" in the context of U.S. interests.[58]

Most independent analysts appear to agree that, so long as Taliban forces enjoy "sanctuary" in Pakistan, their Afghan insurgency will persist. U.S. civilian and military now call for a more comprehensive strategy for fighting the war in Afghanistan, one that will encompass Pakistan's tribal regions.[59] According to the Pentagon, the existence of militant sanctuaries inside Pakistan's FATA represents "the greatest challenge to long-term security within Afghanistan." The commander of NATO forces in Afghanistan has asserted that Pakistan's western tribal regions provide the main pool for recruiting insurgents who fight in Afghanistan. Another senior U.S. military officer estimated that militant infiltration from Pakistan was accounting for about one- third of the attacks on coalition troops in Afghanistan.[60]

Afghan officials continue to accuse Pakistani officials of aiding and abetting terrorism inside Afghanistan. Pakistani officials have sought to allay Afghan leaders' fears that truces in the tribal regions would lead to more cross-border attacks, assuring them that Islamabad makes no distinction between Pakistani and Afghan interests on this issue.[61] Yet Afghan President Karzai has asserted his country's right to defend itself and "cross the border and destroy terrorist nests." He has specifically named Baitullah Mehsud and Maulana Fazlullah among the anti-Afghan militants he wishes to see neutralized. Islamabad rejected the "regrettable" comments and vowed to defend its sovereign territory.[62]

Pakistan's mixed record on battling Islamist extremism includes an ongoing apparent tolerance of Taliban elements operating from its territory.[63] The "Kandahari clique" reportedly operates not from Pakistan's tribal areas, but from populated areas in and around the Baluchistan provincial capital of Quetta. Many analysts believe that Pakistan's intelligence services know the whereabouts of these Afghan Taliban leadership elements and likely even maintain active contacts with them at some level as part of a hedge strategy in the region. Some reports indicate that elements of Pakistan's major intelligence agency and military forces aid the Taliban and other extremists forces as a matter of policy. Such support may even include providing training and fire support for Taliban offensives (see also "Questions About Pakistan's Main Intelligence Agency" below).[64] Other reports indicate that U.S. military personnel have been unable to count on the Pakistani military for battlefield support and do not trust Pakistan's Frontier Corps, whom some say are active facilitators of militant infiltration into Afghanistan. At least one senior U.S.

Senator has questioned the wisdom of providing U.S. aid to a group that is ineffective, at best, and may even be providing support to "terrorists."[65]

As pressure on Islamabad to curtail the cross-border attacks has increased, Pakistani officials more openly contend that the problem is essentially internal to Afghanistan and has its roots in the inability of the Kabul government to effectively extend its writ, and in the lack of sufficient Afghan and Western military forces to defeat the Taliban insurgents. This view is supported by some independent analyses.[66] Pakistani leaders insist that Afghan stability is a vital Pakistani interest. They ask interested partners to enhance their own efforts to control the border region by undertaking an expansion of military deployments and checkposts on the Afghan side of the border, by engaging more robust intelligence sharing, and by continuing to supply the counterinsurgency equipment requested by Pakistan. Islamabad touts the expected effectiveness of sophisticated technologies such as biometric scanners in reducing illicit cross-border movements, but analysts are pessimistic that such measures can meaningfully address militant infiltration, as such elements generally skirt border checkposts, in any case.[67]

U.S./NATO supply routes

With roughly three-quarters of supplies for U.S. troops in Afghanistan moving either through or over Pakistan, insurgents in 2008 began more focused attempts to interdict NATO supply lines, especially near the historic Khyber Pass connecting Peshawar with Jalalabad, Afghanistan. Such efforts included a March 2008 attack that left 25 fuel trucks. In November, scores of masked militants hijacked a supply convoy of 13 trucks, capturing loads of wheat along with two Humvees. Weeks later, insurgents set fire to nearly 100 trucks, destroying at least 50 cargo containers and killing several Pakistani drivers in the process. At year's end, the Pakistani military reportedly launched a major offensive in the Khyber agency aimed at securing the supply route, which was temporarily closed during the height of the fighting. Despite the Pakistani effort, sporadic interdiction attacks continue to date.[68]

After a U.S. special forces raid in the FATA in early September, Pakistani officials apparently closed the crucial Torkham highway in response. The land route was opened less than one day later, but the episode illuminated how important Pakistan's cooperation is to sustaining multilateral military efforts to the west. A Pentagon official subsequently said the U.S. military was increasing its tests of alternative supply routes.[69] In mid-December, a rally organized by one of Pakistan's leading Islamist political parties brought more than 10,000 demonstrators into the streets of Peshawar demanding that Islamabad close the supply route entirely.[70]

U.S. military officials has claimed that such attacks have a negligible effect on combat operations in Afghanistan, with only about 1% of the cargo moving from the Karachi port into Afghanistan being lost to such attacks, and with stockpiled supplies that could last 60-90 days in the event of a severing of the supply chain.[71] Nevertheless, the search for alternative supply routes continued, concentrating especially on routes from Central Asia and Russia. Moscow agreed in late 2008 to allow non-lethal NATO supplies to Afghanistan to cross Russian territory, but apparently has declined to allow passage of troops as sought by NATO. In January 2009, the Centcom commander reported that alternative routes had been secured, but it is not yet clear whether these can carry the kind of heavy traffic seen in Pakistan.[72]

Pakistani military operations

The Pakistan army has deployed upwards of 100,000 regular and paramilitary troops to western Pakistan in response to the surge in militancy there. Their militant foes appear to be employing heavy weapons in more aggressive tactics, making frontal attacks on army outposts instead of the hit-and-run skirmishes of the past. The army also has suffered from a raft of suicide bomb attacks and the kidnaping of hundreds of its soldiers. Such setbacks damage the army's morale and caused some to question the organization's loyalties and capabilities.[73] Pakistan has sent major regular army units to replace Frontier Corps soldiers in some areas near the Afghan border and has deployed elite, U.S.-trained and equipped commandos to the tribal areas.[74]

Months-long battles with militants have concentrated on three fronts: the Swat valley, and the Bajaur and South Waziristan tribal agencies. Yet the strife has affected other areas of western Pakistan. Taliban forces may also have opened a new front in the Upper Dir valley of the NWFP, where one report says a new militant "headquarters" has been established.[75] In late 2008 and early 2009, Taliban forces also spread their activities into the previously relatively peaceful Orakzai agency, the only in the FATA that does not border Afghanistan.[76] Moreover, an unprecedented January 2009 attack on a Frontier Corps outpost in the Mohmand district by some 600 Taliban militants left 46 combatants dead, including six Pakistani soldiers. The attack represented an unusual reversal in that the militants had crossed into Pakistan from Afghanistan, thus signaling increased coordination by Taliban units spanning the border.[77]

In mid-2008, Pakistani paramilitary forces had launched offensive operations against Islamist militants in the Khyber tribal agency near Peshawar, with more than 1,000 Frontier Corps troops attacking positions held by fighters loyal to tribal leader Mangal Bagh. U.S. officials were encouraged by the energetic Pakistani military action. The government reported major gains in pushing militants out of previous strongholds and, by early July, authorities were claiming to have reached a peace agreement with tribal elders.[78] In mid-July, government forces launched another offensive, this time in the Hangu region of the NWFP. By month's end, a senior Islamist commander was reported killed in ongoing fighting and the still nominally obtaining truce was teetering on the brink of failure. Some observers called these government offensives a staged drama designed to placate both a nervous Pakistani public and a Washington audience that seeks more forceful action against religious militancy.[79]

More recently, Pakistani ground troops have undertaken operations against militants in the Bajaur agency beginning in August. The ongoing battle has been called especially important as a critical test of both the Pakistani military's capabilities *and* intentions with regard to combating militancy, and it was welcomed by Defense Secretary Gates as a reflection of the new Islamabad government's willingness to fight.[80] Some 8,000 Pakistani troops are being backed by helicopter gunships and ground attack jets. The Frontier Corps' top officer has estimated that militant forces in Bajaur number about 2,000, including foreigners. Battles have included a series of engagements at the strategic tunnel Kohat tunnel, a key link in the U.S. military supply chain running from Karachi to Afghanistan.[81] The fighting apparently has attracted militants from neighboring regions and these reinforced insurgents have been able to put up surprisingly strong resistance, complete with sophisticated tactics, weapons, and communications systems, and reportedly make use of an elaborate network of tunnels in which they stockpile weapons and ammunition. Still, Pakistani military officials report having killed more than 1,500 militants in the Bajaur fighting in 2008.[82]

Fierce combat with well-entrenched militants continues to date in Baj aur, where Pakistan army commanders may have underestimated the capabilities of their opponents. Pessimistic analysts view the gains from such operations as temporary and predict that widespread militant presence in Bajaur and neighboring regions is likely to continue. Moreover, as of early 2009, the Afghan insurgency continues apace: According to one NATO commander battling the Taliban in southern Afghanistan, "The borders are wide open."[83] In late January, a jirga of more than 500 tribal elders and Islamist politicians met in the Punjabi city of Multan and issued a declaration demanding that military operations in western Pakistan be halted and peace talks commenced.[84]

The Pakistani military effort in Baj aur has included airstrikes on residential areas occupied by suspected militants who may be using civilians as human shields. The use of fixed-wing aircraft continued and reportedly has killed some women and children along with scores of militants. The strife is causing a serious humanitarian crisis. In August, the U.S. government provided emergency assistance to displaced families. The United Nations estimates that hundreds of thousands of civilians have fled from Bajaur, with about 20,000 of these moving into Afghanistan. International human rights groups have called for international assistance to both Pakistani and Afghan civilians adversely affected by the fighting. Some 300,000 refugees reportedly have fled Bajaur and are living in makeshift camps near Peshawar.[85]

Tribal militias

Autumn 2008 saw an increase in the number of *lashkars*—tribal militias—being formed in the FATA. These private armies may represent a growing popular resistance to Islamist militancy in the region, not unlike that seen in Iraq's "Sunni Awakening." A potential effort to bolster the capabilities of tribal leaders near the Afghan border would target that region's Al Qaeda elements and be similar to U.S. efforts in Iraq's Anbar province. Employing this tack in Pakistan presents new difficulties, however, including the fact that the Pakistani Taliban is not alien to the tribal regions but is, in fact, comprised of the tribals' ethnolinguistic brethren.[86] Still, with as many as 20 suspected pro-government tribals being killed by Islamist extremists every week in western Pakistan, tribal leaders may be increasingly alienated by the violence and so more receptive to cooperation with the Pakistan military.[87]

The Pakistan army reportedly backs these militias and the NWFP governor has expressed hope that they could turn the tide against Taliban insurgents. Islamabad reportedly plans to provide small arms to these anti-Taliban tribal militias, which are said to number some 14,000 men in Bajaur and another 11,000 more in neighboring Orakzai and Dir. No U.S. government funds will be involved.[88] Some reporting indicates that, to date, the lashkars have proven ineffective against better-armed and more motivated Taliban fighters. Intimidation tactics and the targeted killings of pro-government tribal leaders continue to take a toll, and Islamabad's military and political support for the tribal efforts is said to be "episodic" and "unsustained." Some analysts worry that, by employing lashkars to meet its goals in the FATA, the

Islamabad government risks sparking an all-out war in the region.[89] The militias, when conceived as small private armies, represent a form of outsourcing of security by the state and often prove unreliable as well as ineffective.[90]

Questions about Pakistan's main intelligence agency

The Inter-Services Intelligence Directorate (ISI) is Pakistan's main foreign intelligence agency. Close U.S. links with the ISI date back at least to the 1980s, when American and Pakistani intelligence officers oversaw cooperative efforts to train and supply Afghan "freedom fighters" who were battling the Soviet Army. Yet mutual mistrust has been ever-present and, in the summer of 2008, long-standing doubts about the activities and aims of the ISI compounded.[91] Some analysts label the ISI a "rogue" agency driven by Islamist ideology that can and does act beyond the operational control of its nominal administrators. Yet many observers conclude that the ISI, while sometimes willing to "push the envelope" in pursuing Pakistan's perceived regional interests, is a disciplined organization that obeys the orders of its commanders in the Pakistani military.[92] In an episode that only brought embarrassment for Pakistan's newly seated civilian government, a July effort to bring the ISI under the formal control of the Interior Ministry was reversed only hours its announcement, fueling speculation that the Pakistani military does not intend to relinquish its traditionally primary role in foreign and national security policy making. U.S. officials reportedly continue to quietly criticize the new civilian government for its alleged "lack of supervision" of the ISI.[93]

The Kabul government claims to have evidence of ISI complicity in both an April assassination attempt on Afghan President Karzai and in the July bombing of India's Kabul Embassy. The Indian government joined Kabul in issuing accusations of ISI involvement in the latter event. Islamabad counters that, despite repeated Pakistani demands, neither neighbor has provided any evidence supporting the "unsubstantiated allegations."[94] A June 2008 think-tank report on insurgency in Afghanistan included the finding that, "There is some indication that individuals within the Pakistan government—for example, within the Frontier Corps and the ISI—were involved in assisting insurgent groups" inside Afghanistan.[95]

In July 2008, a top U.S. intelligence official reportedly presented evidence to Pakistani officials that ISI agents were providing assistance to militant elements who undertake attacks in Afghanistan. Specifically mentioned was an alleged relationship between ISI agents and members of the Haqqani network believed based in FATA and named as responsible the Kabul embassy bombing. U.S. counterterrorism officials reportedly do not believe that top Pakistani military or intelligence officials have sanctioned aid to the Haqqani network, but suspect that local and retired ISI operatives are complicit.[96] Islamabad angrily rejected such reports as "baseless and malicious," but Pakistan's federal information minister did concede that some individuals within ISI "probably" remain "ideologically sympathetic to the Taliban" and act out of synch with government policy.[97]

President Bush himself was reported to have bluntly asked the visiting Pakistani Prime Minister who was controlling the ISI, and also to have expressed concern that Pakistani intelligence officers were leaking operational information to militants which could allow those elements to evade militarized efforts against them.[98] When asked about the ISI's command structure, Prime Minister Gillani assured an American audience the agency "is under the Prime Minister" and "will do only what I want them to do." The claim was met with skepticism and U.S. pressure on Islamabad to control the ISI persists.[99]

There may be apprehension in Pakistani military circles that President Zardari will seek to impose his will on the army by shuffling its leadership, a move that could bring direct confrontation with the country's security establishment. At least some elements of Pakistan's security services are said to find Zardari too compromising with the United States.[100] In September, the Islamabad government named a new ISI chief, Lt. Gen. Ahmed Shuja Pasha, who had served as director general of military operations since 2005. Pasha, said to be close with Army Chief Gen. Kayani, is identified as a professional soldier who takes the threat of Islamist extremism seriously. Although little is known about the new intelligence chief, his appointment was met with cautious optimism by the Bush Administration.[101] In November, the civilian government disbanded the ISI's political wing, which was widely suspected of manipulating domestic political outcomes over a period of decades. Foreign Minister Qureshi said the move will free the ISI to concentrate on counterterrorism efforts.[102] When asked about control over his own organization and lingering Islamist sentiments among its officers, Pasha in January 2009 said, "Many may think in a different direction ... but no one can dare to disobey a command or even do something that was not ordered."[103]

U.S.-Pakistan Counterterrorism Cooperation

Increasing Islamist militancy in Pakistan has elicited acute U.S. government attention and multiple high-level visits. Some of President Bush's top military and intelligence aides reportedly sought and, in July, won his authorization for more energetic direct U.S. military action on Pakistani soil, perhaps to include sending special forces units into the FATA. Pentagon officials are said to be increasingly frustrated by the allegedly feckless counterinsurgency efforts of the internally squabbling Islamabad government.[104] The *New York Times* reports that, since 2004, the U.S. military has used secret authority to carry out covert attacks against Al Qaeda and other militants in several countries, including Pakistan.[105] Some reports suggest that U.S. officials are frustrated by signs that the Pakistani military is slow to shift away from a conventional war strategy focused on India, and they have made clear the United States stands ready to assist Pakistan in "reorienting" its army for counterinsurgency efforts. Some U.S. military commanders in Afghanistan are reported to be deeply skeptical that Islamabad will use future U.S. military assistance for its intended purposes.[106] Adm. Mullen himself has called for a "calm" approach to building effective teamwork with the Pakistanis, saying their military leaders understand the nature of the threat.[107] Many analysts warn that allowing tensions to grow in the U.S.-Pakistan bilateral military relationship only helps Al Qaeda and other extremist groups by fueling anti-American sentiments.[108]

The explicit U.S. readiness to increase bilateral counterterrorism cooperation is described by some as being expressed to Islamabad in the form of "pressure." Former President Musharraf rejected suggestions that U.S. troops could be more effective than Pakistanis in battling Islamist militants, asserting that a direct U.S. military presence in Pakistan is neither necessary nor acceptable. Upon assuming the Pakistani presidency, Asif Zardari warned that Pakistan "will not tolerate the violation of [its] sovereignty and territorial integrity by any power in the name of combating terrorism." He, too, insisted that, with the provision of U.S. intelligence, Pakistani forces are better suited to tracking and capturing terrorists in the border region.[109] Many independent commentators warn that a U.S. policy shift toward increased military incursions on Pakistani territory is unlikely to contribute meaningfully to the stabilization of Afghanistan and could badly damage the U.S.-Pakistan relationship, perhaps even leading to a curtailment of bilateral military and intelligence cooperation, which themselves may be the key to long-term success in the fight against Pashtun and other insurgents.[110]

The United States has built a new coordination and intelligence-sharing centers on the Afghan side of the shared border near the Khyber Pass. Another such site is under construction and four more reportedly are being considered. Hundreds of millions of dollars of U.S. aid is slated to go toward training and equipping more than 8,000 paramilitary Frontier Corps (FC) troops by mid-2010; some two dozen U.S. trainers began work in October. The Chairman of the Senate Armed Services Committee, Senator Carl Levin, who returned from a May 2008 trip to the region with serious doubts about the intentions of the Pakistani government, may seek to condition future FC aid funds on Pakistan's demonstrated commitment to halting cross-border infiltration. Several fellow Senators are said to support such conditionality.[111]

In late 2008, U.S. and Pakistani military forces reportedly were improving their coordination and intelligence sharing efforts, perhaps reflecting a greater willingness by Pakistan to combat militants on its side of the border with Afghanistan. Pakistani officers are now allowed to view video feeds from unmanned American drones and to access U.S. intercepts of militants' communications.[112] Vice President Biden returned from a trip to the region and reported seeing "a great deal more cooperation" between the U.S. and Pakistani militaries in the border area. ISAF Commander U.S. Gen. David McKiernan has lauded improved tactical-level coordination that has allowed for joint operations along the border.[113]

Yet some reporting is more discouraging and suggests that progress on cooperation and coordination remains hampered by language barriers, tensions between Pakistani and Afghan officials, and pervasive mistrust among the U.S., Pakistani, and Afghan militaries. For example, the $3 million Border Coordination Center (BCC) at Torkham opened in March 2008, but operations were delayed by logistical problems and political wrangling. During the period, the number of insurgent attacks in the region increased sharply, reportedly delaying construction of a second BCC to the southeast.[114]

U.S. military incursions into Pakistan—especially those involving ground troops—put tremendous pressure on both Islamabad's civilian government and on the country's military. Some observers fear the attacks will undermine both the civilian government, whose legitimacy depends in part on a perception that it is serving the national interest, as well as the military, which comes under pressure to protect not only Pakistani territory, but also its own reputation.[115] Others see such actions as potentially leading to the curtailment of Pakistan's military cooperation with the United States, something Islamabad's opposition parliamentarians have already threatened.[116] Moreover, Pakistan's Ambassador to the United States warns that such attacks are counterproductive to the extent that they turn Pakistani public opinion against the counterterrorism effort. Many Pakistani editorialists echo this concern, with one offering that, "If you bomb a moderate sensibility often enough it has a tendency to lose its sense of objectivity and to feel driven in the direction of extremism."[117] One former Bush State Department official assesses that unilateral U.S. military activity on Pakistani territory can be "profoundly counterproductive" by empowering Pakistani elements who already distrust U.S. intentions.[118] Even President Bush's Deputy Secretary of State conceded that, "Unilateral actions are probably not a durable or a viable solution over a prolonged period of time" and suggested that trilateral cooperation among the United States, Pakistan, and Afghanistan was the best way forward.[119]

Cross-border coordination and U.S. military action

American commanders in Afghanistan reportedly have sought greater leeway to attack indigenous Pakistani militants on Pakistani soil. Permission for U.S.-led attacks on forces under the command of militant leaders such as Sirajuddin Haqqani and Baitullah Mehsud is not overtly forthcoming to date.[120] By one account, top Bush Administration officials in late 2007 drafted a secret plan to facilitate U.S. Special Operations force missions in western Pakistan, a plan that the U.S. President may have approved in July 2008. Pakistan's army chief strongly denied that his country had agreed to any new rules of engagement that would permit U.S. ground forces to operate inside Pakistan. As part of the Joint Statement issued following a September 2008 session of the U.S.-Pakistan Strategic Dialogue, the United States reiterated "support for Pakistan's sovereignty, independence, unity, and territorial integrity."[121]

U.S.-led coalition forces at times come under artillery fire launched on the Pakistani side of the border. Mid-2008 reports of a major buildup of U.S.-led coalition forces in eastern Afghanistan triggered alarm in Pakistan, where fears of a "foreign invasion" are exacerbated by cross-border military action. According to a NATO spokesman, "There is no planning for, no mandate for, an incursion of NATO troops into Pakistan."[122] Airstrikes and rumors of potential U.S. ground incursions "seriously undermine" the Pakistani people's support for the Islamabad government, according to the NWFP governor.[123] There is in Pakistan no shortage of conspiracy theorists, some of whom are convinced that the true intent of U.S. policy is to dismantle the world's only Muslim state with nuclear weapons.[124]

June frontier corps deaths

In June 2008, a unit of Pakistani paramilitary soldiers was caught up in a firefight between Taliban militants and U.S.-led coalition forces at the border Pakistan-Afghanistan border in the Mohmand tribal agency. U.S. air assets, apparently targeting fleeing insurgents, delivered 12 gravity bombs on Pakistani territory and killed 11 Frontier Corps soldiers. Islamabad strongly condemned the airstrike, calling it "unprovoked" and "a gross violation of the international border" that "tends to undermine the very basis of our cooperation." A Pakistani military statement called the airstrike "cowardly," and some in Pakistan believe the country's troops were intentionally targeted. The Bush Administration expressed regret for the deaths of Pakistani soldiers.[125] The findings of separate investigations reportedly were incompatible, with U.S. analysts claiming the border post in question was erroneously omitted from an American database used to prevent accidental attacks on friendly forces, a claim was rejected by the Pakistani military.[126] The incident served to inflame already sensitive bilateral ties.[127]

September U.S. special forces raid

In September 2008, U.S. special forces troops apparently staged a helicopter raid in the South Waziristan village of Angoor Adda, where at least 20 people were reported killed, women and children among them. The Pakistani government strongly condemned the "completely unprovoked act of killing" and lodged formal protests with the U.S. Embassy for the "gross violation of Pakistan's territory" and "grave provocation." Both chambers of the Pakistani Parliament issued unanimous resolutions strongly condemning the "cowardly" attack. The U.S. government did not comment on the reports.[128] In a strongly-worded statement, Army Chief Gen. Kayani said, "The sovereignty and territorial integrity of the country will be defended at all cost and no external force is allowed to conduct operations inside Pakistan.... There is no question of any agreement or understanding with the Coalition Forces whereby they are allowed to conduct operations on our side of the border." According to Pakistan's national security advisor, the incursion had a "double negative effect" by eliciting greater scrutiny on and opposition to aerial attacks by pilotless U.S. drones, which he called counterproductive "spoilers."[129] Plans for further U.S. ground incursions reportedly were suspended to allow the Pakistani military to press its own attacks, although some observers say the Pentagon had underestimated the strength of the Pakistani response to cross-border raids. The backlash may have caused U.S. officials to focus only on an intensified Predator missile strike campaign.[130]

Aerial drone attacks

Missile strikes in Pakistan launched by armed, unmanned American Predator aircraft have been a controversial, but sometimes effective tactic against Islamist militants in remote regions of western Pakistan. Pakistani press reports suggest that such drones "violate Pakistani airspace" on a daily basis. Three Predators are said to be deployed at a secret Pakistani airbase and can be launched without specific permission from the Islamabad government (Pakistan officially denies the existence of any such bases).[131] Predator attacks have killed a reported 263 people, most of them alleged militants, in at least 30 separate strikes since August 2008.[132] The Centcom Commander Gen. Petraeus claims that such strikes in western Pakistan are "extremely important" and have killed at least three top extremist leaders in that region.[133]

By some accounts, U.S. officials reached a quiet January 2008 understanding with then-President Musharraf to allow for increased employment of U.S. aerial surveillance and Predator strikes on Pakistani territory.[134] Musharraf's successor, President Zardari, may even have struck a secret accord with U.S. officials involving better bilateral coordination for Predator attacks and a jointly approved target list. Reports citing unnamed senior officials from both countries have claimed that a tacit agreement on drone attacks was reached in September 2008; these reports are officially denied by Islamabad. Nevertheless, Secretary of Defense Gates has assured Congress that the U.S. intent to continue with such strikes has been conveyed to the Pakistani government.[135] Neither Washington nor Islamabad offers official confirmation of Predator strikes on Pakistani territory. Pentagon officials eager to increase the use of armed drones in Pakistan reportedly meet resistance from State Department diplomats who fear that Pakistani resentments built up in response to sovereignty violations and to the deaths of civilians are harmful to U.S. interests, outweighing potential gains.

Officially, Pakistan's Foreign Ministry calls Predator attacks "destabilizing" that are "helping the terrorists." Strident Pakistani government reaction has included summoning the U.S. Ambassador to lodge a strong protest, and condemnation of missile attacks that Islamabad believes "undermine public support for the government's counterterrorism efforts" and should be "stopped immediately." During his first visit to Pakistan as Centcom chief in early November, Gen. Petraeus reportedly was met with a single overriding message from Pakistani interlocutors: cross- border U.S. military strikes in the FATA are counterproductive. Pakistan's defense minister warned Gen. Petraeus that the strikes were creating "bad blood" and contribute to anti-American outrage among ordinary Pakistanis.[136]

A flurry of suspected Predator drone attacks on Pakistani territory in the latter months of 2008 suggested a shift in tactics in the effort to neutralize Al Qaeda and other Islamist militants in the border region. Analysts see the increasing number and effectiveness of these attacks as having forced Al Qaeda members to keep an especially low profile, thus hampering their ability to operate. At the same time, complaints abound that such strikes provide Taliban forces with a rallying cry and detract from Islamabad's efforts to characterize counterinsurgency operations as indigenous, especially when civilians are harmed.[137] The apparently increasing accuracy of such attacks has triggered a redoubled scramble by Taliban forces to weed out "U.S. spies" suspected of providing the requisite intelligence.[138]

In mid-November, the first suspected Predator strike beyond the FATA was recorded when missiles hit a village in the Bannu district—well inside Pakistan's "settled areas"—and five foreign militants were reported killed. This attack spurred Islamabad to issue a strong protest to the U.S. Ambassador, and Pakistan's army chief called for an end to such strikes.[139] Yet, only two days later, fugitive British militant Rashid Rauf was reported killed in a missile strike in North Waziristan. Pakistani military officials then responded by issuing thinly-veiled threats to shoot down any American drones flying over Pakistani territory.[140] Yet no such efforts are known to have been undertaken and December saw at least four more Predator strikes on FATA targets leaving a reported 18 people dead. A January 1 missile strike reportedly killed two senior Al Qaeda fugitives, both Kenyan nationals believed to have perpetrated the 1998 bombings of U.S. embassies in East Africa, along with the September bombing of the Islamabad Marriott.[141]

President Zardari called on then-President-Elect Obama to re-assess the Bush Administration policy of employing aerial attacks on Pakistani territory. Yet dual Predator strikes apparently took place just days after President Obama took office: Up to 20 people, including five foreign militants, were killed in January 23 strikes on targets in both North and South Waziristan. Some accounts had President Obama personally approving of the strikes. Islamabad again expressed its sense that such attacks are counterproductive in the effort to combat militancy.[142]

The Mumbai Terrorist Attack and Deteriorated Relations with India[143]

Pre-November 26 Engagement

Among the top goals of Indian officials in 2008 was gauging the new civilian Pakistani government's commitment to the bilateral peace process. Within this modest context, the outcome of February national elections was viewed as generally positive. However, ensuing months saw a marked deterioration of India-Pakistan relations. In May, India accused Pakistan of committing multiple cease-fire and territorial violations along the Kashmiri Line of Control (LOC). Reported violations continued and Indian officials suspect the Pakistani military was renewing its alleged practice of providing cover fire for militant infiltrations into Indian Kashmir.[144] June visits to Islamabad by the Indian foreign minister and later by Foreign Minister Qureshi to New Delhi were cordial and appeared to get the peace process back on track, but produced no new initiatives. Then, on July 7, a suicide car bomb killed 58 people, including 4 Indian nationals, at the Indian Embassy in Kabul, Afghanistan. Afghan and Indian officials claimed that Pakistan's intelligence agency was complicit, a charge later echoed by Washington.[145]

Later in July, Pakistan's foreign secretary met with his Indian counterpart in New Delhi to launch the fifth round of the bilateral Composite Dialogue. Following the meeting, the Indian diplomat warned that recent events—culminating in the embassy bombing—had brought the peace process "under stress." Blunt language again followed another high-level meeting, when the same Indian official suggested that Pakistan-India relations were at a four-year low ebb.[146] Along with the Kabul Embassy bombing, Indians widely suspected Pakistani complicity in July terrorist attacks inside India, and India's Prime Minister has warned that such terrorism could bring the bilateral peace process to a halt. Moreover, New Delhi's progress in an initiative that would allow India to purchase nuclear materials and technologies on the international market spurred Islamabad to warn of a potential new nuclear arms race on the Asian subcontinent.[147]

Renewed violence in India's Jammu and Kashmir state in August further exacerbated bilateral tensions. When the Pakistani Senate passed a resolution on the increasingly incendiary situation, an Indian official called the move "gross interference" in India's internal affairs. The exchange was soon repeated when the Foreign Minister Qureshi decried "excessive and unwarranted use of force" in Kashmir by the Indian government, a charge rejected as unhelpful by New Delhi. The Islamabad government conveyed "deep concern" at reports of perceived human rights violations in Indian Kashmir.[148] Later in August, a senior Indian official expressed worry at the possibly imminent removal from office of Pakistani President Musharraf, saying such a development would "leave radical extremist outfits with freedom to do what they like" in the region.[149]

Still, senior government officials in both capitals sought to press ahead with engagement. The new Pakistani President met with the Indian prime Minister in New York City in September, where the two leaders formally stated their intent to restart the waning peace process by scheduling the fifth round of composite dialogue talks.[150] In October, the Pakistani national security advisor was in New Delhi for meetings with top Indian officials. He and his Indian counterpart had "very cordial" and "most productive" talks on matters of mutual concern. Yet, within days, Indian officials were again accusing Pakistan of violating thc Kashmir cease-fire after five suspected separatist militants were killed as they tried to cross the LOC into Indian Kashmir, the third reported infiltration attempt in an eight-day period. Meanwhile, the Islamabad government continued to criticize New Delhi's Kashmir policies, calling the summer uprising in Indian Kashmir "entirely indigenous" and urging India to "restrain its security forces" and "bring the atrocities against Kashmiris to an end."[151]

In late November, a fifth round of Home/Interior Secretary-level talks on terrorism and drug trafficking was held in Islamabad and, mere hours before the November 26 Mumbai terrorist attacks began, Foreign Minister Qureshi was in New Delhi to review progress in the latest composite dialogue round, which Indian leaders expected to be "productive and fruitful." Thus, on the brink of yet another serious derailing of the peace process caused by a major terrorist attack, many observers were sanguine about the outlook for improving relations.[152]

Terrorism in Mumbai and Islamabad's response[153]

On the evening of November 26, a number of well-trained militants came ashore from the Arabian Sea on small boats and attacked numerous high-profile targets in Mumbai, India, with automatic weapons and explosives. By the time the episode ended some 62 hours later, about 165 people, along with nine terrorists, had been killed and hundreds more injured. Among the multiple sites attacked in the peninsular city known as India's business and entertainment capital were two luxury hotels—the Taj Mahal Palace and the Oberoi-Trident—along with the main railway terminal, a Jewish cultural center, a café frequented by foreigners, a cinema house, and two hospitals. Six

American citizens were among the 26 foreigners reported dead. Indian officials concluded that the attackers numbered only ten, one of whom was captured and later confirmed to be a Pakistani national.

The audacious, days-long attack on India's most populous city deeply affected the Indian people and their government. Because the attackers appear to have come from, and received training and equipment in, neighboring Pakistan, the episode has led to renewed bilateral tensions. In the U.S. Congress, H.Res. 1532, agreed to by unanimous consent on December 10, condemned the attacks, offered condolences and support to the people and government of India, and expressed U.S. congressional desire to improve coordination between the United States and India to combat terrorism and advance international security. The resolution also called upon the Pakistani government to cooperate fully with India in bringing the culprits to justice and to prevent Pakistan's territory from "serving as a safe-haven and training ground for terrorists."[154]

The investigation into the attacks remains incomplete, but press reporting, statements from U.S. and Indian authorities, and a "dossier" of purported evidence compiled by New Delhi strongly suggest that all of the attackers came to India from neighboring Pakistan, and that the perpetrators likely were members and acting under the orchestration of the Pakistan-based Lashkar-e-Taiba (LeT) terrorist group. The LeT—originally a Kashmiri-separatist-oriented militant organization that later developed broader jihadi aspirations and that has links to Al Qaeda—is widely believed to have past ties with Pakistan's military and intelligence services. By some accounts, these links are ongoing, leading to suspicions, but no known evidence, of involvement in the attack by Pakistani state elements.

Many observers saw the Mumbai attack as presenting a "moment of truth" for the civilian government in Islamabad, one in which both their mettle and sincerity would be t]ested.[155] The attacks brought sharp attention to the ongoing problem of Islamism terrorism that emanates from Pakistan. Pakistani President Zardari faces the difficult task of avoiding open conflict with India while at the same time not alienating Pakistan's powerful military and intelligence services. Some analysts believe this balancing act may be doomed.[156] The U.N. Secretary-General and the British foreign secretary are among the world figures who have pressed Islamabad to promptly and fully cooperate with India and investigate the attack.[157]

Over the course of December, Pakistani officials slowly began to acknowledge evidence that the attack had links to Pakistani soil and nationals. By mid-January, they were declaring that the entire Pakistan-based leadership of LeT, a total of 124 people, was in custody. Later they reported that all assets and property of the Jamaat-ud-Dawa (JuD)—a nominally charitable organization that is identified as a continuation of the LeT with a new name—were under Punjabi government control.[158] In early January, Assistant Secretary of State Richard Boucher expressed approval of the steps taken by Islamabad to date while also asserting that there was "a long way to go" in efforts to eliminate militant Islamist threat from Pakistani soil.[159] In early February, senior Indian officials were again intimating that the ISI had close links with the perpetrators of the Mumbai attack. Islamabad called the accusation "yet another manifestation of undisguised hostility and global smear campaign being conducted by India against Pakistan."[160] Leaks prior to Pakistan's official response to the Indian "dossier" suggested that Islamabad was set to conclude that the attack was planned in a third-country, perhaps Bangladesh. However, on February 9, Pakistani officials made moves toward filing formal charges in a Pakistani court, even as they insisted that further evidence would be required for successful prosecution.[161]

Fallout for bilateral relations

The Islamabad government strongly condemned the Mumbai terrorism and offered New Delhi its full cooperation with the ongoing investigation, but mutual acrimony clouds such an effort, and the attacks have brought into question the viability of a nearly five-year-old bilateral peace process between India and Pakistan, which New Delhi current says is in a "pause." In the face of domestic pressure from their respective publics, the leadership of both India and Pakistan have visibly sought to keep the situation from escalating. Yet political posturing could yet polarize the situation and reverse years of increasingly positive bilateral interactions.[162] New Delhi welcomed Islamabad's December crackdown while also pressing Pakistan to "shut down" the LeT entirely, along with the JuD. In December, in response to a formal Indian request, the U.N. Security Council sanctioned the JuD for its alleged links to terrorism.

Tensions remained high throughout December, with reports of military activity on both sides of the shared border exacerbating the sometimes fraught rhetoric of national leaders.[163] Yet Indian leaders shied from explicit saber-rattling and many analysts have concluded that circumstances present New Delhi with few viable options other than pursuing a diplomatic offensive against Islamabad. In this effort, India has won considerable international support, but Islamabad has had some success in obfuscating the issue with troop movements away from the Afghan border and by protesting the threat of

Indian military retaliation.[164] In early January, the ISI chief stated flatly that there would not be a war with India as a result of the Mumbai attack, saying, "We may be crazy in Pakistan, but we are not completely out of our minds. We know full well that terror is our enemy, not India."[165]

The Indian government has maintained that the attackers not only collaborated and came from Pakistani territory, but that official Pakistani elements are almost certainly complicit. On January 5, New Delhi released a "dossier" of what it called evidence linking the Mumbai attackers to Pakistan; copies of this document were sent to the U.S., Pakistani, and other governments. Among the evidence was information gained through interrogation of the sole captured gunman, along with telephone transcripts, details on weapons and other captured equipment, and records from GPS instruments and satellite phones. In releasing the material, India's foreign secretary said it "beggared the imagination" to think that the perpetrators could act without the knowledge of Pakistani establishment elements, and he asserted that Pakistan was obligated to extradite the "criminals" on Pakistani soil. Prime Minister Singh himself said, "There is enough evidence to show that, given the sophistication and military precision of the attack, it must have had the support of some official agencies in Pakistan."[166]

Islamabad rejects such "unfortunate allegations" and criticizes New Delhi for "ratcheting up tensions" with "hostile propaganda." It termed the dossier's contents as "information" rather than "evidence."[167] Two days after the dossier's release Islamabad did, however, issue a first-ever public admission that the captured gunman was, in fact, a Pakistani national.

Indian leaders have at times expressed displeasure with a perceived lack of sufficient diplomatic pressure on Pakistan from the U.S. and other Western governments.[168] In their efforts to maintain diplomatic pressure on Islamabad, top Indian officials continued to issue sometimes harsh rhetoric. For example, in January, India's defense minister voiced long-standing doubts that Islamabad's leaders were taking meaningful action against anti-India militants in Pakistan, saying he saw no noticeable change in their attitude.[169] The Indian external affairs minister later said the Mumbai attack "put a very large question mark over the achievements of the composite dialogue process" and lamented what he called "the absence of a sincere and transparent position on terrorism" in Islamabad, saying this has "significantly eroded" popular support for the peace process among Indians.[170] The Indian Prime Minister himself has used strong and direct language:

> During the past year, we faced a severe challenge from terrorist groups operating from outside our country. Many of them act in association with hostile intelligence agencies in these countries. ... Terrorism ... is largely sponsored from outside our country, mainly Pakistan, which has utilized terrorism as an instrument of state policy.[171]

In mid-January, New Delhi took concrete action by canceling previously scheduled talks on the Sir Creek dispute with Pakistan.[172]

The Pakistani position is captured in a mid-January statement from its Foreign Ministry:

> India has placed a "pause" on the Composite Dialogue. Pakistan believes that sustained engagement and dialogue is necessary to allay each other's concerns. Breakdown of dialogue only works to the advantage of the terrorists. Conflict, confrontation and tensions is exactly what the terrorists want. We should not walk into their trap. It is important to show statesmanship.[173]

At the time of this writing, Islamabad is vowing to soon release the preliminary findings of its own investigation. Some press reports indicate that these findings include what would be a controversial assertion that the attack was planned outside of Pakistan.[174]

Implications for U.S. Interests

U.S. regional policy focuses foremost on fostering stability and precluding open conflict between two nuclear-armed powers; neutralizing the threat posed by religious extremists; democratization; and economic development. The Bush Administration had responded to the Mumbai attacks by reaffirming its commitment to close and supportive relations with India. Given the perspective of senior Obama Administration officials and top U.S. military commanders that success in efforts to stabilize Afghanistan may require an easing of India-Pakistan tensions, fallout from the Mumbai terrorist attacks has further complicated U.S. policy in South Asia. In a stark example of the sensitive dynamics involved, in December an unnamed senior Pakistani security official reportedly said Pakistan would respond to any Indian military mobilization along their shared border by withdrawing "all troops" from its border with Afghanistan and redeploying them along the frontier with India, as was done during the 2002 India-Pakistan crisis. Such a move by Pakistan would almost certainly derail militarized efforts to combat Islamist militancy in the Pakistan-Afghanistan border region.

Selected Commentary on U.S. Policy Options

Numerous observers are identifying Pakistan as being among the most important foreign policy issues facing President Obama. In addressing the several policy dilemmas posed by Pakistan, most analyses urge a greater U.S. emphasis on diplomacy and development aid; many include a corresponding call for de-emphasizing strictly militarized approaches to regional issues. Some notable recent commentary includes:

- *A New Course for Pakistan*, from the Center for Strategic and International Studies, bases its recommendations for U.S. policy on the findings of more than 200 personal interviews in Pakistan during April 2008. In concluding that Pakistanis broadly recognized early 2008 as a critical moment in the country's history, the authors endorse a more strategic U.S. approach to Pakistan that would include decreasing reliance on the Pakistani military. They urge a closer U.S. focus on strengthening rule of law and governance in Pakistan, as well as on stabilizing that country's economy and ensuring security both along the Pakistan- Afghanistan border and across the country.[175]
- The Pakistan Policy Working Group, comprised of 13 Washington-based experts, released a major report on the future of U.S.-Pakistan relations, which argues that, "Pakistan may be the single greatest challenge facing the next American President." The report offers a series of key recommendations for U.S. policy, including exhibiting patience with Islamabad's new civilian leadership while working to stabilize their government with economic aid and diplomacy.[176]
- In a late 2008 *Foreign Affairs* article, two senior regional analysts warn that neither adding more U.S. and Western troops in Afghanistan nor increasing cross- border attacks into Pakistan is likely to improve the regional security situation. Instead, they argue for political and diplomatic initiatives that would distinguish between local militants and global jihadists such as Al Qaeda, offer inclusion to a wide array of reconcilable insurgent elements in both Afghanistan and Pakistan, and include a major development initiative to boost living standards there. They view a U.S. policy of "pressuring"

Pakistan to be inherently flawed in the absence of efforts to address Islamabad's fundamental sources of insecurity.[177]

- One Carnegie Endowment-based analyst offered the next U.S. presidential administration a five-point strategy, urging it to: (1) strengthen Islamabad's civilian government so as to consolidate democracy and convey respect for the wishes of the Pakistani people; (2) invest in improving Pakistan's human capital and support its civil society with a focus on education and health services; (3) help Pakistan in its struggle against terrorism and radicalism with security assistance that improves counterinsurgency capabilities; (4) encourage reconciliation between Pakistan and India; and (5) foster South Asian economic integration.[178]
- *Partnership for Progress*, from the Center for American Progress, reviewed the challenges and new opportunities presented by Pakistan, and recommended pursuit of U.S. policies that recognize the regional aspects of Pakistan's security orientation; better integrate international support; move beyond a narrow focus on military and intelligence cooperation; encourage democratization and civilian governance oversight in Islamabad; enhance transparency and accountability in U.S. assistance efforts; reform U.S. national security institutions so as to strengthen non-military tools; and create a long-term and proactive engagement with Pakistan.[179]
- A 2009 report on the FATA from a noted Pakistani specialist asserts a need for long-term U.S. engagement with Pakistan and its people, "shifting from a transactional relationship to one built on strategic considerations and respect for Pakistan's political and development needs." It offers U.S. policy makers near- and medium-term recommendations for dealing with militancy in the FATA, including defining an exit strategy from Afghanistan and accelerating funding for economic development in western Pakistan. For the U.S. military, it urges a rebuilding of trust with Pakistani counterparts, increased provision of helicopters and other equipment for counterinsurgency operations, and the establishment of tripartite training and exercises with Afghan, Pakistani, and U.S. forces, among others.[180]

Setting and Regional Relations

Historical Setting

The long and checkered Pakistan-U.S. relationship has its roots in the Cold War and South Asia regional politics of the 1950s. U.S. concerns about Soviet expansionism and Pakistan's desire for security assistance against a perceived threat from India prompted the two countries to negotiate a mutual defense assistance agreement in 1954. By 1955, Pakistan had further aligned itself with the West by joining two regional defense pacts, the South East Asia Treaty Organization and the Central Treaty Organization (or "Baghdad Pact"). As a result of these alliances, Islamabad received nearly $2 billion in U.S. assistance from 1953 to 1961, one-quarter of this in military aid, making Pakistan one of America's most important security assistance partners of the period. President Dwight D. Eisenhower famously called Pakistan America's "most allied ally in Asia." Differing expectations of the security relationship long bedeviled bilateral ties, however. During and immediately after the Indo-Pakistani wars of 1965 and 1971, the United States suspended military assistance to both sides, resulting in a cooling of the Pakistan-U.S. relationship and a perception among many in Pakistan that the United States was not a reliable ally.

In the mid-1970s, new strains arose over Pakistan's efforts to respond to India's 1974 underground nuclear test by seeking its own nuclear weapons capability. U.S. aid was suspended by President Jimmy Carter in 1979 in response to Pakistan's covert construction of a uranium enrichment facility. However, following the Soviet invasion of Afghanistan later that year, Pakistan again was viewed as a frontline ally in the effort to block Soviet expansionism. In 1981, the Reagan Administration pledged for Islamabad a five-year, $3.2 billion aid package. Pakistan became a key transit country for arms supplies to the Afghan resistance, as well as home for millions of Afghan refugees, many of whom have yet to return.

Despite this renewal of U.S. aid and close security ties, many in Congress remained troubled by Pakistan's nuclear weapons program. In 1985, Section 620E(e) (the Pressler amendment) was added to the Foreign Assistance Act, requiring the President to certify to Congress that Pakistan does not possess a nuclear explosive device during the fiscal year for which aid is to be provided. With the Soviet withdrawal from Afghanistan, Pakistan's nuclear activities again came under intensive U.S. scrutiny and, in 1990, President George H.W.

Bush again suspended aid to Pakistan. Under the provisions of the Pressler amendment, most bilateral economic and all military aid ended, and deliveries of major military equipment ceased. In 1992, Congress partially relaxed the scope of sanctions to allow for food assistance and continuing support for nongovernmental organizations. Among the notable results of the aid cutoff was the nondelivery of F-16 fighter aircraft purchased by Pakistan in 1989. Nine years later, the United States agreed to compensate Pakistan with a $325 million cash payment and $140 million worth of surplus wheat and soy, but the episode engendered lingering Pakistani resentments.

U.S. disengagement from Pakistan (and Afghanistan) after 1990 had serious and lasting effects on Pakistani perceptions. Former Pakistani Army Chief and President Musharraf himself repeatedly voiced a narrative in which Pakistan joined the United States to "wage a jihad" in Afghanistan in the 1980s, only to see "disaster" follow when the "military victory was bungled up" and the United States then left the region "abandoned totally." When combined with ensuing sanctions on U.S. aid, this left many Pakistanis with the sense they had been "used and ditched."[181] The succeeding Pakistani President, Asif Zardari, has taken up a similar narrative, writing in January 2009 that, "Frankly, the abandonment of Afghanistan and Pakistan after the defeat of the Soviets in Afghanistan in the 1980s set the stage for the era of terrorism that we are enduring."[182]

During the 1990s, with U.S. attention shifted away from the region, Islamabad further consolidated its nuclear weapons capability, fanned the flames of a growing separatist insurgency in neighboring Indian-controlled Kashmir, and nurtured the Taliban movement in Afghanistan, where the radical Islamist group took control of Kabul in 1996. After this more than one decade of alienation, U.S. relations with Pakistan were once again transformed in dramatic fashion, this time by the September 2001 terrorist attacks on the United States and the ensuing enlistment of Pakistan as a pivotal ally in U.S.-led counterterrorism efforts. A small trickle of foreign assistance to Pakistan again became a prodigious flow and, in a sign of renewed U.S. recognition of the country's importance, President George W. Bush designated Pakistan as a major non-NATO ally of the United States in 2004. A Congressional Pakistan Caucus was formed the same year to facilitate dialogue among Pakistani-Americans and their political representatives in Congress, and to improve and strengthen bilateral relations between Pakistan and the United States.

Today, U.S. diplomatic engagement with Pakistan continues to be deep and multifaceted. Then- President Bush traveled to Pakistan in March 2006 for the first such presidential visit in six years, and numerous high-level governmental meetings ensued. During his visit, President Bush and President Musharraf issued a Joint Statement on the U.S.-Pakistan "strategic partnership" calling for a "strategic dialogue" and "significant expansion" of bilateral economic ties.[183] As President- elect, Barack Obama stated his intention to create an "effective, strategic partnership with Pakistan" that will "make both countries safer."[184]

Political Setting[185]

Pakistan's political history is a troubled one, marked by tripartite power struggles among presidents, prime ministers, and army chiefs. Military regimes have ruled Pakistan for more than half of its 61 years of existence, interspersed with periods of generally weak civilian governance.[186] From 1988 to 1999, Islamabad had democratically elected governments, and the army appeared to have moved from its traditional role of "kingmaker" to one of power broker. Benazir Bhutto (leader of the Pakistan People's Party) and Nawaz Sharif (leader of the Pakistan Muslim League) each served twice as prime minister during this period. The Bhutto government was dismissed on charges of corruption and nepotism in 1996, and Sharif won a landslide victory in ensuing elections, which were judged generally free and fair by international observers. Sharif moved quickly to bolster his powers by curtailing those of the president and judiciary, and he emerged as one of Pakistan's strongest-ever elected leaders. Critics accused him of intimidating the opposition and the press (in fact, many observers hold Pakistan's civilian political leaders at least as responsible as the army for the anemic state of the country's governance institutions).

Musharraf's 1999 Coup d'Etat

In October 1999, in proximate response to Prime Minister Sharif's attempt to remove him, Chief of Army Staff Gen. Pervez Musharraf overthrew the government, dismissed the National Assembly, and appointed himself "chief executive." In the wake of this military overthrow of the elected government, Islamabad faced considerable international opprobrium and was subjected to automatic coup-related U.S. sanctions under Section 508 of the annual foreign assistance appropriations act (Pakistan was already under nuclear-related U.S. sanctions). Musharraf later assumed the title of president following a controversial 2002 referendum. National elections were held in October of that year, as ordered by the Supreme Court. A new civilian government was seated—Prime Minister M.Z. Jamali was replaced with Musharraf ally Shaukat Aziz in mid2005—but it remained weak. In contravention of democratic norms, Musharraf continued to hold the dual offices of president *and* army chief. Many figures across the spectrum of Pakistani society at first welcomed Musharraf, or at least were willing to give him the benefit of the doubt, as a potential reformer who would curtail corruption and the influence of religious extremists. Yet his domestic popularity suffered following numerous indications that, as with Pakistan's previous president-generals, expanding his own power and that of the military would be his central goal.

In September 2007, President Musharraf promoted Gen. Ashfaq Pervez Kayani, a highly- regarded, ostensibly pro-Western figure, to the position of Vice Chief of Army Staff. Kayani then succeeded Musharraf in the powerful role of army chief upon Musharraf's subsequent resignation from the army. In assuming his new office, Kayani vowed to press ahead with Pakistan army efforts to root out extremists from western Pakistan. He appeared to become a new locus of U.S. hopes for Pakistani democratization, with U.S. officials reportedly seeing an opportunity for him to manage a peaceful transition to civilian rule while maintaining a disinterest in pursuing his own political power.[187]

The 2008 democratic revival

President Bush had predicted that Pakistan's long-anticipated polls, originally slated for late 2007, would be "an important test of Pakistan's commitment to democratic reform" and, during his 2006 visit to Islamabad, said President Musharraf understood the elections "need to be open and honest." Secretary of State Rice repeated the admonition in late 2007, saying the expected polls would be "a real test" of the Islamabad government's commitment to democratization and that the U.S. government was "pressing that case very hard." The then-Chairman of the Senate Foreign Relations Committee, Senator Joe Biden, later warned Musharraf there would be "consequences" if slated elections were not fair and open, saying U.S. aid levels could be decreased.[188] Musharraf himself stood for—and controversially won—reelection as president in October 2007 (under the Pakistani system, the president is indirectly elected by an Electoral College comprised of the membership of all national and provincial legislatures).

In February 2008, Pakistan held elections to seat a new National Assembly and all four provincial assemblies. Analysts had foreseen a process entailing rampant political-related violence and electoral rigging in favor of the incumbent, Musharraf-friendly Pakistan Muslim League-Q (PML-Q) faction. Despite weeks of bloodshed leading up to the polls, the day itself was surprisingly calm. Moreover, fears of large-scale rigging were proven unfounded, as the PML-Q was swept from power in a considerable wave of support for Pakistan's two leading opposition parties, the Pakistan People's Party (PPP), now overseen by Benazir Bhutto's widower, Asif Zardari, and the Pakistan Muslim League-Nawaz (PML-N) of former Prime Minister Sharif. The two largely secular, moderate parties proceeded to form a ruling parliamentary coalition in Islamabad, and also took charge of coalition governments in the two most populous of the country's four provinces.

As a perceived referendum on President Musharraf's rule, the polls reflected a widespread popular rejection of his policies. They also forwarded arguments that the Pakistani populace supports moderate political parties without explicitly religious manifestos. At the same time, the results were seen by many analysts as compounding difficulties for U.S. policy makers who may have placed too much faith in the person of Musharraf, an increasingly isolated figure whose already damaged status was further weakened.

Election results and coalition politics

The 2008 elections saw the PPP win a clear plurality of seats (121 of 342) in the National Assembly. The PML-N of Nawaz Sharif took another 91 seats. The incumbent PML-Q won only 54. This outcome provided the country's two main secular opposition parties with a near two- thirds majority. They were joined in a new national ruling coalition by the secular Pashtun nationalist Awami National Party (ANP) and the Islamist Jamiat Ulema-i-Islam faction of Fazl-urRehman (JUI-F), both of which find their main strength in the Pashtun-majority North West Frontier Province (NWFP). The PPP also won an outright majority in the provincial parliament of Sindh, the Bhuttos' ancestral homeland, but still moved to form a ruling provincial coalition with the regional Muttahida Quami Movement (MQM), which dominates Karachi's political landscape (in 2009, the MQM joined the federal coalition). In the wealthy and densely populated Punjab province, Sharif's PML-N thrashed the PML-Q in their heartland to take nearly half the provincial assembly seats. Sharif's brother Shabaz is serving again as Punjab chief minister, overseeing a coalition with the PPP. Voters in the NWFP roundly rejected the previously incumbent Islamist coalition and awarded the ANP a resounding comeback after its virtual shutout in 2002. The PPP and ANP agreed to share power in the NWFP, with the chief minister and most cabinet ministers coming from the ANP. Only in sparsely populated Baluchistan did the PML-Q win a plurality of seats, but the Quetta-based assembly is managed by a grand alliance under a PPP chief minister.

Musharraf's post-election status. Following the election of an opposition alliance, President Musharraf rejected repeated calls for his resignation and claimed to maintain the support of the powerful army. He expressed a willingness to work with the new Parliament, even as he recognized the potential for a two-thirds opposition majority to reverse many of the changes made during his rule. Such a super-majority could even have moved to impeach him, but for months the PPP put a damper on impeachment talk and instead appeared to seek a "dignified exit" for the embattled Musharraf. Although the Pakistani president's power and status were much eroded, he remained a potent political player in Islamabad, given especially his lingering support from the military and from some foreign governments, including the United States. Many observers suspected Musharraf engaged in behind-the-scenes efforts to weaken the new civilian coalition with a special eye toward marginalizing Nawaz Sharif and the PML-N.[189]

Coalition building and government formation. In March 2008, PPP leader Zardari and PML-N leader Sharif issued a written declaration of their intention to share power at the center (along with the ANP) under a PPP Prime Minister and in the Punjab under a PML-N Chief Minister.[190] In a major show of opposition unity, the accord notably vowed to seek restoration of deposed judges to office within 30 days of the new government's seating. Many viewed this "Murree Declaration" as an historic rejection of military-bureaucratic rule in Islamabad. Sindhi businesswoman Fahimda Mirza—a PPP stalwart and close associate of Zardari—became Pakistan's first-ever female National Assembly Speaker.

Zardari announced the prime ministerial candidacy of Yousaf Raza Gillani, a party stalwart from the Punjab province. Gillani was National Assembly Speaker during Benazir Bhutto's second government (1993-1996) and spent five years in prison (200 1-2006) after being sentenced by an anti-corruption court created under President Musharraf.[191] In March 2008, Gillani became Pakistan's 22nd Prime Minister. Of his 24 cabinet ministers, 11 were from the PPP and 9 from the PML-N. Important new federal ministers included Foreign Minister Shah Mehmood Qureshi, who hails from a land-owning family in southern Punjabi city of Multan and has been a PPP lawmaker since 1985, serving as a Punjab provincial minister during the 1990s; and Defense Minister Chaudhry Ahmed Mukhtar, an industrialist from the Gujrat region of Punjab, who served as federal commerce minister in Benazir Bhutto's second government and who won his parliamentary seat in 2008 by defeating PML-Q leader Chaudhry Shujaat Hussein. The de facto Interior Minister, Rehman Malik, is a PPP member and former bureaucrat who headed the Federal Investigation Agency during Bhutto's second government.

Coalition politics. Never before in Pakistan's history had the country's two leading political parties come together to share power. While many observers praised the Murree Declaration as representing a potentially new conciliatory style of party politics, others noted that the PPP and PML-N spent most of the 1990s as bitter enemies. The history of mutual party animosity in fact dates to 1972, when Benazir's father, Prime Minister Zulfikar Ali Bhutto, nationalized industries owned by Nawaz Sharif's father.[192] Opposition to Musharraf's continued power united these parties for a time, but with Musharraf fanning the flames of party competition—and with his possibly imminent departure from power removing the key unifying factor between them— analysts were pessimistic that an accommodation could last.

In May 2008, Zardari announced that a constitutional reforms package had been completed, saying this proposed "18th Amendment" would reverse changes to the constitution made under Musharraf and so "walk [Musharraf] away rather than impeach him away." The PPP transmitted to the PML-N an 80-point draft proposal that would restore the deposed judges while greatly reducing the power of the presidency. Proposed amendments would, *inter alia*, remove the president's powers to declare war, dismiss the Parliament, and appoint governors and military service chiefs. The bill faced a lengthy period of assessment before legislative action was expected. Critics of the bill decried its alleged indemnification of President Musharraf's November 2007 actions and in its provisions that could make the Pakistani judiciary subordinate to the executive. In June, Zardari and Sharif met to create a consensus on outstanding issues, including the judges' restoration and the possible impeachment of the president, but no breakthroughs were announced. Sharif reportedly refused to see his party lieutenants rejoin the federal cabinet until the judicial benches were restored through executive order (see below). Still, both leaders vowed to keep the coalition intact.

Restoration of deposed judges

During the six-week-long state of emergency launched by President Musharraf on November 3, 2007, seven Supreme Court justices, including the Chief Justice, and about 56 High Court judges refused to take a new oath of office and were dismissed. The Supreme Court was then reconstituted with justices appointed by Musharraf himself. The question of whether and how to restore the Chief Justice and other deposed judges remained a key divisive issue. In declaring an intention to restore the pre-November 3 Supreme Court, the new civilian dispensation appeared to set itself on a collision course with Musharraf. Reseating that court likely would have lead to Musharraf's removal from office, as the justices had appeared close to finding his October reelection unconstitutional. Many Pakistanis suspect the U.S. government of hindering restoration efforts. Asif Zardari has sought to assure those agitating for the judges' reinstatement that restoration would come "in due course of time," but that other political variables dictate patience in this regard. Nawaz Sharif himself accused the U.S. government of actively discouraging such restoration.[193] Many observers argue that respect for judicial independence is a key requirement for sustaining and strengthening Pakistan's democratic transition.[194]

Pakistan's federal law minister has stated that, because Musharraf's November 2007 actions were validated by the Supreme Court, only that court can undo the changes. In late August 2008, eight judges who had been sacked from the Sindh High Court took a new oath of office and were reappointed in a move criticized by the leader of the "lawyer's movement," who said the action implicitly accepted their original removal as having been constitutional. Shortly after, three deposed Supreme Court justices were reinstated after taking a new oath. The PPP leadership continues to vow that all sacked judges will be restored, but they do not provide a deadline for such reinstatement. Pakistani cynics see Zardari behaving similarly to Musharraf in his efforts to prevent a truly independent judiciary from taking shape.[195]

The "Lawyers' Movement." The "lawyer's movement" that arose in response to Musharraf's March 2007 dismissal of Chief Justice Iftikhar Chaudhry (who was reseated in July of that year and dismissed again in the November emergency) was a vital facet of the pro-rule of law, antiMusharraf sentiment that spread in Pakistan during 2007. It has not faded away: lawyers continue to boycott many courts and the movement remains able to mobilize significant street protests, which Chaudhry continues to publicly support. Aitzaz Ahsan, the Supreme Court Bar Association president and PPP Senator who lead the successful effort to have Chaudhry reseated in mid-2007, has been at the forefront of efforts to restore the pre-emergency judiciary.[196] His subsequent detention attracted the attention of some in the U.S. Congress, who called for his immediate release. Ahsan has criticized Washington for callousness regarding Musharraf's crackdown on the Supreme Court, claiming that U.S. policy is "deaf and oblivious" to the voice of ordinary Pakistanis.[197] Nawaz Sharif himself has declared an intention to personally participate in "lawyers' movement" efforts to restore deposed judges to office, which are slated to include a March 2009 "long march" on the Pakistani capital.

Coalition discord. The original April 30, 2008, deadline for the judge's restoration passed without action. Despite Sharif's apparent optimism that a resolution would be reached, subsequent meetings with Zardari in London again failed to break the deadlock. In May, Sharif announced that his party would withdraw from its seats in the federal cabinet while still supporting the PPP-led national coalition on an "issue by issue basis." Nine PML-N ministers subsequently handed in resignations. A legal advisor to Sharif reportedly held the Bush Administration partly responsible for the negotiation's breakdown, given an alleged U.S. concern that President Musharraf be "protected" and allowed a "safe exit" sometime near the end of 2008. His claims reflected widely held suspicions among Pakistanis about U.S. "meddling" in their country's coalition politics.[198] In a July visit to Islamabad, the lead U.S. diplomat for South and Central Asia urged Pakistan's political leaders to concentrate their energies on addressing critical issues such as religious militancy, rising food costs, and energy shortages rather than fixating on efforts to remove President Musharraf. Sharif was said to have flatly rejected the advice, countering that Musharraf's impeachment was a necessary step toward consolidation of the country's democratization.[199]

Impeachment plans and Musharraf's resignation

On August 5, 2008, PPP leader Zardari and PML-N leader Sharif agreed in principle to seek the impeachment of President Musharraf. Three days later, the four-party ruling coalition said it would launch impeachment proceedings "immediately" (under Pakistan's Constitution, impeachment of the president requires a two-thirds majority vote by the combined 442-seat membership of Parliament's two chambers.) Musharraf's aides vowed that the president would fight the effort, but some former political allies began urging Musharraf to resign rather than further polarize the country. Prime Minister Gillani expressed confidence that the military leadership was pro-democracy and would not intervene to protect Musharraf.[200] Cynical observers saw the two major party leaders valuing their own political fortunes over the health of the Pakistani nation. Such cynicism only deepened with the later news that Zardari would present himself as candidate to be Pakistan's next president.[201]

The first aspect of the federal coalition's plan to remove the president involved passing antiMusharraf resolutions in each of the country's four provincial assemblies. The Punjab assembly overwhelmingly passed the first such resolution; the NWFP, Sindh, and Baluchistan assemblies followed within days. With signs that the military brass would not come to his aid, the besieged president appeared to have no allies remaining, and a flood of reports indicated that Musharraf's resignation was imminent.[202] On August 18, President Musharraf delivered a resignation address to the nation in which he claimed responsibility both for turning around Pakistan's economy and for introducing the "essence of democracy" there. He blamed the new civilian government for the country's current economic and political instability, rejected the "charge sheet" that had been brought against him, explained his decision to resign as an effort to avoid confrontation and further instability, and placed his fate in the hands of the Pakistani people.[203]

Coalition collapse and PPP consolidation

Almost instantly upon Musharraf's resignation, serious rifts again appeared in the ruling coalition, with Nawaz Sharif reportedly delivering an ultimatum to the PPP that the Chief Justice be restored to office within 72 hours or the PML-N would withdraw support. Moreover, the PPP's announcement that Zardari himself would be a candidate for the presidency violated Sharif's understanding that the new president would be a nonpolitical figure.[204] On August 25, Sharif responded to what he saw as a series of broken promises by withdrawing his party's support for the ruling coalition and joining the opposition benches in Parliament. The end of the five-monthlong accommodation between the PPP and PML-N did not lead to new elections, as Zardari's party collected enough smaller party support to remain in power. Yet the development triggered numerous analysts to predict even more political instability in Islamabad, and the fractiousness of Pakistan's governance setting cast a further pall over prospects for the country's new civilian leadership to deal effectively with Pakistan's urgent economic and security problems.[205]

Asif Zardari's candidacy to replace Musharraf suggested that the presidency's constitutional powers would not be amended in the foreseeable future. With support from the influential regional MQM party based in Karachi, Zardari won the September 6 presidential election with 481 out of 702 votes in the electoral college. Allegations of corruption still haunt Zardari, and reports arose that cast doubt on his recent mental health.[206] Zardari's controversial record led many analysts to decry his candidacy as a "disaster" for both Pakistan and its democratic institutions.[207] According to some reports, the Pakistani security establishment was dead-set against a Zardari presidency and put its full weight behind the PML-N candidate.[208]

Zardari himself posed the presidential election as a culmination of his assassinated wife's efforts, and he vowed to "bring back into balance the powers of the presidency," reconstitute judicial independence through the reinstatement of judges deposed by Musharraf, and carry on the fight against Taliban and other religious extremists.[209] In his inaugural speech, Zardari called for an all- parties committee to "revisit" the 17th Amendment and Article 58(2)b of the Constitution, which gives the President the power to dismiss Parliament. Prime Minister Gillani has said his government is committed to revoking the article.[210] As the largest opposition party, the PML-N has threatened to launch its own effort to repeal the 17th Amendment if the PPP fails to do so.

Confidence in the civilian leadership has been harmed by seemingly worsening security and economic crises, leaving both ordinary Pakistanis and foreign diplomats uneasy about its capacity. The latest major embarrassment for the PPP government came with the January 2009 firing of National Security Advisor Mahmood Durrani, a former army general, Ambassador to the United States, and proponent of improved relations with India. Durrani, who had confirmed for the press that the sole captured Mumbai attacker was a Pakistani national, was dismissed by Prime Minister Gillani for giving interviews without prior consultation, but many observers suspected ulterior motives. Durrani himself said he was fired because the Prime Minister had been "ignorant" with regard to the decision to confirm the gunman's nationality.[211]

Pakistani disappointment in President Zardari and his PPP-led government appears to be pervasive. Many analysts have concluded that Zardari and his top advisors no longer intend to reduce the powers of the presidency as they had previously promised to do. There also is much skepticism about previous promises by PPP leaders to see the judiciary fully restored to its pre-November 2007 state. More generally, critics see the PPP-led government as lacking both expertise and direction.[212] An opinion survey conducted in October 2008 found 88% of Pakistanis saying the country was headed in the wrong direction. Zardari's approval rating was a mere 19%, and support for the PPP had plummeted from 32% in June to only 19%.[213]

Role of the Pakistani military

The army's role as a dominant and overt political player in Pakistan may be changing. Following President Musharraf's November 2007 resignation as army chief, the new leadership showed signs of distancing itself from both Musharraf and from direct involvement in the country's governance. The president's handpicked successor, Gen. Kayani, issued orders barring officers from holding unauthorized meetings with civilian leaders; dictated that all active officers holding posts in civilian agencies resign from those positions; and announced that the military's only role in the electoral process would be maintenance of security. He later called for a "harmonized relationship between various pillars of state, as provided in the Constitution." In March 2008, Kayani exerted further influence by making his first major new appointments, replacing two of the nine corps commanders appointed by Musharraf. To date, Kayani reportedly has removed about 3,000 active or retired military personnel from civilian government posts. In November 2008, he allowed the disbanding of both the political wing of the country's main intelligence agency and the dissolution of the National Security Council established under former President Musharraf, a body that critics had said facilitated the military's ongoing involvement in Pakistan's governance.[214] Many analysts see Gen. Kayani as motivated to improve the institutional image of the military after a serious erosion of its status under Musharraf. His dictates and rhetoric have brought accolades from numerous commentators.[215] According to Pakistan's envoy to the United States, the country's "national consensus on democracy" is fully supported by the Pakistani military, which is "scrupulously" avoiding any overt or covert role in the country's politics.[216]

U.S. Policy

Pakistan's relatively credible 2008 polls allowed the Bush Administration to issue a determination that a democratically elected government had been restored in Islamabad after a 101-month hiatus. This permanently removed coup-related aid sanctions that President Bush had been authorized to waive annually.[217] The Administration recognized Pakistan's 2008 political shift as a renewed opportunity to assist in efforts to consolidate the country's democratic institutions. Both before and after the elections, U.S. officials expounded a desire to see "moderate forces" within Pakistani politics come together to sustain their country's political and economic reforms and to carry on the fight against religious extremism and terrorism. The Bush White House anticipated Pakistan's continued cooperation in this regard.[218]

After meeting with myriad Pakistani officials Islamabad in March 2008, then-Deputy Secretary of State Negroponte said the U.S.-Pakistan partnership "remains strong" and "we envision a continued close, productive alliance that benefits both countries."[219] By some accounts, however, the U.S. government sought and may continue seeking to influence Islamabad's internal political processes. Most Pakistanis expressed a keen sensitivity to signs of U.S. attempts to influence the post-election coalition-building negotiations. Some observers suspected the Bush Administration remained wedded to a policy that would have keep the embattled Musharraf in power despite his weakness and lack of public support. During June 2008, speculation was rife in Pakistan that the United States was steering the PPP leadership toward implementing whatever agreements were made between Benazir Bhutto and Musharraf in 2007.[220]

Still, senior Bush Administration officials appeared to be recognizing the importance of a broader array of political figures in Islamabad. In what was taken to be a clear indication of shifting U.S. policy, Deputy Secretary Negroponte—who had in late 2007 described the Pakistani president as an "indispensable ally" of the United States—offered little public defense of Musharraf in early 2008, calling his future status a matter to be determined by "the internal Pakistani political process." The White House also said Pakistanis themselves must determine the outcome.[221]

By removing the single most important interlocutor in Islamabad, Musharraf's resignation presented yet another challenge for U.S. officials in their dealings with Pakistan. Despite the Bush Administration's official noninterference posture, many reports had the U.S. government urging a "soft landing" for Musharraf. Still, in the end, the Bush Administration watched quietly as its key Pakistani ally was marginalized, apparently concluding that Musharraf's time was up and that any further overt U.S. support for the discredited ex-general would only stoke visceral anti-American sentiments in Pakistan. Both major party U.S. presidential candidates welcomed Musharraf's exit as a step toward ending Pakistan's political crisis.[222]

Regional Relations

Pakistan-India Rivalry

Three full-scale wars—in 1947-1948, 1965, and 1971—and a constant state of military preparedness on both sides of their mutual border have marked six decades of bitter rivalry between Pakistan and India. The acrimonious partition of British India into two successor states in 1947 and the unresolved issue of Kashmiri sovereignty have been major sources of tension. Both countries have built large defense establishments at significant cost to economic and social development. The Kashmir problem is rooted in claims by both countries to the former princely state, divided since 1948 by a military Line of Control (LOC) into the Indian state of Jammu and Kashmir and Pakistan-held Azad [Free] Kashmir. India blames Pakistan for supporting a violent separatist rebellion in the Muslim-dominated Kashmir Valley that has taken up to 66,000 lives since 1989. Pakistan admits only to lending moral and political support to the rebels, and it criticizes India for human rights abuses in "Indian-occupied Kashmir." New Delhi continues to blame Pakistan for maintaining an "infrastructure of terror" and for actively supporting terrorist groups that are held responsible for attacks inside India.[223] For many analysts, efforts to ameliorate Pakistan's "obsession" with India could be key to normalizing South Asian politics and ending Islamabad's historic and ambivalent links to religious extremism.[224] Some call on New Delhi to reach out to the new Islamabad government with conciliatory gestures that could facilitate the consolidation of democratization in Pakistan.[225]

India held Pakistan responsible for late 2001 terrorist attacks in Kashmir and on the Indian Parliament complex in New Delhi. The Indian response, a massive military mobilization, was mirrored by Pakistan and within months some one million heavily-armed soldiers were facing off at the international frontier. During an extremely tense 2002 another full-scale war seemed a real and even likely possibility, and may have been averted only through international diplomatic efforts, including multiple visits to the region by top U.S. officials. A spring 2003 peace initiative brought major improvement in the bilateral relationship, allowing for an autumn cease-fire agreement initiated by Pakistan. The process led to a January 2004 summit meeting in Islamabad and a joint agreement to re-engage a "Composite Dialogue" to bring about "peaceful settlement of all bilateral issues, including Jammu and Kashmir, to the satisfaction of both sides."[226]

Since this new initiative was launched, mid-level meetings, normalized diplomatic relations, and increased people-to-people contacts have brought modest, but still meaningful progress toward stable relations. Regular dialogue continued in 2005 and a third round of Composite Dialogue talks was held in 2006. Notable confidence-building measures are in place—in particular travel and commerce across the Kashmiri LOC for the first time in decades—and bilateral trade has increased. Yet militarized territorial disputes over Kashmir, the Siachen Glacier, and the Sir Creek remain unresolved, and Pakistani officials regularly express unhappiness that more substantive progress, especially on the "core issue" of Kashmir, is not occurring.

Following July 11, 2006, terrorist bombings in Mumbai, India, New Delhi postponed planned foreign secretary-level talks, bringing into question the continued viability of the already slow- moving process. However, after meeting on the sidelines of a Nonaligned Movement summit in Cuba, President Musharraf and Indian Prime Minister Singh announced a resumption of formal peace negotiations and also approved implementation of a joint anti-terrorism mechanism. The Composite Dialogue then resumed after a four-month hiatus. No progress was made on outstanding territorial disputes, and India is not known to have presented evidence of Pakistani involvement in the "7/11" bombings, but the two officials did give shape to the proposed joint anti-terrorism mechanism. A notable step came in late 2006, when the two sides agreed to conduct a joint survey of the disputed Sir Creek region.

In January 2007, then-Foreign Minister Kasuri hosted his Indian counterpart, Pranab Mukherjee, in Islamabad for the first such visit in more than a year. The two men gave a favorable review to past progress and planned a fourth Composite Dialogue round. In February, two bombs exploded on an Indian segment of the Samjhauta [Friendship] Express train linking Delhi, India, with Lahore, Pakistan. Resulting fires killed 68 people, most of them Pakistanis. Days later, Kasuri traveled to New Delhi, where he and Mukherjee reaffirmed a bilateral commitment to the peace process despite the apparent effort to subvert it.

The new joint anti-terrorism mechanism met for the first time in Islamabad in March 2007, producing a joint statement in which both governments agreed to use the forum for exchanging information about investigations of and/or efforts to prevent terrorist acts on either side of the shared border. Hopes that the Samjhauta train bombing would provide a fitting "test case" were dashed, however, when India declined to share relevant investigative information. Moreover, Indian officials were unhappy with Islamabad's insistence that the "freedom struggle" underway in Kashmir should not be treated as terrorism under this framework. Still, the engagement even after a major terrorist attack was widely viewed as evidence that the bilateral peace process had gained a sturdy momentum. A new round of dialogue was then initiated when the two foreign ministers met again in Islamabad. No new agreements were reached, but both officials lauded improved bilateral relations and held "the most sustained and intensive dialogue" ever on the Kashmir problem.[227] Political turmoil and uncertainty arose in Islamabad around that same time, however, and led to slowed progress in the bilateral peace process.

A fourth round of bilateral talks on economic and commercial cooperation ended in August 2007 with agreements to facilitate importation of cement from Pakistan and tea from India, among others. Pakistani and Indian officials also held technical-level talks on the modalities of cross- border movement, and separate talks on the Tubal navigation project/Wullar barrage water dispute ended without progress. In September, Pakistan issued a formal protest and expressed "deep concern" in response to the Indian government's announced intention to open the disputed territory of the Siachen Glacier to tourism, saying the region was "illegally occupied" by Indian troops in 1984 and its final status has yet to be determined due to an "inflexible Indian attitude."[228] In a more positive sign in October, trucks carrying tomatoes from India to Pakistan crossed the international border for the first time in 60 years. October 2007 also saw mid-level Pakistani and Indian officials meet to discuss both conventional and nuclear confidence-building measures, but no new initiatives were announced. The countries also held a second meeting of their Joint Anti-Terrorism Mechanism in New Delhi, where the two sides shared new information on terrorism and agreed to continue mutual investigatory cooperation.

With President Musharraf's November 2007 imposition of a state of emergency and growing instability and insecurity in Pakistan, the bilateral peace process ground to a temporary halt. India watched Pakistan's turmoil with great interest, but little public comment. A destabilized Pakistan represents a major security concern for New Delhi, but at the same time history shows that as Pakistan's internal difficulties grow, Pakistani interference in Indian affairs tends to decrease.[229]

In February 2008, the head of Pakistan's new coalition-leading PPP, Asif Zardari, caused a stir when he suggested that Pakistan-India relations should not be hindered by differences over Kashmir, thus appearing to contradict a long-standing Pakistani position that Kashmir represents the "core issue" in bilateral relations. Zardari was quoted as saying, "people-to-people contacts should be improved, then trade" and Kashmir "is a situation [on which] we can agree to disagree." India's leadership, for its part, offered to work with the new Pakistani government in the interests of collective security and prosperity.[230] In May, Pakistan's foreign secretary hosted his Indian counterpart in Islamabad, where the two men expressed satisfaction with the progress of the bilateral peace process. The next day, Foreign Minister Qureshi sat with his Indian counterpart to review the fourth round of the Composite Dialogue. Both ministers reaffirmed their commitment to the process and a fifth round of negotiations was launched in July 2008.[231] Yet, as noted above, although some positive developments came in the fall of 2008, the November terrorist attack on Mumbai spurred a breakdown in the bilateral peace process.

The "IPI" Pipeline Project[232]

Islamabad insists it is going forward with a proposed joint pipeline project to deliver Iranian natural gas to Pakistan and possibly on to India. In early 2007, officials from the three countries resolved a long-running price-mechanism dispute, opening the way for further progress. The fourth meeting of the Pakistan-India Joint Working Group on the Iran-Pakistan-India (IPI) pipeline subsequently was held in Islamabad, where the two countries agreed to split equally expected gas supplies. New Delhi's willingness to participate appeared to wane in the later half of 2007, but an April 2008 visit to Islamabad by India's oil minister led to a reiteration of New Delhi's commitment to the project, and the Iranian president's subsequent South Asia visit included stops in both Islamabad and New Delhi, where more positive signals were issued. However, Iran apparently since backed out of previously negotiated price agreements, and security circumstances in Pakistan have only deteriorated further, sparking new pessimism about the project's viability. Doubts about financing the approximately $7 billion project also have many analysts skeptical about fruition.[233]

Senior Pakistani officials have described the IPI pipeline as being critical to Pakistan's economic growth and political stability. Some independent observers and Members of Congress assert that completion of the pipeline would represent a major confidence-building measure in the region and could bolster regional energy security while facilitating friendlier Pakistan-India ties (see, for example, H.Res. 353 in the 109th Congress). In late 2008, a group of senior, U.S.-based Pakistan experts recommended that Washington reconsider its opposition to the pipeline so as "to encourage better ties and more robust economic linkages between India and Pakistan."[234]

As part of its efforts to isolate Iran economically, the Bush Administration had actively sought to dissuade the Islamabad and New Delhi governments from participation in this project, and a State Department official suggested that current U.S. law dictates American opposition: The Iran-Libya Sanctions Act (P.L. 107-24) requires the President to impose sanctions on foreign companies that make an "investment" of more than $20 million in one year in Iran's energy sector. The 109th Congress extended this provision in the Iran Freedom Support Act (P.L. 109-293). No firms have been sanctioned under this act to date.

Afghanistan

Pakistani leaders have long sought access to Central Asia and "strategic depth" with regard to India through friendly relations with neighboring

Afghanistan. Such policy contributed to President-General Zia ul-Haq's support for Afghan mujahideen "freedom fighters" who were battling Soviet invaders during the 1980s and to Islamabad's later support for the Afghan Taliban regime from 1996 to 2001.[235] British colonialists had purposely divided the ethnic Pashtun tribes inhabiting the mountainous northwestern reaches of their South Asian empire with the 1893 "Durand Line." This porous, 1,600-mile border is not accepted by Afghan leaders, who have at times fanned Pashtun nationalism to the dismay of Pakistanis.[236] Both Pakistan and Afghanistan play central roles as U.S. allies in global efforts to combat Islamic militancy. Ongoing acrimony between Islamabad and Kabul is thus deleterious to U.S. interests.

After fleeing Afghanistan during the 1980s and 1990s, millions of refugees have returned home since 2002, but Pakistan remains the setting for more than 80 encampments and about 2.4 million Afghan refugees. Islamabad plans to repatriate these people entirely by the end of 2009, citing extremism and economic stresses.

Following Islamabad's major September 2001 policy shift, President Musharraf consistently vowed full Pakistani support for the government of Afghan President Hamid Karzai and insisted that Pakistan is playing a "totally neutral role" in Afghanistan. Islamabad claims to have arrested many hundreds of Taliban militants and remanded most of them to Afghan custody, and it reportedly has provided $300 million in economic assistance to Kabul since 2001. Nevertheless, Musharraf and Karzai exchanged public accusations and recriminations about the ongoing movement of Islamic militants in the border region, and U.S. officials issued increasingly strong claims about the problems posed by Taliban insurgents and other militants who are widely believed to enjoy safehaven on the Pakistani side of the Durand Line.

Pakistan is wary of signs that India is pursuing a policy of "strategic encirclement," taking note of New Delhi's past support for Tajik and Uzbek militias which comprised the Afghan Northern Alliance, and the post-2001 opening of numerous Indian consulates in Afghanistan. More fundamental, perhaps, than the regime type in Islamabad is the Pakistani geopolitical perspective focused on India as the primary threat and on Afghanistan as an arena of security competition between Islamabad and New Delhi. In the conception of one long-time analyst, "Pakistan's grand strategy, with an emphasis on balancing against Afghanistan and India, will continue to limit cooperation in the war on terrorism, regardless of whether elected civilian leaders retain power or the military intervenes again."[237]

In 2007, an unprecedented joint "jirga," or tribal assembly, was held in Kabul and included nearly 700 delegates from both Pakistan and Afghanistan. The meeting was endorsed by the United States as a means of bringing stability to Afghanistan. President Musharraf, after initially declining to participate (a perceived snub to both Afghan President Karzai and to the U.S. government), attended the jirga's final session. He offered a rare admission that support for militants emanating from Pakistan has caused problems for Afghanistan, saying "There is no doubt Afghan militants are supported from Pakistan soil. The problem that you have in your region is because support is provided from our side." The jirga ended with a declaration that included plans for dialogue with "the opposition," i.e., the Taliban.238

Still, bilateral relations worsened in 2008. The Kabul government claimed to have evidence of Pakistani complicity in both an April 2008 assassination attempt on Karzai and in a July 2008 bombing of India's Kabul Embassy. Afghan resentment over these incidents led the Karzai government to suspend its participation in bilateral and regional meetings that include Pakistan until such time as "bilateral trust is restored."[239] In August, the Kabul government agreed to resume talks with Pakistan and Pakistan substantively re-engaged the Tripartite Commission when Army Chief Gen. Kayani traveled to Kabul to meet with his Afghan counterpart and ISAF Commander U.S. Gen. David McKiernan.

In September 2008, President Zardari and President Karzai reaffirmed a commitment to working together to resolve bilateral tensions and to fight the Taliban insurgency. Following Turkish- sponsored talks between Pakistani and Afghan leaders in December, the two leaders agreed to better collaborate in combating regional terrorism, and a January 2009 Joint Declaration expressed the desire of both governments to open a new chapter in cooperative relations, in part through the maintenance of frequent high-level contacts and of a joint jirga process.[240] The Pakistani and Afghan Ambassadors to the United States have jointly stressed the role of economic development and poverty reduction as counterterrorism tools. In this context, they strongly urged passage of pending U.S. legislation that would create Reconstruction Opportunity Zones in their mutual border regions.[241]

China

Pakistan and China have enjoyed a generally close and mutually beneficial relationship over several decades. Pakistan served as a link between Beijing and Washington in 1971, as well as a bridge to the Muslim world for China during the 1980s. China's continuing role as a major arms supplier for

Pakistan began in the 1960s and included helping to build a number of arms factories in Pakistan, as well as supplying complete weapons systems. After the 1990 imposition of U.S. sanctions on Pakistan, the Islamabad-Beijing arms relationship was further strengthened.[242] Pakistan continues to view China as an "all-weather friend" and perhaps its most important strategic ally.

Islamabad may seek future civil nuclear assistance from Beijing, including potential provision of complete power reactors, especially in light of Washington's categorical refusal of Pakistan's request for a civil nuclear cooperation similar to that planned between the United States and India. The Chinese government has assisted Pakistan in constructing a major new port at Gwadar, near the border with Iran. Islamabad and Beijing aspire to make this port, officially opened in March 2007, a major commercial outlet for Central Asian states. Some Western and Indian analysts are concerned that the port may be used for military purposes and could bolster China's naval presence in the Indian Ocean region.

Analysts taking a realist, power political perspective view China as an external balancer in the South Asian subsystem, with Beijing's material support for Islamabad allowing Pakistan to challenge the aspiring regional hegemony of a more powerful India. Many observers, especially those in India, see Chinese support for Pakistan as a key aspect of Beijing's perceived policy of "encirclement" or constraint of India as a means of preventing or delaying New Delhi's ability to challenge Beijing's region-wide influence. Indian leaders have called the Islamabad-Beijing nuclear and missile "proliferation nexus" a cause of serious concern in New Delhi, and U.S. officials remain seized of this potentially destabilizing dynamic.

In 2005, China's Prime Minister visited Islamabad, where Pakistan and China signed 22 accords meant to boost bilateral cooperation. President Musharraf's five-day visit to Beijing in early 2006 saw bilateral discussions on counterterrorism, trade, and technical assistance. Chinese President Hu's late 2006 travel to Islamabad was the first such visit by a Chinese president in ten years; another 18 new bilateral pacts were inked, including a bilateral Free Trade Agreement. In mid- 2007, Prime Minister Aziz visited Beijing, where Pakistan and China signed 27 new agreements and memoranda of understanding to "re-energize" bilateral cooperation in numerous areas, including defense, space technology, and trade. No public mention was made regarding civil nuclear cooperation. President Musharraf's April 2008 travel to Beijing produced ten new memoranda of understanding and a reiteration of the two countries "special relations."

In the month after he took office, President Zardari paid a visit to Beijing. Speculation on his central motive focused on Pakistan's urgent need for aid to correct its growing balance of payments deficit; China's huge foreign-exchange reserves are a potential source of a major cash infusion. Yet Zardari left Beijing without having secured any Chinese commitment in this area, although reports did suggest that the Chinese had agreed to build two new nuclear power reactors in Pakistan.[243] U.S. congressional opponents of such a development confirmed with the Bush State Department that China's provision of new nuclear reactors to Pakistan would represent a clear violation of its international obligations as members of the NSG..[244] Late 2008 visits to Beijing by senior Pakistani military officers reviewed progress on multiple military hardware deals, including Pakistan's purchase of four new Chinese guided-missile frigates and a fleet of co- produced JF- 17 fighter aircraft.[245]

PAKISTAN-U.S. RELATIONS AND KEY COUNTRY ISSUES

U.S. policy interests in Pakistan encompass a wide range of issues, including counterterrorism, nuclear weapons and missile proliferation, South Asian and Afghan stability, democratization and human rights, trade and economic reform, and efforts to counter narcotics trafficking. Relations have been affected by several key developments, including proliferation- and democracy-related sanctions; a continuing Pakistan-India nuclear standoff and conflict over Kashmir; and the September 2001 terrorist attacks against the United States. In the wake of those attacks, President Musharraf—under intense U.S. diplomatic pressure—offered President Bush Pakistan's "unstinted cooperation in the fight against terrorism." Pakistan became a vital ally in the U.S.-led anti-terrorism coalition. U.S. sanctions relating to Pakistan's 1998 nuclear tests and 1999 military coup quickly were waived and, in October 2001, large tranches of U.S. aid began flowing into Pakistan.

Direct U.S. assistance programs include training and equipment for Pakistani security forces, along with aid for health, education, food, democracy promotion, human rights improvement, counternarcotics, border security and law enforcement, as well as trade preference benefits. The United States also supports grant, loan, and debt rescheduling programs for Pakistan by the various major international financial institutions. In June 2004, President Bush designated Pakistan as a major non-NATO ally of the United States under Section 517 of the Foreign Assistance Act of 1961.

Terrorism

After the September 2001 terrorist attacks on the United States, Pakistan pledged and has provided major support for the U.S.-led global anti-terrorism coalition. According to the U.S. Departments of State and Defense, Pakistan has afforded the United States unprecedented levels of cooperation by allowing the U.S. military to use bases within the country, helping to identify and detain extremists, tightening the border between Pakistan and Afghanistan, and blocking terrorist financing.[246] For most of the Bush Administration's two terms in office, senior U.S. officials regularly praised Pakistani anti-terrorism efforts.

In a landmark January 2002 speech, President Musharraf vowed to end Pakistan's use as a base for terrorism of any kind, and he banned numerous militant groups, including Lashkar-e-Taiba and Jaish-e-Muhammad, both blamed for terrorist violence in Kashmir and India, and both designated as terrorist organizations under U.S. law. In the wake of the speech, thousands of Muslim extremists were detained, though most of these were later released. In the spring of 2002, U.S. military and law enforcement personnel began engaging in direct, low-profile efforts to assist Pakistani security forces in tracking and apprehending fugitive Al Qaeda and Taliban fighters on Pakistani territory. Pakistani authorities claim to have captured some 700 Al Qaeda suspects and remanded most of these to U.S. custody.[247]

Important Al Qaeda-related arrests in Pakistan have included Abu Zubaydah (March 2002), Ramzi bin al-Shibh (September 2002), Khalid Sheik Mohammed (March 2003), and Abu Faraj al-Libbi (May 2005). Other allegedly senior Al Qaeda figures were killed in gunbattles and missile attacks, including in several apparent U.S.-directed attacks on Pakistani territory from armed aerial drones. Yet Al Qaeda fugitives and their Taliban allies remain active in Pakistan, especially in the mountainous tribal regions along the Afghan border. Meanwhile, numerous banned indigenous groups continue to operate under new names. For example, Lashkar-e-Taiba became Jamaat al-Dawat (banned under U.S. law in April 2006) and Jaish-e-Mohammed was re-dubbed Khudam-ul Islam.

Former President Musharraf repeatedly vowed to end the activities of religious extremists in Pakistan and to permanently prevent banned groups from resurfacing there. His policies likely spurred two lethal but failed attempts to assassinate him in 2003. Islamabad declared a four- pronged strategy to counter terrorism and religious extremism, containing military, political, administrative, and development aspects. Nonetheless, analysts have long called the Islamabad government's post-2001 efforts cosmetic, ineffective, and the result of international pressure rather than a genuine recognition of the threat posed. Moreover, there have been indications that Pakistan's intelligence agencies have over time lost control of some of the religious militants they previously had groomed to do their foreign policy bidding. In recent years, some Pakistani nationals and religious seminaries have been linked to Islamist terrorism plots in Western countries, especially the United Kingdom.[248] Reports also indicate that terrorist training camps operate on Pakistani soil.[249]

When asked during a 2007 Senate hearing about the possible source of a hypothetical future Al Qaeda attack on the United States, then-Director of National Intelligence Mike McConnell stated his belief that such an attack "most likely would be planned and come out of the [Al Qaeda] leadership in Pakistan."[250] According to then-Under Secretary of State Burns in mid-2007 testimony before the Senate Foreign Relations Committee,

> We know that the tribal areas of the mountainous border regions inside Pakistan have never been within the effective control of any central government. We know that the regions of North and South Waziristan have become safehavens for violent extremist and terrorist activity.... [W]e would like to see a more sustained and effective effort by the Pakistani government to defeat terrorist forces on its soil.

Although the United States lauded Islamabad's anti-terrorism financing efforts earlier this decade, Burns also encouraged more energetic Pakistani action in this area, expressing particular concern about terrorist groups exploiting charitable donations, and about their tactic of re-forming under new names to evade international prohibitions on donations to terrorist organizations. Burns urged Pakistan to pass an Anti-Money Laundering bill that meets international standards, and to establish a Financial Intelligence Unit within the State Bank of Pakistan.[251]

Also in mid-2007, Pakistan's National Security Council reportedly warned President Musharraf that Islamist militancy was rapidly spreading beyond western tribal areas and that a "policy of appeasement" had emboldened the Taliban. The Council was said to have formulated new plans to address the issue, including shifting more paramilitary troops to the FATA from other parts of Pakistan.[252] From the State Department's *Country Reports on Terrorism 2007* (released April 2008):

> The United States remained concerned that the Federally Administered Tribal Areas (FATA) of Pakistan were being used as a safe haven for Al Qaeda terrorists, Afghan insurgents, and other extremists.... Extremists led by Baitullah Mehsud and other Al Qaeda-related extremists re-exerted their hold in areas of South Waziristan.... Extremists have also gained footholds in the settled areas bordering the FATA.[253]

Congressional analysts identified serious shortcomings in the Bush Administration's FATA policy: In April, the U.S. Government Accountability Office (GAO) issued a report in response to congressional requests for assessment of progress in meeting U.S. national security goals related to counterterrorism efforts in Pakistan's FATA. Their investigation found that, "The United States has not met its national security goals to destroy terrorist threats and close safe haven in Pakistan's FATA," and, "No comprehensive plan for meeting U.S. national security goals in the FATA has been developed." The Chairman of the House Foreign Affairs Committee, Representative Howard Berman, called the report's conclusions "appalling."[254]

President Zardari emphatically declares that "the war on terror is Pakistan's war" and asserts that, as a grieving husband who lost his wife to terrorism, his commitment to the fight is both national and personal. In a thinly veiled response to U.S. pressure, he wrote, "We do not need lectures about terrorism from anyone.... We live it each and every day." He calls for international support for Pakistani democracy and economic viability, saying "a secure Pakistan is the greatest asset in the world's fight against terrorism."[255] U.S. officials take note of Pakistan's successes against militants in the border region even as they continue to encourage Islamabad's leaders to take greater and more concerted action against extremists elsewhere in the country.[256]

Pakistani officials resent criticism and doubt about their commitment to the counterterrorist fight. They aver that Western pressure on Pakistan to "do more" undermines their effort and has in fact fueled instability and violence.[257] Some argue that their "Waziristan problem" is largely traceable to U.S. policies in the region. From this perspective, the United States essentially abandoned the region after infusing it with money and arms during the 1980s, thus "leaving the jihadi baby in Pakistan's lap." Furthermore, the argument goes, a U.S. failure to decisively defeat Afghan Taliban remnants in 2002, a diversion of key resources to the war in Iraq and the recruiting boon that war provided to jihadi groups, and an over-reliance on allegedly ill-equipped

NATO troops all combined to build and sustain in western Pakistan a religious extremist movement that did not previously exist.[258]

Al Qaeda's resurgence in Pakistan

U.S. officials remain concerned that Al Qaeda terrorists operate with impunity on Pakistani territory. Such concern surged following the July 2007 release of a National Intelligence Estimate on terrorist threats to the U.S. homeland, which concluded that Al Qaeda "has protected or regenerated key elements of its Homeland attack capability, including a safehaven in the FATA, operational lieutenants, and its top leadership."[259] In his February 2008 threat assessment for a Senate committee, Director of National Intelligence McConnell offered the conclusions of the U.S. intelligence community:

> Al Qaeda has been able to retain a safehaven in Pakistan's FATA that provides the organization many of the advantages it once derived from its base across the border in Afghanistan, albeit on a smaller and less secure scale. The FATA serves as a staging area for Al Qaeda's attacks in support of the Taliban in Afghanistan as well as a location for training new terrorist operatives, for attacks in Pakistan, the Middle East, Africa, Europe and the United States.[260]

Al Qaeda founder Osama Bin Laden and his lieutenant, Egyptian Islamic radical leader Ayman alZawahri, are believed by many to be hiding somewhere in Pakistan's western border region. Pakistani officials reject such suspicions and generally insist there is no evidence to support them, but numerous U.S. officials have suggested otherwise. In 2006, President Bush said he would order U.S. forces to enter Pakistan if he received good intelligence on bin Laden's location.[261] Islamabad reportedly has remanded to U.S. custody roughly 500 Al Qaeda fugitives to date, including some senior alleged operatives. However, despite clear successes in disrupting extremist networks in Pakistan since 2001, there are numerous signs that Al Qaeda is resurgent on Pakistani territory, with anti-U.S. terrorists appearing to have benefitted from what some analysts call a Pakistani policy of appeasement in western tribal areas near the Afghan border.

By seeking accommodation with pro-Taliban leaders in these areas, the Pakistani government may inadvertently have allowed foreign (largely Arab) militants to obtain safe haven from which they can plot and train for terrorist attacks against U.S. and other Western targets. Moreover, many observers warn that an American preoccupation with Iraq contributed to allowing Al

Qaeda's reemergence in Pakistan.[262] The then-head of the U.S. Central Intelligence Agency portrayed Al Qaeda as being on the defensive in South Asia, claiming that its leadership is losing the battle for hearts and minds in the Muslim world. Some independent analysts agree that Al Qaeda's "grand project" of establishing a militant Islamic caliphate has been a resounding failure, but warn that the group remains potent and serves as a model for global jihadi groups.[263]

Infiltration into Afghanistan

Tensions between the Kabul and Islamabad governments—which stretch back many decades— have at times reached alarming levels in recent years, with top Afghan officials accusing Pakistan of manipulating Islamic militancy in the region to destabilize Afghanistan. Likewise, U.S. military commanders in Afghanistan have since 2003 complained that Islamist insurgents remain able to attack coalition troops in Afghanistan, then escape across the Pakistani frontier. U.S. government officials voice similar worries, even expressing concern that elements of Pakistan's intelligence agency might be assisting members of the Taliban. In 2006, the State Department's top counterterrorism official told a Senate panel that elements of Pakistan's "local, tribal governments" are believed to be in collusion with the Taliban and Al Qaeda, but that the United States had no "compelling evidence" that Pakistan's intelligence agency is assisting militants.[264] Later that year, the Commander of the U.S. European Command told the same Senate panel it was "generally accepted" that the Taliban headquarters is somewhere in the vicinity of Quetta, the capital of Pakistan's southwestern Baluchistan province.[265]

The more than 100,000 Pakistani troops operating in the border region are hampered by limited communications and other counterinsurgency capabilities, meaning their response to provocations can be overly reliant on imprecise, mass firepower. This has contributed to a significant number of civilian casualties. Simultaneously, tribal leaders who cooperate with the federal government face dire threats from the extremists—as many as 500 have been the victims of targeted killings—and the militants have sought to deter such cooperation by regularly beheading accused "U.S. spies."

Pakistan launches internal military operations

In late 2003, President Musharraf made an unprecedented show of force by moving 25,000 Pakistani troops into the traditionally autonomous FATA on the Afghan frontier. The first half of 2004 saw an escalation of Pakistani army operations, many in coordination with U.S. and Afghan forces just across the international frontier.[266] Kabul's October 2004 elections were held without major disturbances, apparently in part due to Musharraf's commitment to reducing infiltrations. Yet concerns sharpened in 2005 and, by the middle of that year, Afghan leaders were openly accusing Islamabad of supporting insurgents and providing their leadership with safe haven. Islamabad denied the charges and sought to reassure Kabul by dispatching additional troops to border areas, bringing the total to 80,000. Still, 2006 was the deadliest year to date for U.S. troops in Afghanistan and, at year's end, there were growing indications that Islamabad's efforts to control the tribal areas were meeting with little success. Former President Musharraf's "carrot and stick" approach of offering amnesty to those militant tribals who "surrendered," and using force against those who resisted, clearly did not rid the region of Islamist militants.

Islamabad shifts strategy

As military operations failed to subdue the militants while causing much "collateral damage" and alienating local residents, Islamabad in 2004 began shifting strategy to arrange truces with Waziri commanders, first at Shakai in South Waziristan in April 2004, then again in February 2005. Officials in Islamabad recognized that the social fabric of the FATA had changed following its role as a staging and recruiting area for the war against the Soviet Army in Afghanistan during the 1980s: the traditional power base was eroded as the influence of religious elements had greatly increased. President Musharraf lambasted the creeping "Talibanization" of the tribal areas and sought to implement a new scheme, shifting over time from an almost wholly militarized approach to one emphasizing negotiation and economic development, as well as re-elevating the role of tribal maliks who would work in closer conjunction with federal political agents. The aim, then, became restoration of a kind of enhanced status quo ante with a limited state writ (maliks would enjoy more pay and larger levies), and the reduction and ultimately full withdrawal of army troops. The U.S. government offered cautious initial support for the new strategy.[267]

Cease-fire and North Waziristan truce

In mid-2006, militants in North Waziristan announced a unilateral cease-fire to allow for creation of a tribal council seeking resolution with government forces. On September 5, 2006, the Islamabad government and pro-Taliban insurgents in Miramshah, North Waziristan, signed a truce to ensure "permanent peace" in the region. A representative of the provincial governor agreed on behalf of the government to end army operations against local tribesmen; release all detainees; lift all public sanctions, pay compensation for property damage, return confiscated vehicles and other goods; and remove all new army checkposts. In turn, two representatives of the "local mujahideen students" (trans. "Taliban") agreed to end their attacks on government troops and officials; halt the cross-border movement of insurgents to Afghanistan; and evict all foreigners who did not agree to live in peace and honor the pact.[268]

News of the truce received lukewarm reception in Washington, where officials took a "wait-andsee" approach. Within weeks there was growing concern among both U.S. government officials and independent analysts that the truce represented a Pakistani "surrender" and had in effect created a sanctuary for extremists, with the rate of Taliban activities in neighboring Afghanistan much increased. Still, Islamabad pressed ahead with a plan to extend a similar truce to the Bajaur tribal agency. Only hours before such a deal was to be struck on October 30, 2006, 82 people were killed in a dawn air attack on a madrassa in Chinghai, Bajaur. The Pakistani military claimed to have undertaken the attack after the school's pro-Taliban leader continued to train terrorists and shelter "unwanted foreigners," yet many observers speculated that U.S. Predator drones were involved. Nine days later, a suicide bomber killed 42 army recruits at a military training camp at Dargai in the NWFP, not far from the sight of the Chinghai attack. The bombing was the most deadly attack on the Pakistani military in recent memory.

The FATA in 2007

Instability in the FATA only increased in 2007, with a large trust deficit between government forces and tribal leaders, and a conclusion by top U.S. officials that President Musharraf's strategy of making truce deals with pro-Taliban militants had failed. In January, the then-director of the U.S. Defense Intelligence Agency told a Senate panel that tribal leaders in Waziristan had not abided by most terms of the September 2006 North Waziristan truce.[269] In March, the then- Undersecretary of Defense for Policy reported to the same panel that there was "an almost immediate and steady increase of cross-border infiltration and attacks" just after that agreement had been reached. Some reports even describe anecdotes of the Pakistani military providing fire support for Taliban units operating in Afghanistan. The now-defunct September 2006 peace deal clearly failed to curb violence and religious militancy in the region and had no apparent effect on the continued cross-border movement of pro-Taliban forces into Afghanistan. Many analysts insist that any such future agreements of this nature are doomed to similar failure in the absence of substantive changes in Pakistan's fundamental regional and domestic policies.[270]

By the close of 2007, U.S. intelligence analysts had amassed considerable evidence that Islamabad's truces with religious militants in the FATA had given Taliban, Al Qaeda, and other Islamist extremists space in which to rebuild their networks. A behind-the-scenes diplomatic effort to prod the Islamabad government on its counterterrorism strategy was ramped up during the course of the year, but it may have only been through more public and strongly-worded U.S. criticisms of Pakistan in July that Islamabad was convinced to be more energetic in its militarized efforts.[271] A spate of militant attacks on Pakistani military targets during that month, apparently in retaliation for the government's armed assault on Islamabad's radical Red Mosque, led Musharraf to further bolster the army's presence in the region. Top Bush Administration officials suggested the tack of seeking accommodation with regional extremist elements should be abandoned.[272] Many analysts insist that only by bringing the tribal areas under the full writ of the Pakistani state and facilitating major economic development there can the FATA problem be resolved.

Infiltration into Kashmir and India

Islamabad has been under continuous U.S. and international pressure to terminate the infiltration of separatist militants across the Kashmiri Line of Control (LOC). Such pressure reportedly elicited a January 2002 promise from President Musharraf to Deputy Secretary of State Armitage that all such movements would cease. Armitage later reportedly received another pledge from the Pakistani president, this time an assurance that any existing terrorist camps in Pakistani Kashmir would be closed. Musharraf assured India that he would not permit any territory under Pakistan's control to be used to support terrorism, and he insisted that his government did everything possible to stop infiltration and shut down militant base camps in Pakistani-controlled territory. Critics contended, however, that Islamabad continued to actively support anti-India militants as a means both to maintain strategically the domestic backing of Islamists who view the Kashmir issue as fundamental to the Pakistani national idea, and to disrupt tactically the state government in Indian Kashmir in seeking to erode New Delhi's legitimacy there.

Positive indications growing from the latest Pakistan-India peace initiative include a cease-fire at the LOC that has held since November 2003 and statements from Indian officials indicating that rates of militant infiltration are down significantly. However, Indian leaders periodically reiterate their complaints that Islamabad has taken insufficient action to eradicate the remaining "infrastructure of terrorism" on Pakistani-controlled territory. With indications that terrorism on Indian soil beyond the Jammu and Kashmir state may have been linked to Pakistan-based terrorist groups, Indian leaders repeat demands that Pakistan uphold its promises to curtail the operations of Islamic militants and violent Kashmiri separatists originating on Pakistani-controlled territory.

Following conflicting reports from Indian government officials about the criminal investigation into July 2006 Bombay terrorist bombings, India's prime minister stated that India had "credible evidence" of Pakistani government complicity in the plot. Islamabad rejected Indian accusations as "propaganda" designed "to externalize an internal [Indian] malaise."[273] Several other terrorist attacks against Indian targets outside of Kashmir have been linked to Pakistan-based groups, including lethal assaults on civilians in Delhi and Bangalore in 2005, in Varanasi in 2006, in Hyderabad in 2007, and in Mumbai in 2008. Indian security officials also routinely blame Pakistan's intelligence service for assisting the infiltration of Islamist militants into India from Nepal, Bangladesh, and Bhutan, as well as across the Kashmiri LOC.[274]

Domestic terrorism

Pakistan is known to be a base for numerous indigenous terrorist organizations, and the country continues to suffer from terrorism at home. Until a March 2006 car bombing at the U.S. consulate in Karachi that left one American diplomat dead, post-2001 attacks on Western targets had been rare, but 2002 saw several acts of lethal anti-Western terrorism, including the kidnaping and murder of reporter Daniel Pearl, a grenade attack on a Protestant church in Islamabad that killed a U.S. Embassy employee, and two car bomb attacks, including one on the same U.S. consulate. These attacks, widely viewed as expressions of militants' anger with the Musharraf regime for its cooperation with the United States, were linked to Al Qaeda, as well as to indigenous militant groups, by U.S. and Pakistani officials. Some analysts believe that, by redirecting Pakistan's internal security resources, an increase in militant violence can ease pressure on Al Qaeda and affiliated groups and so allow them to operate more freely there.

From 2003-2006, Pakistan's most serious domestic terrorism was directed against the country's Shia minority and included suicide bomb attacks that killed scores of people. Indications are that the indigenous Lashkar-e-Jhangvi (LJ) Sunni terrorist group is responsible for the most deadly anti-Shia violence. Two attempts to kill Musharraf in December 2003 and failed efforts to assassinate other top Pakistani officials in 2004 were linked to the LJ and to other Al Qaeda-allied groups, and illuminated the grave and continuing danger presented by religious extremists.

Other Security Issues

Pakistan-U.S. security cooperation

U.S.-Pakistan security cooperation accelerated rapidly after 2001, and President Bush formally designated Pakistan as a major non-NATO U.S. ally in 2004. The close U.S.-Pakistan security ties of the cold war era, which came to a near halt after the 1990 aid cutoff, have been restored as a result of Pakistan's role in the U.S.-led anti-terrorism campaign. In 2002, the United States began allowing commercial sales that enabled Pakistan to refurbish at least part of its fleet of American- made F-16 fighter aircraft and, three years later, Washington announced that it would resume sales of new F-16 fighters to Pakistan after a 16-year hiatus. A revived high-level U.S.-Pakistan Defense Consultative Group (DCG)—moribund from 1997 to 2001—sits for high-level discussions on military cooperation, security assistance, and anti-terrorism; its most recent session came in May 2006. In 2003, a U.S.-Pakistan-Afghanistan Tripartite Commission was established to bring together military commanders for regular discussions on Afghan stability and border security. Officers from NATO's International Security Assistance Force in Afghanistan have since joined the body, which met for the 25th time in January 2009.

Defense Supplies

Major government-to-government arms sales and grants to Pakistan since 2001 have included items useful for counterterrorism operations, along with a number of "big ticket" platforms more suited to conventional warfare. In dollar value terms, the bulk of purchases are made with Pakistani national funds: the Pentagon reports total Foreign Military Sales agreements with Pakistan worth $4.55 billion for FY2002-FY2007 (in-process sales of F-16 combat aircraft and related equipment account for about three-quarters of this). The United States also has provided Pakistan with nearly $1.6 billion in Foreign Military Financing (FMF) since 2001, with a "base program" of $300 million per year beginning in FY2005. These funds are used to purchase U.S. military equipment. Pakistan also has been granted U.S. defense supplies as

Excess Defense Articles (EDA). Major post-2001 defense supplies paid for with FMF include the following:

- eight P-3C Orion maritime patrol aircraft and their refurbishment (valued at $474 million);
- about 5,250 TOW anti-armor missiles ($186 million; 2,007 delivered);
- more than 5,600 military radio sets ($163 million);
- six AN/TPS-77 surveillance radars ($100 million, all delivered and in operation);
- six C-1 30E transport aircraft and their refurbishment ($76 million, all delivered and in operation); and
- 20 AH-1F Cobra attack helicopters granted under EDA, then refurbished ($48 million, 12 delivered, 8 pending refurbishment for up to $115 million more).

Supplies paid for with a mix of Pakistani national funds and FMF include:

- up to 60 mid-life update kits for F-1 6A/B combat aircraft (valued at $891 million, with at least $335 million of this in FMF; Pakistan's current plans are to purchase 46 of these); and
- 115 M-109 self-propelled howitzers ($87 million, with $53 million in FMF).

Notable items paid for entirely with Pakistani national funds include:

- 18 new F-16C/D Block 50/52 combat aircraft, with an option for 18 more (valued at $1.43 billion);
- F-1 6 armaments including 500 AMRAAM air-to-air missiles; 1,450 2,000-pound bombs; 500 JDAM bomb tail kits; and 1,600 Enhanced Paveway laser-guided bomb kits ($667 million);
- 100 Harpoon anti-ship missiles ($298 million, 88 delivered);
- 500 Sidewinder air-to-air missiles ($95 million, 420 delivered);
- six Phalanx close-in naval guns ($80 million).[275]

While the Pentagon has notified Congress to the possible transfer to Pakistan of three P-3B aircraft as EDA grants that would be modified to carry the E-2C Hawkeye airborne early warning suite in a deal worth up to $855 million, negotiations have not progressed beyond the notification stage. If implemented, FMF could be used toward this purchase. Major EDA grants since 2001 include 14 F-16A/B combat aircraft and 16 T-37 military trainer jets (20 more are pending). Pakistan may receive an EDA Oliver Perry-class anti-submarine frigate, the *USS McInerney*, in mid-2010 (the transfer was authorized by Congress in October 2008). Islamabad reportedly has requested $65 million worth of refurbishment and weapons for the 40-year-old vessel.[276] Under Coalition Support Funds (part of the Pentagon budget), Pakistan received 26 Bell 412 utility helicopters, along with related parts and maintenance, valued at $235 million.

The Defense Department has characterized F- 16 fighters, P-3C patrol aircraft, and anti-armor missiles as having significant anti-terrorism applications.[277] The State Department claims that, since 2005, FMF funds have been "solely for counterterrorism efforts, broadly defined."[278] Such claims elicit skepticism from some observers. Moreover, analysts who emphasize the importance of strengthening the U.S.-India strategic partnership call U.S. military aid to Pakistan incompatible with U.S. strategic goals in the region.[279] Pakistan is eager to receive more counterinsurgency equipment for use in western Pakistan, including helicopters, armored personnel carriers, laser target designators, laser-guided munitions, and more night-vision goggles and surveillance gear. By some accounts, Pakistani officials are frustrated by what they see a slow U.S. supply chain that fails to produce some equipment even years after it was promised.[280]

Other security-related programs for Pakistan are said to be aimed especially at bolstering Islamabad's counterterrorism and border security efforts, and have included U.S.-funded road- building projects in the NWFP and FATA; and the provision of night-vision equipment, communications gear, protective vests, and transport helicopters and aircraft. The United States also has undertaken to train and equip new Pakistan Army Air Assault units that can move quickly to find and target terrorist elements. Modest U.S.-funded military education and training programs seek to enhance the professionalism of Pakistan's military leaders, and develop respect for rule of law, human rights, and democratic values. The Pentagon may seek to substantially increase the value of its own assistance program for the Pakistani military by establishing a new Counterinsurgency Capability Fund of perhaps $400 million per year through FY20 15.[281]

Some reports indicate that U.S. military assistance to Pakistan has failed to effectively bolster the paramilitary forces battling Islamist militants in western Pakistan. Such forces are said to remain underfunded, poorly trained, and "overwhelmingly outgunned."[282] However, a July 2008 Pentagon-funded assessment found that Section 1206 "Global Train and Equip" funding was important for providing urgently needed military assistance to Pakistan and that the counterinsurgency capabilities of Pakistani special operations forces were measurably improved by the training and equipment that came through such funding.[283] The Bush Administration launched an initiative to strengthen the capacity of the Frontier Corps (FC), an 65,000-man paramilitary force overseen by the Pakistani Interior Ministry. The FC has primary responsibility for border security in the NWFP and Baluchistan provinces. The Pentagon in 2007 began using its funds to train and equip the FC, as well as to increase the involvement of the U.S. Special Operations Command in assisting with Pakistani counterterrorism efforts. Fewer than 100 Americans reportedly have been engaged in training Pakistan's elite Special Service Group commandos with a goal of doubling that force's size to 5,000.[284]

U.S. security assistance to Pakistan's civilian sector is aimed at strengthening the country's law enforcement capabilities through basic police training, provision of advanced identification systems, and establishment of a new Counterterrorism Special Investigation Group. U.S. efforts may be hindered by Pakistani shortcomings that include poorly trained and poorly equipped personnel who generally are underpaid by ineffectively coordinated and overburdened government agencies.[285] A 2008 think-tank report asserts that Pakistan's police and civilian intelligence agencies are better suited to combating insurgency and terrorism than are the country's regular army. It finds that Pakistan's police forces are "incapable of combating crime, upholding the law, or protecting citizens and the state against militant violence," and places the bulk of responsibility on the politicization of the police forces. The report recommends sweeping reforms to address corruption and human rights abuses.[286]

Renewed F-16 Sales and congressional concerns[287]

In 2005, the State Department announced a renewal of F-16 sales to Pakistan after a 16-year hiatus. A subsequent October 2005 earthquake in northern Pakistan put the F-16 purchase program on hold and led to a sharp reduction in the number of aircraft requested by Pakistan, which originally had been 75. In June 2006, the Pentagon notified Congress of a possible Foreign Military Sale to Pakistan worth up to $5.1 billion. The deal involves 18 newly-built F-16 Block 50/52 aircraft, along with related munitions and equipment, and represents the largest-ever weapons sale to Pakistan (Islamabad later declined an option to purchase 18 additional new aircraft). Associated munitions for new F-16s and for mid-life upgrades on others include 500

AMRAAM air-to-air missiles and thousands of both gravity and "smart" bombs.[288]

Congressional concerns about the sale and displeasure at the Bush Administration's apparently improper notification procedures spurred a July 2006 hearing of the House International Relations Committee. During that session, many Members worried that F-16s were better suited to fighting India than to combating terrorists; some warned that U.S. military technology could be passed from Pakistan to China. The State Department's lead official on political-military relations sought to assure the committee that the sale would serve U.S. interests by strengthening the defense capabilities of a key ally without disturbing the regional balance of power and that all possible measures would be taken to prevent the onward transfer of U.S. technologies. H.J.Res. 93, disapproving the proposed sale, was introduced in the House, but died in committee.

Secretary of State Rice subsequently informed Congress that no F-16 combat aircraft or related equipment would be delivered to Pakistan until Islamabad provided written security assurances that U.S. technology will not be accessible by third parties. Islamabad has denied that any "extraordinary" security requirements were requested; however, congressional concerns appear to have been satisfactorily addressed. After further negotiations on specifics, including a payment process that requires a major outlay from the Pakistani treasury, the United States and Pakistan signed a September 2006 letter of acceptance for the multi-billion dollar F-16 deal. Since then, several major U.S. defense corporations have won contracts worth hundreds of millions of dollars to supply F-16 parts and munitions to Pakistan, including a December 2007 award to Lockheed- Martin worth about $500 million.

F-16 reprogramming

In July 2008, the State Department notified Congress of its intention to shift $227 million in FY2008 FMF funds toward supporting Pakistan's F-16 mid-life update program. The Islamabad government had previously vowed to use its own national funds for the bulk of such upgrades. The proposal was met with anger and dismay by some in Congress who said it would do little to enhance Pakistan's counterterrorism capabilities. A State Department spokesman asserted that Islamabad sought and was granted the consideration so as to provide much-needed financial relief. Two senior House Members, concerned that the proposal would "divert funds from more effective counterterrorism tools," requested a hold be placed on the planned reprogramming and proposed that Congress provide $200 million in budgetary support to Pakistan.[289] The hold request was not honored and $116 million in reprogrammed funds was disbursed in August. More such reprogramming of FMF funds may come in FY2009.

At a subsequent hearing on Pakistan's F-16 program, the chairman of the House Foreign Affairs Subcommittee on the Middle East and South Asia, Representative Gary Ackerman, criticized what he called the Bush Administration's "cavalier discard" of congressional concerns about the appropriate uses of Foreign Military Sales. He and other Members in attendance cast doubt on the efficacy of F-16s as counterinsurgency weapons. The State Department official testifying insisted that, by paying for upgrades to Pakistan's existing F-16s, the United States would both bolster that country's counterterrorism capabilities and ease fiscal pressures on the new civilian government. He said the aircraft had become "an iconic symbol" of the U.S. commitment to Pakistan.[290]

Nuclear weapons and missile proliferation[291]

Many policy analysts consider an apparent arms race between India and Pakistan to be among the most likely potential causes of the future use of nuclear weapons by states. In May 1998, India conducted unannounced nuclear tests, breaking a 24-year, self-imposed moratorium on such testing. Despite U.S. and world efforts to dissuade it, Pakistan quickly followed. The tests created a global storm of criticism and represented a serious setback to two decades of U.S. nuclear nonproliferation efforts in South Asia. Pakistan currently is believed to have enough fissile material, mainly enriched uranium, for 55-90 nuclear weapons; India, with a program focused on plutonium, may be capable of building a similar number. Both countries have aircraft capable of delivering nuclear bombs (U.S.-supplied F-16 combat aircraft in Pakistan's air force reportedly have been refitted to carry nuclear bombs).[292] Pakistan's military has inducted short- and medium-range ballistic missiles (allegedly acquired from China and North Korea), while India possesses short- and intermediate-range missiles. Both countries have tested cruise missiles with radar-evading capabilities. All missiles are assumed to be capable of delivering nuclear warheads over significant distances.

In 2000, Pakistan placed its nuclear forces under the control of a National Command Authority chaired by the President. According to the most recent global threat assessment by the U.S. Director of National Intelligence, "Although both New Delhi and Islamabad are fielding a more mature strategic nuclear capability, they do not appear to be engaged in a Cold War-style arms race for numerical superiority.[293] In late 2008, President Zardari said he favored a no-first-use policy on nuclear weapons, the first-ever such statement by a Pakistani leader. While the informal declaration was widely welcomed globally, it was met with consternation in many Pakistani circles and has not to date appeared in any official Pakistani policy statements.[294]

The A.Q. Khan nuclear proliferation network[295]

Sensitive Pakistani nuclear materials and technologies have been transferred illicitly to third parties. Press reports in late 2002 suggested that Pakistan assisted Pyongyang's covert nuclear weapons program by providing North Korea with uranium enrichment materials and technologies beginning in the mid-1990s. Islamabad rejected such reports as "baseless" and Secretary of State Colin Powell was assured that no such transfers were occurring. Under U.S. law, if such assistance is confirmed by the U.S. President, all non-humanitarian U.S. aid to Pakistan may be suspended, although the President has the authority to waive any sanctions that he determines would jeopardize U.S. national security. In early 2003, the Bush Administration determined that the relevant facts "do not warrant imposition of sanctions under applicable U.S. laws." Press reports during 2003 suggested that both Iran and Libya benefitted from Pakistani nuclear assistance. Islamabad denied any nuclear cooperation with Tehran or Tripoli, although it conceded in December 2003 that certain senior scientists were under investigation for possible "independent" proliferation activities.

The investigation led to the February 2004 "public humiliation" of metallurgist Abdul Qadeer Khan, known as the founder of Pakistan's nuclear weapons program and a national hero, when he confessed to involvement in an illicit nuclear smuggling network. Khan and at least seven associates were said to have sold crucial nuclear weapons technology and uranium-enrichment materials to North Korea, Iran, and Libya. Such technology may have included complete blueprints for an advanced nuclear weapon design.[296] President Musharraf, citing Khan's contributions to his nation, issued a pardon that was later called conditional.[297] The United States has been assured that the Islamabad government had no knowledge of such activities; Washington called the decision to pardon an internal Pakistani matter. Some independent observers insist that Khan's activities were, in fact, well known to top Pakistani authorities and that elements of the U.S. government turned a blind eye to the proliferation while seeking Pakistan's continued cooperation with other foreign policy efforts.[298] Khan himself has alleged that at least one illicit shipment of uranium enrichment equipment to North Korea was supervised by the Pakistani army with the consent of then-Army Chief Musharraf. A spokesman for Musharraf called the allegations "lies."[299]

While President Musharraf did promise President Bush that all information learned about Khan's proliferation network would be shared, Pakistan has refused to allow any direct access to Khan by U.S. or international investigators. In May 2006, days after releasing from detention nuclear scientist and suspected Khan collaborator Mohammed Farooq, the Islamabad government declared the investigation "closed." Some in Congress remained skeptical, however, and a House panel subsequently held a hearing at which three nongovernmental experts urged that U.S. and international investigators be given direct access to Khan, in particular to learn more about assistance given to Iran's nuclear program. Some analysts even claim that Iran's strides in uranium enrichment and the related international crisis are almost wholly attributable to Khan's past assistance to Tehran's nuclear program.[300] No alleged Pakistani participants have faced criminal charges in the case.

In 2007, a London-based think tank released a report on the Khan network, finding that "at least some of Khan's associates appear to have escaped law enforcement attention and could, after a period of lying low, resume their black-market business." Shortly after, a House panel held another hearing on the Khan network; several Members and nongovernmental expert witnesses again called for Pakistan to allow direct access to Khan for U.S. investigators.[301]

In July 2007, Islamabad reportedly eased house arrest restrictions on Khan, although the Foreign Ministry denied any change in Khan's status. A Foreign Ministry spokesman in April 2008 said no foreign countries were seeking access to Khan as, internationally, the issue is "a closed chapter." In May 2008, Khan reneged on his 2004 confession, saying its "false allegations" were made only under pressure from the Musharraf government. In July, the new, civilian-led government relaxed travel and communications restrictions on Khan even as it persuaded a judge to bar Khan from speaking about nuclear proliferation.[302] In January 2009, the U.S. government placed sanctions on 13 people and three firms linked to the Khan network. In February, Khan was released from house arrest on the order of the Islamabad High Court, a development that triggered new worries for both the Obama Administration and in the U.S. Congress.[303] The U.S. government has remained "very concerned" about Khan's smuggling network: In May 2008 a high-ranking U.S. intelligence official called the security of Pakistan's nuclear weapons a "number one" worry for the United States that is tracked as a continuing high priority.[304]

Major new plutonium facilities?

Revelations in 2006 that Pakistan is constructing a major heavy water nuclear reactor at the Khushab complex brought a flurry of concern from analysts who foresee a regional competition in fissile material production, perhaps including China. A subsequent report identified a third plutonium production reactor at Khushab. Upon completion, which could be many years away, two new reactors with combined 1,000-megawatt capacity might boost Pakistan's weapons-grade plutonium production capabilities to more than 200 kilograms per year, or enough for up to 50 nuclear weapons. Moreover, a 2007 report warned that Pakistan may soon be reprocessing weapons-grade plutonium at its Chashma facility, further adding to its potential stockpile and aiding in the development of thermonuclear weapons. While Islamabad does not comment directly on the constructions, government officials there insist that Pakistan will continue to update and consolidate its nuclear program for the purpose of minimum credible deterrence. The Bush Administration responded to the 2006 revelations by claiming it had been aware of Pakistani plans and that it discourages the use of the facilities for military purposes.[305]

Pakistan's nuclear transparency and security[306]

During 2006, Islamabad appeared to launch a public relations effort aimed at overcoming the stigma caused by Khan's proliferation activities. The effort included dispatching to Washington the chief of the country's Strategic Plans Division (SPD), Khalid Kidwai, a retired lieutenant general who attempted to make more transparent Pakistan's nuclear command and control structure, and who acknowledged that Pakistan's past proliferation record had been "poor and indefensible."[307] Among the most urgent concerns of U.S. officials has been the security of Pakistan's nuclear weapons and materials, which could be degraded as instability persists. While the danger of Islamist extremist gaining possession of a nuclear explosive device is considered remote, the risk of rogue scientists or security officials seeking to sell nuclear materials and/or technology is seen to be higher in a setting of deteriorating security conditions.

Most analysts appear to have concluded that the security of Pakistan's nuclear weapons and facilities is much improved in recent years. Some note that periods of interstate crisis between Pakistan and India can be particularly dangerous in the context of nuclear security, when Pakistan's warheads are more likely to be mobilized and so are outside of their heavily-guarded storage sites.[308] More worrisome, many claim, is the possibility that Pakistan's nuclear know-how or technologies could remain prone to leakage.[309] A congressionally-mandated commission on the prevention of WMD proliferation and terrorism issued a December report that highlighted Pakistan as existing at "the intersection of nuclear weapons and terrorism." The report made several recommendations aimed at strengthening stability and governance in Pakistan so as to prevent the use of Pakistani WMD materials or technologies in a potential future terrorist attack on the United States.[310]

India's national security advisor—a figure not expected to downplay the dangers—assessed that Pakistan's nuclear arsenal is "largely safe."[311] Still, in early 2008, IAEA Director-General Mohammed ElBaradei expressed fear that continued "chaos" could lead to Pakistan's nuclear weapons falling into the hands of extremist elements. Unsurprisingly, the Islamabad government angrily rejects such fears as unrealistic, but even some Pakistani commentators aver that such warnings should not be dismissed.[312]

Pakistan reportedly has since 2005 been employing a multilayered system of checks that most prominently includes a Personnel Reliability Program modeled after that used by the United States. The program carefully vets and monitors potential and serving employees at the country's nuclear facilities with a particular emphasis on religious sentiments. Other aspects include biometric scanners and what Pakistani officials call their indigenously developed versions of Permissive Action Links (PALs), sophisticated locks put on U.S. nuclear weapons to prevent their unauthorized use. The United States reportedly has spent nearly $100 million since 2001 on a classified program to help secure Pakistan's strategic weapons. Islamabad claims the amount is closer to $10 million and it emphatically rejects suggestions that the country's nuclear arsenal is anything but fully secure.[313]

The SPD claims that 10,000 soldiers are devoted to the task of guarding the country's nuclear weapons. Reports of U.S. "war-gaming" scenarios to intervene in Pakistan to secure the country's nuclear weapons in a crisis suggest that U.S. options are severely limited and that the cooperation of the Pakistani government and military would be crucial to the success of such efforts. Such reports may themselves antagonize Islamabad.[314] SPD chief Kidwai insists that Pakistan's security systems are foolproof, but serious concerns about laboratory security, the auditing of nuclear fuel, and the ability of Pakistan's nuclear engineers to sell their knowledge continue to be widespread. Of the roughly 70,000 people said to work at Pakistani nuclear installations, 7,000 are scientists, and some 2,000 are labeled by Kidwai himself as holding "critical knowledge."[315]

U.S. nonproliferation policy

The United States has long sought to halt or limit the proliferation of nuclear weapons in South Asia. In May 1998, following the Indian and Pakistani nuclear tests, President Clinton imposed full restrictions on all non-humanitarian aid to both countries as mandated under Section 102 of the Arms Export Control Act. However, Congress and the President acted almost immediately to lift certain aid restrictions and, in October 2001, all remaining nuclear-related sanctions on Pakistan (and India) were removed. Officially, the United States has continued to urge Pakistan and India to join the Nuclear Nonproliferation Treaty (NPT) as non-nuclear weapon states and it offers no official recognition of their nuclear weapons capabilities, which exist outside of the international nonproliferation regime.

During the latter years of the Clinton Administration, the United States set forth nonproliferation "benchmarks" for Pakistan and India, including halting further nuclear testing and signing and ratifying the Comprehensive Test Ban Treaty (CTBT); halting fissile material production and pursuing Fissile Material Control Treaty negotiations; refraining from deploying nuclear weapons and testing ballistic missiles; and restricting any and all exportation of nuclear materials or technologies. The results of U.S. efforts were mixed, at best, and neither Pakistan nor India are signatories to the CTBT or the NPT. The Bush Administration quickly set aside the benchmark framework. However, concerns about onward proliferation, fears that Pakistan could become destabilized by the U.S.-led counterterrorism efforts in Afghanistan, and concern over the issue of political succession in Islamabad have heightened U.S. attention to weapons proliferation in the region. Some Members of Congress have identified "contradictions" in U.S. nonproliferation policy toward South Asia, particularly as related to the Senate's rejection of the CTBT and indications that the United States seeks to build new nuclear weapons. Section 1601 of the Foreign Relations Authorization Act of FY2003 (P.L. 107-228) outlined congressionally mandated U.S. nonproliferation objectives for Pakistan and India.[316]

Pakistan-India tensions and the Kashmir issue

In the interests of regional stability, the United States strongly encourages an ongoing Pakistan- India peace initiative and remains concerned about the potential for long-standing disagreements to cause open hostilities between these two nuclear-armed countries. Relations between Pakistan and India remain deadlocked on the issue of Kashmiri sovereignty, and a separatist rebellion has been underway in the region since 1989. Tensions were extremely high in the wake of the Kargil conflict of 1999, when an incursion by Pakistani soldiers led to a bloody six-week-long battle. Throughout 2000 and 2001, cross-border firing and shelling caused scores of both military and civilian deaths. A July 2001 Pakistan-India summit meeting failed to produce even a joint statement, reportedly due to pressure from hardliners on both sides. Major stumbling blocks were India's refusal to acknowledge the "centrality of Kashmir" to future talks and Pakistan's objection to references to "cross-border terrorism."

The 2002 crisis

Then-Secretary of State Powell visited South Asia in October 2001 in an effort to ease escalating tensions over Kashmir, but a bombing at the Jammu and Kashmir state assembly building later that month was followed by a December assault on the Indian Parliament in New Delhi (both incidents were blamed on Pakistan-based terrorist groups). India mobilized some 700,000 troops along the Pakistan-India frontier and threatened war unless Islamabad ended all "cross-border infiltration" of Islamic militants. This triggered a corresponding Pakistani military mobilization. Under significant international diplomatic pressure (and likely also the threat of India's use of force), President Musharraf in January 2002 gave a landmark address in which he vowed to end the presence of terrorist entities on Pakistani soil, and he outlawed five militant groups, including those most often named in attacks in India: Lashkar-e-Taiba and Jaish-e-Mohammed.[317]

Despite the Pakistani pledge, infiltrations into Indian-held Kashmir continued, and a May 2002 terrorist attack on an Indian army base at Kaluchak killed 34, most of them women and children. This event again brought Pakistan and India to the brink of full-scale war, and caused Islamabad to recall army troops from patrol operations along the Pakistan-Afghanistan border. Intensive international diplomatic missions to South Asia reduced tensions during the summer of 2002 and appeared to have prevented the outbreak of war. Numerous top U.S. officials were involved in the effort and strenuously urged the two countries to renew bilateral dialogue.[318]

The most recent peace process

Pakistan and India began full military draw-downs in October 2002 and, after a cooling-off period, a "hand of friendship" offer to Pakistan by the Indian prime minister in April 2003 led to the restoration of full diplomatic relations. Yet surging separatist violence that summer contributed to an exchange of sharp rhetoric between Pakistani and Indian leaders at the United

Nations, casting doubt on the nascent peace effort. A new confidence-building initiative got Pakistan and India back on a positive track, and a November 2003 cease-fire was initiated after a proposal by Pakistani Prime Minister Z.K. Jamali. President Musharraf later suggested that Pakistan might be willing to "set aside" its long-standing demand for a plebiscite in Kashmir, a proposal welcomed by the United States, but called a "disastrous shift" in policy by Pakistani opposition parties.

Although militant infiltration did not end, New Delhi acknowledged that it was significantly decreased and, combined with other confidence-building measures, relations were sufficiently improved that the Indian prime minister attended a January 2004 summit meeting of the South Asian Association for Regional Cooperation in Islamabad. There Pakistan and India issued a joint "Islamabad Declaration" calling for a renewed "Composite Dialogue" to bring about "peaceful settlement of all bilateral issues, including Jammu and Kashmir, to the satisfaction of both sides."[319] A major confidence-building development came in April 2005, when a new bus service was launched linking Muzaffarabad in Pakistani Kashmir and Srinagar in Indian Kashmir, and a summit meeting produced an agreement to address the Kashmir issue "in a forward looking manner for a final settlement." Still, many Kashmiris reject any settlement process that excludes them.

Even as the normalization of India-Pakistan relations moves forward—and likely in reaction to their apparent marginalization in the face of this development—separatist militants have continued their attacks, and many observers in both India and the United States believe support for Kashmiri militants remains Pakistani state policy. Yet many indicators show positive longterm trends. Steadily reduced rates of infiltration may be attributed to the endurance of the Pakistan-India dialogue. Moreover, President Musharraf made notable efforts to exhibit flexibility, including late 2006 statements that Pakistan is "against independence" for Kashmir, and his offering of a four-point proposal that would lead to "self-governance ... falling between autonomy and independence."[320] This was seen by many analysts as being roughly in line with New Delhi's Kashmir position. Indeed, the Indian prime minister welcomed Musharraf's proposals. Prospects for a government-to-government accommodation may thus be improved. However, political and security crises in Pakistan slowed the process in 2007. Following the seating of a new civilian government in Islamabad in early 2008, dialogue resume in May.

Baluchistan unrest

Pakistan's vast southwestern Baluchistan province is about the size of California and accounts for 44% of the country's land area, but only 5% of its population. The U.S. military has made use of bases in the region to support its operations in neighboring Afghanistan. The province is the proposed setting for a pipeline that would deliver Iranian natural gas to both Pakistan and India, a project which, if brought to fruition, could bring hundreds of millions of dollars in annual transit fees to Islamabad's national treasury, but conflict in Baluchistan reduces the appeal to investors of building a pipeline across the province. The presence in Baluchistan of Jundallah, a trans-border militant group that claims to fight on behalf of Baloch rights, has caused friction between Islamabad and Tehran. More broadly, such problems raise serious questions about Pakistan's internal stability and national cohesion.[321]

Over the decades of Pakistani independence, many of the ethnic Baloch and some of the Pashtun tribes who inhabit this relatively poor and underdeveloped province have engaged in armed conflict with federal government forces, variously seeking more equitable returns on the region's rich natural resources, greater autonomy under the country's federal system, or even outright independence and formation of a Baloch state that might include ethnic brethren and some territories of both Afghanistan and Iran. Non-Baloch (mostly Punjabis) have been seen to benefit disproportionately from provincial mineral and energy extraction projects, and indigenous Baloch were given only a small role in the construction of a major new port at Gwadar. Many Baloch thus complain of being a marginalized group in their own homeland. Long-standing resentments sparked armed conflicts in 1948, 1958, and 1973. The latter insurrection, which lasted four years, involved tens of thousands of armed guerillas and brought much destruction to the province; it was put down only after a major effort by the Pakistan Army, which made use of combat helicopters provided by Iran. Some 8,000 rebels and Pakistani soldiers were killed.

The current conflict

Mid-2004 saw an increase in hit-and-run attacks on army outposts and in the sabotage of oil and gas pipelines. The alleged rape of a Baloch doctor by Pakistani soldiers in 2005 sparked provincial anger and a major spike in separatist violence over the course of the year. In December of that year, rockets were fired at a Baluchistan army camp during a visit to the site by President Musharraf. A Baloch separatist group claimed responsibility and the Pakistani military began major offensive operations to destroy the militants' camps. In the midst of increasingly heavy fighting in January 2006, Musharraf openly accused India of arming and financing militants fighting in Baluchistan. New Delhi categorically rejected the allegations. U.N. and other international aid groups soon suspended their operations in Baluchistan due to security concerns. Shortly after, Baloch militants shot and killed three Chinese engineers and their Pakistani driver, causing disruption in Islamabad-Beijing relations.

Fighting waned in the middle of 2006, with hundreds of rebels surrendering in return for amnesty. The main rebel tribal leader and onetime Baluchistan chief minister, 79-year-old Nawab Akbar Bugti, had gone into hiding and was believed cut off from his own forces. In August, Bugti was located in a cave hideout and was killed by Pakistan army troops in a battle that left dozens of soldiers and rebels dead. Recognizing Bugti's popularity among wide segments of the Baloch populace and of the potential for his killing to provide martyr status, government officials denied the tribal leader had been targeted. Nevertheless, news of his death spurred major unrest across the province and beyond, with hundreds of arrests in the midst of large-scale street demonstrations. Bugti's killing was criticized across the spectrum of Pakistani politicians and analysts, with some commentators calling it a Pakistani Army miscue of historic proportions.[322] Days of rioting included numerous deaths and injuries, but the more dire predictions of spreading unrest and perhaps even the disintegration of Pakistan's federal system did not come to pass. By October 2006, Pakistan's interior minister was claiming a "normalization" and decrease in violence in Baluchistan, although a low-intensity insurgency continued and the overarching problem remained unresolved.[323]

President Musharraf called Baloch rebels "miscreants" and "terrorists;" the Islamabad government officially banned the separatist Baluchistan Liberation Army as a terrorist organization in 2006 and at times suggests that Baloch militants are religious extremists. Yet most rebel attacks are taken against military and infrastructure targets, and—despite an apparent government campaign to link the two movements—Islam appears to play little or no role as a motive for Baloch militancy.[324] Pakistan's new civilian dispensation has undertaken some efforts to peacefully resolve the Baluchistan dispute. In May 2008, the Islamabad government freed a Baloch nationalist leader and former provincial chief minister, Akthar Mengal, who had been imprisoned for two years. The move was seen as a peace gesture toward the troubled province. Yet major mid-2008 skirmishes between Baloch militants and security forces left several dozen people dead, and subsequent reports suggest that the government has failed to keep promises made to the Baloch people, dashing expectations and leaving the troubled province even less secure.[325]

Narcotics[326]

In September 2008, President Bush again named Pakistan (along with both Afghanistan and India) among the world's 20 "major drug transit or major illicit drug producing" countries."[327] Pakistan is a major transit country for opiates that are grown and processed in Afghanistan then distributed worldwide by Pakistan-based traffickers. The State Department indicates that Pakistan's cooperation on drug control "remains strong," and the Islamabad government has made impressive strides in eradicating indigenous opium poppy cultivation. However, the Department's most recent *International Narcotics Control Strategy Report* (issued March 2008) asserted that "the imperative of combating militants in the FATA diverted resources and political attention away from Pakistan's goal of returning to a poppy-free status and Pakistan saw an increase of poppy cultivation in 2007." It also expressed concern that Pakistan's long-anticipated Master Drug Control Plan, expected in early 2007, is yet to be approved.[328]

Opium production spiked in post-Taliban Afghanistan and is at all-time high, supplying more than 90% of the world's heroin.[329] Elements of Pakistan's intelligence agency are suspected of past involvement in drug trafficking; in 2003, a former U.S. Ambassador to Pakistan told a House panel that their role in the heroin trade from 1997-2003 was "substantial."[330] The State Department finds no evidence that the Islamabad government or any of its senior officials are complicit in narcotics trafficking, but concedes that low government salaries and endemic societal corruption contribute to lower-level complicity.[331] The Pakistani criminal network involved in production, processing, and trafficking is described as being "enormous, highly motivated, profit- driven, ruthless, and efficient." Taliban militants are reported to benefit significantly by taxing Afghan farmers and extorting traffickers.[332] Other reports indicate that profits from drug sales are financing the activities of Islamic extremists in Pakistan and Kashmir.

U.S. counternarcotics programs aim to assist Pakistan in fortifying its borders and coast against drug trafficking and terrorism, support expanded regional cooperation, encourage Pakistani efforts to eliminate poppy cultivation, and inhibit further cultivation. The United States also aims to increase the interdiction of narcotics from Afghanistan. Islamabad's own counternarcotics efforts are hampered by lack of full government commitment, scarcity of funds, poor infrastructure, and likely corruption. Since 2002, the State Department's Bureau of International Narcotics and Law Enforcement Affairs has supported Pakistan's Border Security Project by training border forces, establishing border outposts, providing vehicles and surveillance and communications equipment, transferring helicopters and fixed-wing aircraft to the Interior Ministry's Air Wing, and road-building in western tribal areas. Congress funded such programs with roughly $22 million in FY2008.

Islamization, Anti-American Sentiment and Madrassas

With some 168 million citizens, Pakistan is the world's second-most populous Muslim country, and the nation's very foundation grew from a perceived need to create a homeland for South Asian Muslims in the wake of decolonization. However, religious-based political parties traditionally have fared poorly in national elections. An unexpected outcome of the country's 2002 polls saw the Muttahida Majlis-e-Amal (MMA or United Action Front), a coalition of six Islamic parties, win 11% of the popular vote. It also gained control of the provincial assembly in the North West Frontier Province (NWFP) and led a coalition in the Baluchistan assembly. These Pashtun-majority western provinces border Afghanistan, where U.S.-led counterterrorism operations are ongoing. In 2003, the NWFP provincial assembly passed a Shariat (Islamic law) bill. In both 2005 and 2006, the same assembly passed a Hasba (accountability) bill that many feared could create a parallel Islamic legal body. Pakistan's Supreme Court, responding to petitions by the central government, rejected most of this legislation as unconstitutional, but in 2007 it upheld most of a modified Hasba bill re-submitted by the NWFP assembly. Such developments alarm Pakistan's moderates and the Pakistani President himself decried any attempts to "Talibanize" regions of Pakistan.[333] The Islamist coalition was ousted from power in Peshawar and suffered major electoral losses nationwide when February 2008 polls saw the secular Pashtun nationalist Awami National Party take over the NWFP government. Still, in the latter months of 2008, nearly two-thirds of Pakistanis reported believing that Sharia law should play a greater role in the country's governance.[334]

Pakistan's Islamists are notable for expressions of anti-American sentiment, at times calling for "jihad" against the existential threat to Pakistani sovereignty they believe alliance with Washington entails. Most analysts contend that two December 2003 attempts to assassinate President Musharraf were carried out by Islamist militants angered by Pakistan's post-September

2001 policy shift. The "Pakistani Taliban" that has emerged in western tribal areas has sought to impose bans on television and CD players, and has instigated attacks on girls schools and nongovernmental organization-operated clinics, obstructing efforts to improve female health and education. Some observers identify a causal link between the poor state of Pakistan's public education system and the persistence of xenophobia and religious extremism in that country.[335]

Anti-American sentiment is not limited to Islamic groups, however. Many across the spectrum of Pakistani society express anger at U.S. global foreign policy, in particular when such policy is perceived to be unfriendly or hostile to the Muslim world (as in, for example, Palestine and Iraq).[336] In 2004 testimony before a Senate panel, a senior U.S. expert opined: "Pakistan is probably the most anti-American country in the world right now, ranging from the radical Islamists on one side to the liberals and Westernized elites on the other side."[337] In a 2005 interview, President Musharraf conceded that "the man on the street [in Pakistan] does not have a good opinion of the United States." He added, by way of partial explanation, that Pakistan had been "left high and dry" after serving as a strategic U.S. ally during the 1980s. When asked about anti-American sentiment in Pakistan during his maiden July 2008 visit to the United States as head of government, Prime Minister Gillani offered that the impression in Pakistan is that "America wants war."[338]

A Pew poll taken shortly before Pakistan's catastrophic October 2005 earthquake found only 23% of Pakistanis expressing a favorable view of the United States, the lowest percentage for any country surveyed. That percentage doubled to 46% in an ACNielsen poll taken after large-scale U.S. disaster relief efforts in earthquake-affected areas, with the great majority of Pakistanis indicating that their perceptions had been positively influenced by witnessing such efforts. However, a January 2006 missile attack on Pakistani homes near the Afghan border killed numerous civilians and was blamed on U.S. forces, renewing animosity toward the United States among segments of the Pakistani populace. Another noteworthy episode in 2006 saw Pakistani cities hosting major public demonstrations against the publication in European newspapers of cartoons deemed offensive to Muslims. These protests, which were violent at times, included strong anti-U.S. and anti-Musharraf components, suggesting that Islamist organizers used the issue to forward their own political ends. Subsequently, a June 2006 Pew Center poll found only 27% of Pakistanis holding a favorable opinion of the United States, and this dropped to 19% in a September 2007 survey by the U.S.-based group Terror

Free Tomorrow, suggesting that public diplomacy gains following the 2005 earthquake had receded.

In December 2008, the Washington-based International Republican Institute (IRI) released a survey of public opinion in Pakistan taken in October. The findings indicated that significant resentment toward and distrust of the United States persist among large segments of the Pakistani public, which appears split on the issue of Pakistani military efforts to combat extremists:

- Nearly two-thirds opposed Pakistan's cooperation with the United States in the so-called war on terrorism;
- nearly three-quarters opposed U.S. military incursions in Pakistan's tribal areas;
- one in three Pakistanis reported believing that either the U.S. or Pakistani government was responsible for the September Marriott bombing; only 7% blamed the Taliban or terrorists;
- fully half said they opposed Pakistan army operations in western Pakistan; and
- a majority continued to express support for peace deals with religious extremists.[339]

A late 2008 Gallup survey found only one in seven Pakistanis holding the opinion that counterterrorism cooperation with the United States had benefitted their country. Yet, in more encouraging findings, three in five respondents to the IRI poll believed that religious extremism represented a "serious problem" for Pakistan, with a majority saying the Al Qaeda and Taliban presence in Pakistan was part of this. Moreover, a subsequent Gallup poll showed 60% of Pakistanis saying their government should take a tougher stance in efforts to rid the country of terrorist activities. Support for a harder line was found to be markedly higher in Punjab.[340]

Pakistan's religious schools (Madrassas)[341]

Afghanistan's Taliban movement itself began among students attending Pakistani religious schools (madrassas). Among the more than 15,000 madrassas training some 1.5 million children in Pakistan are a small percentage that have been implicated in teaching militant anti-Western, anti-American, anti-Hindu, and even anti-Shia values. Former Secretary of State Powell once identified these as "programs that do nothing but prepare youngsters to be fundamentalists and to be terrorists."[342] Contrary to popularly held conceptions, however, research indicates that the great majority of

Pakistan's violent Islamist extremists does not emerge from the country's madrassas, but rather from the dysfunctional public school system or even from private, English- medium schools. One study found that less than one in five international terrorists sampled had Islamic education backgrounds.[343] However, a senior leader of the secular Awami National Party that now leads a coalition government in the North West Frontier Province said in mid-2008 that many Pakistani madrassas encourage militancy and are breeding grounds for terrorism. He appealed to international donors to help Pakistan establish modern educational institutions.[344]

Many of Pakistan's madrassas are financed and operated by Pakistani Islamist political parties such as the JUI-F (closely linked to the Taliban), as well as by multiple unknown foreign entities, many in Saudi Arabia.[345] As many as two-thirds of the seminaries are run by the Deobandi sect, known in part for traditionally anti-Shia sentiments and at times linked to the Sipah-e-Sahaba terrorist group. In its 2007 report on international religious freedom, the U.S. State Department said, "Some unregistered and Deobandi-controlled madrassas in the FATA and northern Baluchistan continued to teach extremism" and that schools run by the Jamaat al-Dawat, considered to be a front organization of the proscribed Lashkar-e-Taiba terrorist group, serve as recruitment centers for extremists. President Musharraf himself has acknowledged that a small number of seminaries were "harboring terrorists" and he has asked religious leaders to help isolate these by openly condemning them.[346]

Global attention to Pakistan's religious schools intensified during the summer of 2005 after Pakistani officials acknowledged that suspects in London terrorist bombings visited Pakistan during the previous year and may have spent time at a madrassa near Lahore. While the Islamabad government repeatedly has pledged to crack down on the more extremist madrassas in his country, there continues to be little concrete evidence that it has done so.[347] Some observers speculate that President Musharraf's alleged reluctance to enforce reform efforts was rooted in his desire to remain on good terms with Pakistan's Islamist political parties, which were seen to be an important part of his political base.[348] When asked in late 2007 about progress in reforming the country's madrassa system, Musharraf made a rare admission of "lack of achievement," but went on to call the registration campaign and efforts to mainstream the curriculum successful.[349]

A key aspect of madrassas' enduring appeal to Pakistani parents is the abysmal state of the country's public schools. Pakistan's primary education system ranks among the world's least effective. Congress, the Bush

Administration, and the 9/11 Commission each have identified this issue as relevant to U.S. interests in South Asia. In the lead-up to Pakistan's February 2008 elections, 16 of the country's major parties committed to raising the federal education budget to 4% of GDP, up from the current 2.4%. The U.S. Congress has appropriated many millions of dollars to assist Pakistan in efforts to reform its education system, including changes that would make madrassa curriculum closer in substance to that provided in non-religious schools. About $256 million has been allocated for education-related aid programs since 2002. In 2006, the U.S.- Pakistan Education dialogue was launched in Washington to bolster further engagement. In April 2008, USAID launched a new $90 million project to bolster the effectiveness of Pakistan's public education sector. Requested funding for FY2009 includes a total of $166 million for basic and higher education programs in Pakistan.[350]

Democratization and Human Rights

Democracy and governance[351]

The status and development of Pakistan's democratic institutions are key U.S. policy concerns, especially among those analysts who view representative government in Islamabad as being a prerequisite for reducing religious extremism and establishing a moderate Pakistani state. There had been hopes that the October 2002 national elections would reverse Pakistan's historic trend toward unstable governance and military interference in democratic institutions. Such hopes were eroded by ensuing developments, including President Musharraf's imposition of major constitutional changes and his retention of the position of army chief. International and Pakistani human rights groups continued to issue reports critical of Islamabad's military-dominated government throughout the Musharraf-dominated era. In 2008, and for the ninth straight year, Freedom House rated Pakistan as "not free" in the areas of political rights and civil liberties.

Pakistan's military-dominated government, 2002-2008

General Musharraf's assumption of the presidency ostensibly was legitimized by a controversial April 2002 referendum marked by evidence of fraud.[352] In August 2002, Musharraf announced sweeping constitutional changes to bolster the president's powers, including provisions for presidential dissolution of the National Assembly. The United States expressed concerns that the changes could make it more difficult to build democratic institutions in Pakistan. The 2002 elections nominally fulfilled Musharraf's promise to restore the National Assembly that was dissolved in the wake of his extra-constitutional seizure of power. The pro-military PML-Q party won a plurality of seats, while a coalition of Islamist parties made a surprisingly strong showing.

The civilian government was hamstrung for more than a year by fractious debate over the legitimacy of constitutional changes and by Musharraf's continued status as army chief *and* president. A surprise December 2003 agreement between Musharraf and the MMA Islamist opposition ended the deadlock by bringing the constitutional changes before Parliament and by eliciting a promise from Musharraf to resign his military commission before 2005. Non-Islamist opposition parties unified under the Alliance for the Restoration of Democracy (ARD) accused the MMA of betrayal and insisted that the new arrangement merely institutionalized military rule in Pakistan. Further apparent reversals for Pakistani democratization came in 2004, including the sentencing of ARD leader and PML-N stalwart Javed Hashmi to 23 years in prison for sedition, mutiny, and forgery (Hashmi was released in 2007), and the "forced" resignation of Prime Minister Jamali for what numerous analysts called his insufficient deference to President Musharraf. Musharraf "shuffled" prime ministers to seat his close ally, Finance Minister Shaukat Aziz. Aziz was seen to be an able financial manager and technocrat favored by the military, but he had no political base in Pakistan. In the final month of 2004 Musharraf chose to continue his role as army chief beyond the stated deadline. Moreover, nominally non-party 2005 municipal elections saw major gains for candidates favored by the PML-Q and notable reversals for Islamists, but were also marked by widespread accusations of rigging. The Bush Administration made no public comment on reported irregularities.

One senior Pakistani scholar offered a critical summary of the country's political circumstances under President Musharraf's rule:

> [T]he "Musharraf model of governance," is narrow and suffers from a crisis of legitimacy. Its major features are: a concentration of power in the presidency, with backup from its army/intelligence and bureaucratic affiliates; induction of retired and serving military officers into important civilian institutions and thus an undermining of the latter's autonomy; co-option of a section of the political elite, who are given a share of power and patronage in return for mobilizing civilian support, on President Musharraf's terms; a reluctant partnership with the Islamic parties, especially the MMA,

and soft-peddling towards Islamic groups; and manipulation of the weak and divided political forces and exclusion of dissident political leaders.[353]

Many analysts have opined that, despite being a self-professed "enlightened moderate," Musharraf in practice strengthened the hand of Pakistan's Islamist extremist forces and that, despite rhetoric about liberalizing Pakistani society, his choice of political allies suggested he was not serious.[354] In the meantime, the Pakistan army further entrenched itself in the country's corporate sector, generating billions of dollars in annual profits from businesses ranging from construction to breakfast cereal. One estimate has this "milbus" (military business) accounting for fully 6% of the country's gross domestic product.[355]

Some observers argue that much of the criticism leveled at President Musharraf was unfair and that he had been a relatively benign "military dictator." Such analyses will, for example, point out that Musharraf's policies vis-à-vis India allowed for a reduction of bilateral tensions and an ongoing peace dialogue, that he appeared to have an extent clamped down on Kashmiri militancy, and that he did not come under fire for corruption, as did Bhutto and other civilian leaders.[356]

During their years of marginalization, the leadership of the country's leading moderate, secular, and arguably most popular party—the Pakistan People's Party—sought greater U.S. support for Pakistani democratization and warned that the space in which they were being allowed to operate was so narrow as to bring into question their continued viability as political forces.[357] They also typically identify a direct causal link between nondemocratic governance and the persistence of religious militancy in Pakistan. In an opinion piece composed shortly before her 2007 assassination, Benazir Bhutto argued that the all the countries of the world had a direct interest in Pakistani democratization, reiterating her long-held view that dictatorship had fueled extremism in her country and that credible elections there were a necessary condition for the reduction of religion militancy.[358]

U.S. Policy

While the United States maintains a keen interest in Pakistani democratization, the issue was widely seen as having become a secondary consideration as counterterrorism concerns grew after 2001. As stated by Assistant Secretary of State Boucher in a 2007 statement to a Senate panel:

> The United States wants to see Pakistan succeed in its transition to an elected civilian-led democracy, to become a moderate, democratic, Muslim nation committed to human rights and the rule of law. All of our assistance programs are directed toward helping Pakistan achieve these goals. This is a long-term undertaking that will require years to accomplish.[359]

Bush Administration officials repeatedly emphasized that democratization is key to the creation of a more moderate and prosperous Pakistan. However, many critics of their policies asserted that the Islamabad government was for more than five years given a "free pass" on the issue of representative government, in part as a means of enlisting that country's continued assistance in U.S.-led counterterrorism efforts.[360] U.S. congressional committees long expressed concern with "the slow pace of the democratic development of Pakistan" (S.Rept. 109-96) and "the lack of progress on improving democratic governance and rule of law" there (H.Rept. 109-486). Secretary of State Rice argued that strong Bush Administration support for Pakistan's democratization process was a "very well kept secret," and she rejected as untrue claims that the U.S. supported a military government in Islamabad without attention to democracy.[361]

Many commentators criticized the Bush Administration's perceived over-emphasis on relations with President Musharraf and the Pakistani military at the expense of positive ties with the broader Pakistan society. As articulated by a scholar who would later become Pakistan's Ambassador to Washington,

> The United States made a critical mistake in putting faith in one man—General Pervez Musharraf—and one institution—the Pakistani military—as instruments of the U.S. policy to eliminate terrorism and bring stability to the Southwest and South Asia. A robust U.S. policy of engagement with Pakistan that helps in building civilian institutions, including law enforcement capability, and eventually results in reverting Pakistan's military to its security functions would be a more effective way of strengthening Pakistan and protecting United States policy interests there.[362]

The U.S. State Department's *Country Report on Human Rights Practices 2006*, issued by the Bureau of Democracy, Human Rights, and Labor in 2007, did not use the word "democracy" or any of its derivatives in discussing Pakistan, but did note that "restrictions on citizens' right to change their government" represented a "major problem."[363] Leading opposition political figures in Islamabad warned that unconditional U.S. support for Musharraf's military-dominated government contributed to an anti-American backlash among Pakistan's moderate forces. Yet others opine that overt U.S. conditionality is unlikely to be effective and may only foster antiU.S. resentments in Pakistan.[364]

Human rights problems

Pakistan is the setting for numerous and serious perceived human rights abuses, some of them perpetrated and/or sanctioned by the state. According to the Department of State, the Islamabad government is known to limit freedoms of association, religion, and movement, and to imprison political leaders. The Department's most recent *Country Report on Human Rights Practices* (issued March 2008) determined that the human rights situation in Pakistan "worsened" during 2007, due primarily to President Musharraf's six-week-long imposition of emergency powers and the attendant suspension of the constitution and dismissal of Supreme and High Provincial Courts. Along with concerns about these anti-democratic practices, the report lists extrajudicial killings, torture, and disappearances; "widespread" government and police corruption; lack of judicial independence; political violence; terrorism; and "extremely poor" prison conditions among the major problems.[365] The most recent State Department report on trafficking in persons (issued June 2008) again said, "Pakistan does not fully comply with the minimum standards for the elimination of trafficking; however, it is making significant efforts to do so." It again placed Pakistan at "Tier 2" due to Islamabad's "limited efforts to combat trafficking in persons over the last year, particularly in the area of law enforcement."[366]

In June 2007, the House Appropriations Committee (H.Rept. 110-197) expressed concern about the Pakistani government's apparent lack of respect for human rights. Senate reports have aired similar concerns. The Human Rights Commission of Pakistan and international human rights groups regularly issue reports critical of Pakistan's lack of political freedoms, lawlessness in many areas (especially the western tribal agencies), and of the country's perceived abuses of the rights of women and minorities. For example, in reviewing the country's human rights circumstances, the Lahore-based Joint Action Committee for People's Rights asserted that,

> On the one hand policies of Musharaf and his civilian partners have fanned religious extremism and intolerance, sectarian divisions resulting in violence, provincial disharmony that has weakened the federation, and created a climate of impunity that has heightened the sense of insecurity in every Pakistani. On the other, their ham-handedness in combating terrorism

has resulted in serious violations of human rights and international humanitarian law.

The group strongly urged Pakistan's civilian government to distinguish itself from the previous regime by promoting and protecting basic human rights.[367] That government did in April 2008 ratify or sign three key international human rights conventions, a move lauded by London-based Amnesty International. The move was lauded by international human rights groups even as a lack of judicial independence and continued "disappearances" are identified as ongoing problems.[368]

Gender discrimination

Discrimination against females is widespread in Pakistan and traditional constraints—cultural, legal, and spousal—keep women in a subordinate position in society. In 2005, Pakistani gang rape victim Mukhtaran Mai—and Islamabad's (mis)handling of her case—became emblematic of gender discrimination problems in Pakistan. The Hudood Ordinance promulgated during the rule of President General Zia ul-Haq is widely criticized for imposing stringent punishments and restrictions under the guise of Islamic law. Among its provisions, the ordinance criminalizes all extramarital sex and makes it extremely difficult for women to prove allegations of rape (those women who make such charges without the required evidence often are jailed as adulterers). In 2006, the Hudood laws were amended in the Women's Protection Act. President Musharraf supported the changes and the ruling PML-Q party joined with the opposition PPP to overcome fierce resistance by Islamist parties. The step was viewed as a landmark in efforts to create more a moderate Pakistani state. However, in 2008, the State Department, while acknowledging that the Women's Protection Act had improved conditions, noted that rape, domestic violence, and abuse against women, such as honor crimes and discriminatory legislation that affected women, remain serious problems. Reported acts of violence against women more than doubled in Pakistan in 2007 as compared to the previous year.[369]

Religious freedom

The State Department's most recent *International Religious Freedom Report* (issued September 2008) again found that in practice the Islamabad government imposes limits on the freedom of religion in Pakistan:

> The Government took some steps to improve its treatment of religious minorities during the period covered by this report, but serious problems remained. Law enforcement personnel abused religious minorities in custody. Security forces and other government agencies did not adequately prevent or address societal abuse against minorities. Discriminatory legislation and the Government's failure to take action against societal forces hostile to those who practice a different faith fostered religious intolerance, acts of violence, and intimidation against religious minorities. Specific laws that discriminate against religious minorities include anti-Ahmadi and blasphemy laws that provide the death penalty for defiling Islam or its prophets.[370]

The State Department has rejected repeated U.S. Commission on International Religious Freedom recommendations that Pakistan be designated a "country of particular concern." The Commission's most recent annual report (May 2008) asserts that,

> [A]ll of the serious religious freedom concerns on which the Commission has reported in the past persist. Sectarian and religiously motivated violence continues, particularly against Shia Muslims, Ahmadis, Christians, and Hindus, and the government's response continues to be insufficient and not fully effective.

The Commission finds that Pakistani government officials provide the country's religious minorities with inadequate protections against societal violence.[371]

Press freedom

Press freedom and the safety of journalists recently have become major concerns in Pakistan, spurred especially by the 2006 discovery of the handcuffed body of Pakistani journalist Hayatullah Khan in a rural area of North Waziristan. Khan, who had been missing for more than six months, was abducted by unknown gunmen after he reported on an apparent U.S.-launched missile attack in Pakistan's tribal region. Khan's family is among those who suspect the involvement of Pakistani security forces; an official inquiry into the death was launched. Other journalists have been detained and possibly tortured, including a pair reportedly held incommunicado without charges for three months after they shot footage of the Jacobabad airbase that was used by U.S. forces. Paris-based Reporters Without Borders placed Pakistan 152nd out of 169 countries in its most recent annual ranking of world press freedom.[372]

Pakistani journalists have taken to the streets to protest perceived abuses. In May 2007, the New York-based Committee to Protect Journalists placed Pakistan sixth in a list of the ten countries where press freedom had most deteriorated since 2002.[373] In early June, in apparent reaction to media coverage of rallies in support of Pakistan's suspended Chief Justice, the Musharraf government issued an ordinance allowing the Pakistan Electronic Media Regulatory Agency to impose strict curbs on television and radio station operations. Human Rights Watch later called the decree a "disgraceful assault on media freedom."[374] Implementation of the ordinance subsequently was halted. In September 2007, the U.S. Embassy in Islamabad expressed concern about recent incidents in which Pakistani journalists were subject to assaults and harassment.[375] In its March 2008 human rights report, the State Department asserted that there was an increase in government arrests, harassment, and intimidation of journalists during 2007.[376]

"Disappeared" persons

According to the U.S. State Department, there was an increase of politically motivated disappearances in Pakistan in 2006 which continued in 2007, with police and security forces holding prisoners incommunicado and refusing to provide information on their whereabouts, particularly in terrorism and national security cases. In late 2006, Pakistan's Supreme Court ordered the government to disclose the whereabouts of 41 suspected security detainees who had "disappeared." Human rights groups claim to have recorded more than 400 cases of such secret detentions since 2002.[377] Amnesty International has criticized Islamabad for human rights abuses related to its cooperation with the U.S.-led "war on terror," including the arbitrary detention, enforced disappearance, and torture of hundreds of people. In late 2007, Pakistan's military and intelligence agencies reportedly released from detention nearly 100 terrorism suspects without charges. No official explanation for the releases was offered and some analysts assert that the primary motive was avoiding the embarrassment of having to reveal that the suspects were being held "on flimsy evidence in [a] secret system."[378] The Islamabad government formally denies involvement in extralegal detentions. It also has denied that any Pakistani citizens had been remanded to U.S. custody for imprisonment at Guantanamo Bay, saying that any Pakistani nationals held in that facility were arrested outside Pakistan, mostly in Afghanistan.[379]

Economic Issues[380]

Overview

Pakistan is a poor country, but the national economy gathered significant positive momentum in the new century, helped in large part by the government's pro-growth policies and by post-2001 infusions of foreign aid. Overall growth averaged 6.6% from 2002-2007. However, poverty remains widespread, and presently high rates of domestic inflation and a serious balance of payments crisis have many analysts concerned about the country's macroeconomic stability. According to the World Bank, nominal GDP per capita in 2007 was only $855, even as poverty rates dropped from 34% to 24% in the first half of the current decade. Severe human losses and property damage from an October 2005 earthquake in northern Pakistan have had limited follow- on economic impact, given a large influx of foreign aid and the stimulus provided by reconstruction efforts.

Pakistan's political crises in 2007 harmed what had been a generally strong national economy. The country's main stock market lost nearly 5% of its value when trading opened following the November emergency imposition and the country's attractiveness for foreign investors almost certainly has suffered with ensuing instability. In the wake of Bhutto's killing, the market again fell by nearly 5%. Food prices have spiked, contributing to inflationary pressures that have in turn sapped exports.[381] Rising fuel costs and food subsidies have spurred the new government to order "massive cuts" in federal spending, including that for the military, and to seek $4-5 billion from international lenders to reverse a sharp deterioration on the current account of its balance of payments. Pakistan also faces a shortfall of some 4,000 megawatts of electricity and scheduled blackouts now affect homes and businesses many hours each day.[382]

Despite these negative signs, the long-term economic outlook for Pakistan is improved since 2001, even as it remains clouded in a country still dependent on foreign lending and the importation of basic commodities. Substantial fiscal deficits and dependency on external aid have been chronic (public and external debt equal nearly three-fifths of GDP), counterbalancing a major overhaul of the tax collection system and what have been major gains in the Karachi Stock Exchange, which nearly doubled in value as the world's best performer in 2002 and was up by 40% in 2007. Along with absolute development gains in recent years, Pakistan's relative standing has also improved: The U.N. Development Program ranked Pakistan 136th out of 177 countries on its

2007/2008 human development index (between Laos and Bhutan), up from 144th in 2003.[383]

Pakistan's real GDP grew by 5.8% in the fiscal year ending June 2008, driven by a booming service sector. Output from this and the manufacturing sector has grown substantially since 2002, but the agricultural sector continues to lag considerably (in part due to droughts), slowing overall growth. Agricultural labor accounts for nearly half of the country's work force, but only about one-fifth of national income and 2% of tax revenue. Expanding textile production and the government's pro-growth measures had most analysts foreseeing solid expansion ahead, but political and security turmoil in 2008 have caused previously optimistic predictions to drop below 5% for the next two years. A relatively small but rapidly growing entrepreneurial class has boosted the consumption of luxury goods.[384]

Pakistan stabilized its external debt at about $33 billion by 2003, but this rose to about $46 billion in 2008. Still, such debt is only slightly more than one-quarter of GDP today, down about one- half in 2000. The country's reported total liquid reserves reached $13.7 billion by May 2007, an all-time high and a nearly five-fold increase since 1999, but were rapidly depleted in 2008. Foreign remittances have exceeded $4 billion annually since 2003 (at around $5.5 billion in FY2006/2007), up from slightly more than $1 billion in 2001. High oil prices and high food commodity prices have driven inflationary pressures, resulting in year-on-year consumer rates above 25% in August 2008. Inflationary pressures are projected to remain strong into 2009; many analysts call rising prices the single most important obstacle to future growth. Pakistan's resources and comparatively well-developed entrepreneurial skills may hold promise for more rapid economic growth and development in coming years. This is particularly true for the country's textile industry, which accounts for two-thirds of all exports (and up to 90% of exports to the United States).

Analysts press for further broadening the country's tax base in order to provide increased revenue for investment in improved infrastructure, health, and education, all prerequisites for economic development. Political insecurity appears to fuel a patronage system of excessive spending without sufficient revenue enhancement efforts.[385] Serious environmental degradation also retards growth: a 2007 World Bank report conservatively estimated that at least 6% of Pakistan's GDP is lost to illness and premature mortality caused by air pollution (both outdoor and indoor); diseases caused by inadequate water supplies, sanitation, and hygiene; and reduced agricultural productivity due to soil degradation.[386]

Attempts at macroeconomic reform historically have floundered due to political instability, but the Musharraf government had notable successes in effecting such reform. Rewards for participation in the post-September 2001 anti-terror coalition eased somewhat Pakistan's severe national debt situation, with many countries, including the United States, boosting bilateral assistance efforts and large amounts of external aid flowing into the country. According to the Asian Development Bank's *Outlook 2008*:

> Improved economic fundamentals have enhanced the resilience of the economy and helped it absorb shocks, including higher global oil prices and 2005's devastating earthquake. But growth has generated a heavy imbalance in the external current account, which could affect economic momentum. The current account deficit has been financed largely by strong incoming foreign investment. External sources have also been employed, increasingly, to finance the fiscal deficit. Issues of long-term sustainability therefore arise, especially in a context of high global oil and commodity prices and domestic political uncertainties.[387]

A 2008 report from the World Bank urged major efforts to strengthen Pakistan's water, power, and transport infrastructure, finding that major inefficiencies were costing the country several percentage points in economic growth each year.

Even as the bulk of criticism of President Musharraf focused on the authoritarian aspects of his rule, many ordinary Pakistanis were unhappy with his government's economic policies, which were seen to have benefitted only a fraction of the country's people. Pakistan's new government took office lambasting the Musharraf regime's alleged mismanagement of the national economy and warning that the country would be unable to meet its economic targets for FY2007/20008.[388] World Bank economist and former Pakistani Finance Minister Shahid Javed Burki is among those who asserted that high rates of growth were not sustainable. He also faulted Islamabad for maintaining a weak regulatory structure that has not constrained private sector expansion nor regulated emerging monopolies, thus spurring sharp price increases, especially in the telecommunications, real estate, and construction sectors. This, according to him, partly explains why Pakistan's impressive economic growth has brought little benefit to the country's poor.[389]

Trade and Investment

Pakistan's primary exports are cotton, textiles and apparel, rice, and leather products. Although China is the country's leading trade partner (based on more than $5 billion worth of exports to Pakistan in 2007), the United States is by far Pakistan's leading export market, accounting for about one-quarter of the total. During 2008, total U.S. imports from Pakistan were worth an estimated $3.6 billion (virtually unchanged from 2007). Some 90% of the 2007 value came from purchases of textiles and apparel. U.S. exports to Pakistan during 2008 were worth an estimated $2.1 billion (up 1% from 2007). Civilian aircraft and associated equipment accounted for about one-quarter of the 2007 value; raw cotton has been another notable U.S. export.[390] Pakistan was the 59th largest export market for U.S. goods in 2007.

According to the *2008 National Trade Estimate* of the U.S. Trade Representative (USTR), Pakistan has "progressively and substantially reduced tariffs and liberalized its import policies" over the past decade, though a number of trade barriers remain. While estimated trade losses due to copyright piracy in Pakistan were notably lower in 2005, business software and book piracy remains serious concerns.[391] Pakistan also has been a world leader in the pirating of music CDs and has appeared on the USTR's "Special 301" Watch List for 18 consecutive years. In 2004, continuing violations caused the USTR to move Pakistan to the Priority Watch List (improved intellectual property rights protection saw it lowered back to the Watch List in 2006, but this status lasted only two years). From the USTR report:

> The government of Pakistan continued to take noticeable steps during 2006 and 2007 to improve copyright enforcement, especially with respect to optical disc piracy. Nevertheless, Pakistan does not provide adequate protection of all intellectual property. Book piracy, weak trademark enforcement, lack of data protection for proprietary pharmaceutical and agricultural chemical test data, and problems with Pakistan's pharmaceutical patent protection remain serious barriers to trade and investment.[392]

In 2007, the USTR again named Pakistan to its Special 301 Watch List, lauding Islamabad for progress on intellectual property rights enforcement, but also expressing ongoing concerns about Pakistan's lack of effective protections in the pharmaceutical sector. In 2008, citing a lack of progress on pharmaceuticals, the USTR put Pakistan back on the Priority Watch List.[393]

According to Pakistan's Ministry of Finance, total foreign direct investment in Pakistan exceeded $6 billion for the year ending June 2008, but many investors remain wary of the country's uncertain political-security circumstances.[394] More than one-third of the foreign investment value comes from U.S.-based investors; much of the remainder originates in Saudi Arabia and other Persian Gulf states. Islamabad is eager to finalize a pending Bilateral Investment Treaty (BIT) and reach a Free Trade Agreement with the United States, believing that its vital textile sector will be bolstered by duty-free access to the U.S. market.[395] The establishment of Reconstruction Opportunity Zones that could facilitate development in Pakistan's poor tribal regions, an initiative of President Bush during his March 2006 visit to Pakistan, was considered by the 110th Congress (S. 2776 and H.R. 6387), but no action was taken.

The Heritage Foundation's *2009 Index of Economic Freedom*—which some say may overemphasize the value of absolute growth and downplay broader quality-of-life measurements—again rated Pakistan's economy as being "mostly unfree" and ranked it 102nd out of 179 countries. The index identified restrictive trade policies, a heavy fiscal burden, weak property ownership protections, and limited financial freedoms as issues.[396] Corruption is another serious problem: for 2008, Berlin-based Transparency International placed Pakistan 135th out of 180 countries in its annual ranking of world corruption levels.[397]

U.S. Aid and Congressional Action

U.S. Assistance

A total of about $16.5 billion in direct, overt U.S. aid went to Pakistan from 1947 through 2007, including some $4.5 billion for military programs. Since the 2001 renewal of large U.S. assistance packages and reimbursements for militarized counterterrorism efforts, Pakistan by the end of FY2008 had received about $12 billion, the majority of this in the form of coalition support reimbursements, with another $3.1 billion for economic purposes and nearly $2.2 billion for security-related programs (see **Table 1**). U.S. assistance to Pakistan is meant primarily to maintain that country's ongoing support for U.S.-led counterterrorism efforts. It also seeks to

> encourage Pakistan's participation in international efforts to prevent the spread of weapons of mass destruction and support in the development of a moderate, democratic, and civilian government which promotes respect for human rights and participation of its citizens in government and society.[398]

Table 1. Overt U.S. Aid and Military Reimbursements to Pakistan, FY2002-FY2009 (rounded to the nearest millions of dollars)

Program or Account	FY2002	FY2003	FY2004	FY2005	FY2006	FY2007	FY2008 (est.)	FY2002 FY2008 Total	FY2009 (req.)
1206	—	—	—	—	23	14	53	90	[a]
CN	—	—	—	8	29	39	55	131	[a]
CSF[b]	1,169[c]	1 , 247	705	964	862	731	920[d]	6,599	200e
FC	—	—	—	—	—	—	75	75	25[a]
FMF	75	225	75	299	297	297	298	1,566	300
IMET	1	1	1	2	2	2	2	11	2
INCLE	91	31	32	32	38	21	22	267	47
NADR[f]	10	1	5	8	9	10	10	53	11
Total Security-Related	1,346	1,505	818	1,313	1,260	1,115	1,435	8,792	585
CSH	14	16	26	21	28	22	30	157	28
DA	10	35	49	29	38	95	30	286	—
ESF[g]	615	188	200	298	337	389	347	2,374	588[h]
Food Aid[i]	5	28	13	32	55	—	42	175	37
HRDF	1	—	2	2	1	11	—	17	—
MRA	9	7	6	6	10	4	—	42	—
Total Economic-Related	654	274	296	388	539[j]	521	449	3,12 1j	653
Grand Total	2,000	1,779	1,114	1,701	1,799	1,636	1,884	11,913	1,238

Sources: U.S. Departments of State, Defense, and Agriculture; U.S. Agency for International Development.

Abbreviations:

1206: Section 1206 of the National Defense Authorization Act (NDAA) for FY2006 (P.L. 109-163, global train and equip; Pentagon budget) CN: Counternarcotics Funds (Pentagon budget)

CSF: Coalition Support Funds (Pentagon budget)

CSH: Child Survival and Health

DA: Development Assistance

ESF: Economic Support Funds

FC: Section 1206 of the NDAA for FY2008 (P.L. 110-181, Pakistan Frontier Corp train and equip; Pentagon budget) FMF: Foreign Military Financing

HRDF: Human Rights and Democracy Funds

IMET: International Military Education and Training

INCLE: International Narcotics Control and Law Enforcement (includes border security)

MRA: Migration and Refugee Assistance

NADR: Nonproliferation, Anti-Terrorism, Demining, and Related[f]

Notes:

a. This funding is "requirements-based for "urgent and emergent threats and opportunties." Thus, there are no pre-allocation data. The NDAA for FY2009 (P.L. 110-417) limits FY2009 FC funding to $25 million.

b. CSF is Pentagon funding to reimburse Pakistan for its support of U.S. military operations. It is not officially designated as foreign assistance, but is counted as such by many analysts.

c.Includes $220 million for Peacekeeping Operations reported by the State Department.

d. Includes CSF payments made or pending for support provided through August 2008. The Consolidated Appropriations Act, 2008 (P.L. 110-161), and the Supplemental Appropriations Act, 2008 (P.L. 1 10-252), appropriated a total of $1 .1 billion for FY2008 CSF payments to key cooperating nations, including Pakistan , which historically has received about 80% of such funds.

e. The Bush Administration requested $900 million for continuing CSF payments in FY2009. To date, Congress has appropriated $200 million for such purposes (P.L. 110-252).

f. The great majority of NADR funds allocated for Pakistan are for anti-terrorism assistance.

g. Congress authorized Pakistan to use FY2003 and FY2004 ESF allocations to cancel a total of $1 .5 billion in concessional debt to the U.S. government. From FY2005- FY2007, $200 million per year in ESF was delivered in the form of "budget support"—cash transfers to Pakistan. Such funds are being "projectized" from FY2008 on.

h. Includes a "bridge" supplemental ESF appropriation of $150 million (P.L. 110-252), $15 million of which the Administration later transferred to I NCLE for developing the capacity of an elite police force in Pakistan's North West Frontier Province.

i. L.480 Title I (loans), P.L.480 Title II (grants), and Section 4 16(b) of the Agricultural Act of 1949, as amended (surplus agricultural commodity donations). Food aid totals do not include freight costs.

j. Includes $70 million in FY2006 International Disaster and Famine Assistance funds for Pakistani earthquake relief.

Consulting fees and administrative overhead can account for a large proportion of appropriated aid, meaning large sums may never reach the people they are meant to benefit.[399]

In 2003, President Bush hosted President Musharraf at Camp David, Maryland, where he vowed to work with Congress on establishing a five-year, $3 billion aid package for Pakistan. Annual installments of $600 million each, split evenly between military and economic aid, began in FY2005.[400] When additional funds for development assistance, law enforcement, and other programs are included, the estimated non-food aid allocation for FY2008 is $976 million. FY2007 was the first year of the Administration's new plan to devote $750 million in U.S. development aid to Pakistan's tribal areas over a five-year period. The new civilian government seated in Islamabad in early 2008 has urged the United States to further boost its aid as a means of strengthening democracy in Pakistan.[401]

In July 2008, the Enhanced Partnership With Pakistan Act of 2008 (S. 3263) was introduced in the Senate. The act sought to "affirm and build a sustained, long-term, multifaceted relationship with Pakistan," in part by tripling non-military U.S. assistance to $1.5 billion per year for FY2009-FY20 13, and by establishing a sense of Congress that such aid levels should continue through FY20 18. It also would have conditioned further military assistance and arms transfers to Pakistan on an annual certification that the security forces of Pakistan were making "concerted efforts" to prevent Al Qaeda, Taliban, and associated militant groups from operating on Pakistani territory, and that such security forces were "not materially interfering" in Pakistan's political or judicial processes. In introducing the act, the co-sponsoring Chairman and Ranking Member of the Senate Foreign Relations Committee expressed a desire to move away from the "transactional" dynamic they believe has characterized U.S.-Pakistan relations and to reverse a pervasive Pakistani sentiment that the United States is not a reliable ally.[402]

FATA development plan and ROZs

As noted above, Pakistan's tribal areas are remote, isolated, poor, and very traditional in cultural practices. The social and economic privation of the inhabitants is seen to make the region a particularly attractive breeding ground for violent extremists. The U.S.-assisted development initiative for the Federally Administered Tribal Areas, launched in 2003, seeks to improve the quality of education, develop healthcare services, and increase opportunities for economic growth and micro-enterprise specifically in Pakistan's western tribal regions.[403] A senior USAID official estimated that, for FY2001-FY2007, about 6% of U.S. economic aid to Pakistan has been allocated for projects in the FATA.[404] The Bush Administration urged Congress to continue funding a proposed five-year, $750 million aid plan for the FATA initiated in FY2007. The plan supports Islamabad's own ten-year, $2 billion Sustainable Development effort there. Skepticism has arisen about the potential for the new policy of significantly boosted funding to be effective. Corruption is endemic in the tribal region and security circumstances are so poor that Western nongovernmental contractors find it extremely difficult to operate there. Moreover, as much as half of the allocated funds likely will be devoted to administrative costs.[405] Islamabad insists that implementation is carried out wholly by Pakistani civil and military authorities and that U.S. aid, while welcomed, must come with no strings attached.[406]

The related establishment of Reconstruction Opportunity Zones (ROZs) that could facilitate further development in the FATA (and neighboring Afghanistan), an initiative of President Bush during his March 2006 visit to Pakistan, ran into political obstacles in the 110th Congress. The ROZ program would provide duty-free access into the U.S. market for certain goods produced in approved areas and potentially create significant employment opportunities. While observers are widely approving of the ROZ plan in principle, many question whether there currently are any products with meaningful export value produced in the FATA. One senior analyst suggests that the need for capital and infrastructural improvements outweighs the need for tariff reductions. A Pakistani commentator has argued that an extremely poor law and order situation in the region will preclude any meaningful investment or industrialization in the foreseeable future.[407] In March 2008, more than two years after the initiative was announced, S. 2776, which would provide duty-free treatment for certain goods from designated ROZs in Afghanistan and Pakistan, was introduced in the Senate. A related bill, H.R. 6387, was referred to House subcommittee four months later. Both failed to emerge from committee.

A major July 2008 report from the Council on Foreign Relations presented a cooperative, incentives-based strategy for U.S. engagement in the FATA that would bolster the Pakistani government's capacity while building mutual confidence in the bilateral relationship. The report urges policy makers to weigh the potential gains of unilateral U.S. actions in the FATA—whether military, political, or economic in nature—against the likely costs in the context of fostering mutual trust. It emphasizes that tactical security gains in the region are likely to be ephemeral if not accompanied by rapid political change and economic incentives that comprise what it labels a "generational challenge."[408]

Economic support funds

The Foreign Assistance Act authorizes the President to furnish foreign assistance in order to promote stability. The Economic Support Funds (ESF) requested under this authorization have represented a significant proportion of post-2001 U.S. assistance to Pakistan. Immediately following the September 2001 terrorist attacks on the United States, the 2001 Emergency Supplemental Appropriations Act for Recovery from and Response to Terrorist Attacks on the United States (P.L. 107-38) included appropriation of $600 million in cash transfers for Pakistan under ESF. Congress subsequently authorized Pakistan to use the FY2003 and FY2004 ESF allocations to cancel about $1.5 billion in concessional debt to the U.S. government.

Within the Administration's FY2005-FY2009 assistance plan for Pakistan it was agreed that $200 million of ESF each year (two-thirds of the program total) would be delivered in the form of "budget support": cash transfers meant to enable the Islamabad government to spend additional resources on education, improving macroeconomic performance, and the quality of and access to healthcare and education. (In the Administration's FY2008 request for foreign operations, Pakistan was to be one of only three countries, along with Jordan and Lebanon, to receive ESF in this form.) These funds were to be used for purposes spelled out in mutually agreed "Shared Objectives" based on goals Pakistan set for itself in its Poverty Reduction Strategy Paper, which is the reference widely used by the donor community. While the State Department and USAID insisted that use of the funds was carefully monitored, criticisms arose that poor oversight and the fungibility of money could allow Pakistan's military-dominated government to use them for purposes other than those intended. In late 2007, the State Department appeared to agree in announcing that budget support for Pakistan would henceforth be "projectized to ensure the money is targeted at the most urgent priorities."[409]

Coalition support funds (CSF)

At the Bush Administration's behest, Congress appropriated billions of dollars to reimburse Pakistan and other nations for their operational and logistical support of U.S.-led counterterrorism operations. These "coalition support funds" (CSF) have accounted for the bulk of U.S. financial transfers to Pakistan since 2001. As of January 2009, more than $8.3 billion had been appropriated or authorized for FY2002-FY2009 Pentagon spending for CSF for "key cooperating nations." Pentagon documents show that disbursements to Islamabad—at some $6.7 billion or an average of $79 million per month—account for roughly four-fifths of these funds. The amount is equal to about one-quarter of Pakistan's total military expenditures. According to Secretary of Defense Gates, CSF payments have been used to support approximately nearly 100 Pakistani army operations and help to keep some 100,000 Pakistani troops in the field in northwest Pakistan by paying for food, clothing, and housing. They also compensate Islamabad for coalition usage of Pakistani airfields and seaports.[410]

Concerns have grown in Congress and among independent analysts that standard accounting procedures were not employed in overseeing these large disbursements from the U.S. Treasury. The State Department claims that Pakistan's requests for CSF reimbursements are carefully vetted by several executive branch agencies, must be approved by the Secretary of Defense, and ultimately can be withheld through specific congressional action. However, a large proportion of CSF funds may have been lost to waste and mismanagement, given a dearth of adequate controls and oversight. Senior Pentagon officials reportedly have taken steps to overhaul the process through which reimbursements and other military aid is provided to Pakistan, and the Bush Administration may have concluded in late 2008 that Pakistan diverted much of the funds toward a military buildup focused on India.[411] The National Defense Authorization Act for FY2008 (P.L. 110-181) for the first time required the Secretary of Defense to submit to Congress itemized descriptions of coalition support reimbursements to Pakistan.

The Government Accountability Office (GAO) was tasked to address oversight of coalition support funds that go to Pakistan. Its June 2008 report found that, until about one year before, only a small fraction of Pakistani requests were disallowed or deferred. In March 2007, the value of rejected requests spiked considerably, although it still represented one-quarter or less of the total. The apparent increased scrutiny corresponded with the arrival in Islamabad of a new U.S. Defense Representative, an army major general who reportedly has played a greater role in the oversight process. GAO concluded that increased oversight and accountability was needed over Pakistan's reimbursement claims for coalition support funds.[412] In August 2008, the leader of Pakistan's ruling party, now-President Asif Zardari claimed, without providing evidence, that as president Pervez Musharraf had been passing only a fraction of the funds over to the Pakistani military, leaving some $700 million of reimbursements per year "missing."[413]

Possible Adjustments to U.S. Assistance Programs

Critics contend that many of the stated institutional and development goals of U.S. assistance to Pakistan remain largely unmet in part due to a perceived U.S. over-reliance on security-related aid. One major study found that only about one-tenth of U.S. aid was being directed toward development, governance, and humanitarian programs.[414] For numerous Pakistan-watchers, a policy of "enhanced cooperation and structured inducements" is viewed as likely to be more effective than a policy based on pressure and threats.[415] Many argue that it could be useful to target U.S. assistance programs in such a way that they more effectively and more directly benefit the country's citizens. Some analysts call for improving America's image in Pakistan by making U.S. aid more visible to ordinary Pakistanis.[416] A costly downside of the perceived focus on security-related aid is that it can empower illiberal forces in Pakistan, namely, the country's military and intelligence agencies, which are seen to have stunted the growth and development of democratic institutions and the rule of law.

One idea commonly floated by analysts is the "conditioning" of aid to Pakistan, perhaps through the creation of "benchmarks." For example, in 2003, a task force of senior American South Asia watchers issued a report on U.S. policy in the region that included a recommendation that the extent of U.S. support for Islamabad should be linked to that government's own performance in making Pakistan a more "modern, progressive, and democratic state." Specifically, the task force urged directing two-thirds of U.S. aid to economic programs and one-third to security assistance, and conditioning increases in aid amounts to progress in Pakistan's reform agenda.[417] Some commentators emphasize that, to be truly effective, conditionality should be applied by many donor countries rather than just the United States and should be directed toward the Pakistani leadership—especially the military—to the exclusion of the general public.[418] In the wake of political crises and deteriorating security circumstances in Pakistan in 2007, some senior Members of Congress were more vocal in calling for conditions on further U.S. assistance in lieu of improvements in these areas.[419]

Many analysts, however, including those who made policy for the Bush Administration, have contended that conditioning U.S. aid to Pakistan has a past record of failure and likely would be counterproductive by reinforcing Pakistani perceptions of the United States as a fickle and unreliable partner. From this perspective, putting additional pressure on an already weak Islamabad government might lead to significant political instability in Pakistan.[420] One senior Washington-based analyst who advocates against placing conditions on U.S. aid to Pakistan instead offered an admittedly modest and "not entirely satisfying" approach that would modify current U.S. policy through more forceful private admonitions to Islamabad to better focus its own counterterrorism efforts while also targeting Taliban leadership, increased provision of U.S. counterinsurgency technologies and training to Pakistani security forces, and the establishment of benchmarks for continued provision of coalition support funding.[421] Private admonitions are considered by some analysts to be meaningless in the absence of public consequences, however.

For Pakistanis themselves, aid conditionality in U.S. congressional legislation can raise unpleasant memories of 1985's Pressler Amendment, which led to a near-total aid cutoff in 1990. Islamabad's sensitivities are thus acute: in 2007, the Pakistan Foreign Ministry said aid conditions legislated in the Implementing the 9/11 Commission Recommendations Act of 2007 (P.L. 110-53) "cast a shadow" on existing U.S.-Pakistan cooperation and create linkages that "did not serve the interest of bilateral cooperation in the past and can prove to be detrimental in the future."[422] Calls for further conditionality from some in Congress led Islamabad to again warn that such moves could harm the bilateral relationship and do damage to U.S. interests. Nevertheless, the State Department reported being "comfortable" with congressional conditions and "confident" that required reports could be issued.[423]

Analysts have also issued criticisms of the programming of aid to Pakistan within the security- related portions. Foremost among these are assertions that the Pakistani military maintains an institutional focus on conventional war-fighting capabilities oriented toward India and that it has used U.S. security assistance to bolster these capabilities while paying insufficient attention to the kinds of counterinsurgency capacity that U.S. policy makers might prefer to see strengthened. For example, of the nearly $1.6 billion in Foreign Military Financing provided to Pakistan from FY2002-FY2008, more than half has been used by Islamabad to purchase weapons of limited use in the context of counterterrorism. These include maritime patrol aircraft, anti-armor missiles, surveillance radars, upgrade kits for F-16 combat aircraft, and self-propelled howitzers. Counterarguments contend that such purchases facilitate regional stability and allow Pakistan to feel more secure vis-à-vis India, its more powerful neighbor.

Pervasive anti-American sentiment in Pakistan has led the U.S. government to minimize its "footprint" when providing aid in certain regions, especially the FATA region bordering Afghanistan. This has meant that some projects are conducted in ways similar to covert operations under the cover of

Pakistani government agencies. Although such an approach facilitates delivery of aid, public diplomacy gains can be sacrificed when aid beneficiaries are unaware of the origin of the assistance they are receiving. Because development of Pakistan's tribal areas is identified as a key U.S. national security goal in and of itself, such costs may be considered acceptable. Instability in Pakistan has led to increased calls for more and better-spent U.S. assistance there. While support for the "Biden-Lugar" plan (S. 3263), or something similar, is widespread among analysts, some warn that Pakistan's crises are so urgent that the country requires large infusions of aid in the nearer-term.[424]

Coup-Related Legislation

Pakistan's 1999 military coup triggered U.S. aid restrictions under Section 508 of the annual foreign assistance appropriations act. Post-September 2001 circumstances saw Congress take action on such restrictions. P.L. 107-57 waived coup-related sanctions on Pakistan through FY2002 and granted presidential authority to waive them through FY2003. In issuing the waiver, the President was required to certify that doing so "would facilitate the transition to democratic rule in Pakistan" and "is important to United States efforts to respond to, deter, or prevent acts of international terrorism." President Bush exercised this waiver authority six times. Pakistan's relatively credible 2008 polls spurred the Bush Administration to issue an April 2008 determination that a democratically elected government had been restored in Islamabad after a 101-month hiatus. This determination permanently removed coup-related aid sanctions.[425]

Proliferation-Related Legislation

Through a series of legislative measures, Congress incrementally lifted sanctions on Pakistan resulting from its nuclear weapons proliferation activities.[426] After the September 2001 terrorist attacks on the United States, policymakers searched for new means of providing assistance to Pakistan. President Bush's issuance of a final determination that month removed remaining sanctions on Pakistan (and India) resulting from the 1998 nuclear tests, finding that restrictions were not in U.S. national security interests. Some Members of the 108th Congress urged reinstatement of proliferation-related sanctions in response to evidence of Pakistani assistance to third-party nuclear weapons programs. However, the Nuclear Black-Market Elimination Act (H.R. 4965) died in committee. Legislation in the 109th Congress included the Pakistan Proliferation Accountability Act of 2005 (H.R. 1553), which sought to prohibit the provision of military equipment to Pakistan unless the President could certify that Pakistan has verifiably halted all proliferation activities and is fully sharing with the United States all information relevant to the A.Q. Khan proliferation network. This bill also did not emerge from committee.

In the 110th Congress, the House-passed version of the Implementing the 9/11 Commission Recommendations Act of 2007 (H.R. 1) included provisions to suspend all arms sales licenses and deliveries to any "nuclear proliferation host country" unless the President certifies that such a country is, *inter alia*, fully investigating and taking actions to permanently halt illicit nuclear proliferation activities. Related Senate-passed legislation (S. 4) contained no such language and the provisions did not appear in the subsequent law (P.L. 110-53).

9/11 Commission Recommendations

The 9/11 Commission Report released in 2004 identified the government of President Musharraf as the best hope for stability in Pakistan and Afghanistan, and it recommended that the United States make a long-term commitment to provide comprehensive support for Islamabad so long as Pakistan itself was committed to combating extremism and to a policy of "enlightened moderation." In the Intelligence Reform and Terrorism Prevention Act of 2004 (P.L. 108-458), Congress broadly endorsed this recommendation by calling for U.S. aid to Pakistan to be sustained at a minimum of FY2005 levels and requiring the President to report to Congress a description of long-term U.S. strategy to engage with and support Pakistan. A 2005 follow-on report by Commissioners gave a "C" grade to U.S. efforts to support Pakistan's anti-extremism policies and warned that the country "remains a sanctuary and training ground for terrorists." In the 109th Congress, H.R. 5017 and S. 3456 sought to insure implementation of the recommendations of the 9/11 Commission. The bills contained Pakistan-specific language, but neither emerged from committee.

A new Democratic majority took up the issue again in 2007. The premiere House resolution of the 110th Congress, the Implementing the 9/11 Commission Recommendations Act of 2007, contained discussion of U.S. policy toward Pakistan. The resultant law (P.L. 110-53) included conditions on U.S. aid to Pakistan for the first time in the post-9/11 era.

SELECTED PAKISTAN-RELATED LEGISLATION IN THE 110TH CONGRESS

P.L. 110-53: The Implementing the 9/11 Commission Recommendations Act of 2007 (became Public Law on August 3, 2007):

- Would have ended U.S. military assistance and arms sales licensing to Pakistan in FY2008 unless the President reported to Congress that Islamabad was "undertaking a comprehensive military, legal, economic, and political campaign" to "eliminating from Pakistani territory any organization such as the Taliban, al Qaeda, or any successor, engaged in military, insurgent, or terrorist activities in Afghanistan," and was making progress toward eliminating support or safe haven for terrorists."
- Required the President report to Congress a long-term U.S. strategy for engaging Pakistan.
- Provided an extension of the President's authority to waive coup-related sanctions through FY2008.

P.L. 110-161: The Consolidated Appropriations Act, 2008 (became Public Law on December 26, 2007):

- Provided $250 million in FY2008 Foreign Military Financing for Pakistani counterterrorism activities. Another $50 million would be provided for such purposes after the Secretary of State reported to Congress that Pakistan is "making concerted efforts" to combat both Al Qaeda and Taliban forces on Pakistani territory and is "implementing democratic reforms."
- Appropriated $300 million for FY2008 coalition support reimbursements to Pakistan and other key cooperating nations.

P.L. 110-181: The National Defense Authorization Act (NDAA) for FY2008 (became Public Law on January 28, 2008):

- Authorized up to $75 million in FY2008 Section 1206 funding to enhance the counterterrorism capabilities of Pakistan's paramilitary Frontier Corp. Such assistance is to be provided in a manner that "promotes respect for human rights and fundamental freedoms and respect for legitimate civilian authority within Pakistan."

- Authorized up to $1.2 billion in FY2008 Pentagon coalition support reimbursements to "any key cooperating nation" in connection with U.S. military operations in Iraq or Afghanistan.
- Would have withheld coalition support reimbursements to Pakistan unless the Secretary of Defense submitted to Congress a report on enhancing security and stability along the Afghanistan-Pakistan border. The report required a "detailed description" of Pakistan's efforts to "eliminate safe havens for the Taliban, Al Qaeda and other violent extremists on the national territory of Pakistan" and to "prevent the movement of such forces across the border of Pakistan into Afghanistan.... "
- Required the Secretary of Defense to submit to Congress itemized descriptions of coalition support reimbursements to Pakistan for the period February 2008- September 2009.

P.L. 110-417: The National Defense Authorization Act for FY2009 (became Public Law on October 14, 2008):

- Extended Section 1206 authority to build the capacity of Pakistan's Frontier Corps through FY2009 and limits the authorized funding for such assistance to $25 million.
- • Amended the NDAA for FY2008 (P.L. 110-181) by requiring additional Administration reporting on efforts to enhance security and stability along the Pakistan-Afghanistan border.

P.L. 110-429: The Naval Vessel Transfer Act of 2008 (became Public Law on October 15, 2008):

- Authorized the President to transfer to Pakistan the guided missile frigate *USS McInerney* as an excess defense article as per H.R. 5916.

S. 2776: The Afghanistan and Pakistan Reconstruction Opportunity Zones Act of 2008 (referred to Senate committee on March 13, 2008; a related bill, **H.R. 6387**, was referred to House subcommittee on July 9, 2008):

- Would have provided duty-free treatment for certain goods from designated Reconstruction Opportunity Zones in Afghanistan and Pakistan.

S. 3263: The Enhanced Partnership With Pakistan Act of 2008 (reported unanimously out Senate committee on September 26, 2008, and placed on the Senate calendar):

- Would have made it the policy of the United States to "affirm and build a sustained, long-term, multifaceted relationship with Pakistan."
- Would have tripled non-military U.S. assistance to Pakistan to $1.5 billion per year for FY2009-FY20 13, and established a sense of Congress that such aid levels should continue through FY20 18.
- Would have conditioned further military assistance and arms transfers to Pakistan on an annual certification by the Secretary of State that the security forces of Pakistan were making "concerted efforts" to prevent Al Qaeda, Taliban, and associated militant groups from operating on Pakistani territory, and that such security forces were "not materially interfering" in Pakistan's political or judicial processes.
- Would have expressed the sense of Congress that coalition support payments to Pakistan are a "critical component" of the global counterterrorism effort and that increased oversight and accountability was needed over Pakistan's reimbursement claims for such funds.
- Would have required the Secretary of State to develop a "comprehensive, cross- border strategy" for Afghanistan and Pakistan and report to Congress a detailed description of such a strategy.

Source: Map Resources. Adapted by CRS.

Figure 1. Map of Pakistan

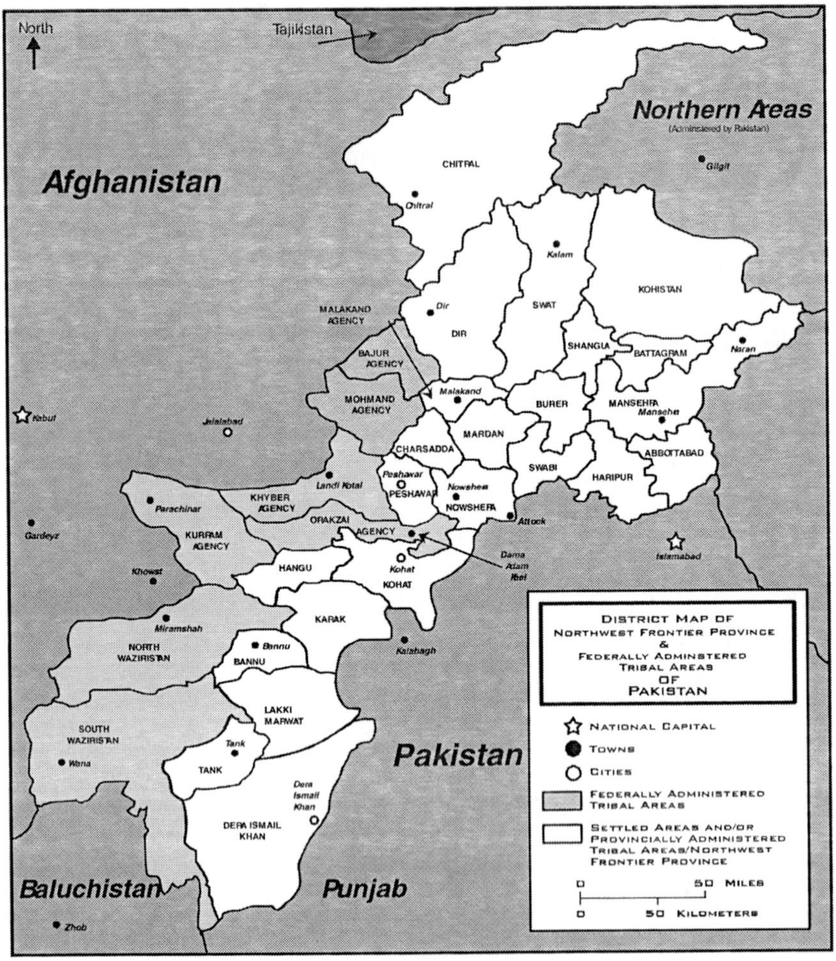

Figure 2. District Map of Pakistan's North West Frontier Province and Federally Administered Tribal Areas

End Notes

[1] Bruce Riedel, "Pakistan and Terror: The Eye of the Storm," *Annals of the American Academy of Political and Social Science,* 618, 31, July 2008.
[2] Kenneth Ballen, "Bin Laden's Soft Support," *Washington Monthly*, May 2008.
[3] See http://islamabad.usembassy.gov/pr_03272008.html.
[4] Talat Masood, "Managing Pakistan-U.S. Relations" (op-ed), *Hindu* (Chennai), June 25, 2008.

[5] "Pakistanis Hope U.S. Under Obama Will Be Less Bossy," *Reuters*, November 5, 2008.

[6] See http://www.whitehouse.gov/news/releases/2008/07/20080728-5.html. Gillani's visit was panned by many analysts, who saw the new Pakistani leader failing to impress audiences in both Washington and Islamabad, thus further straining already tense bilateral relations (see, for example, "Gilani's Poor Show in the US," *Jane's Foreign Report*, August 12, 2008).

[7] See http://www.state.gov/r/pa/prs/ps/2008/sept/110444.htm.

[8] See http://www.state.gov/r/pa/prs/ps/2008/sept/110353.htm.

[9] See http://www.mofa.gov.pk/Press_Releases/2008/Nov/PR_345_08.htm.

[10] "Pakistan Leaders Were to Meet at Hotel, Official Says," *Wall Street Journal*, September 23, 2008; "Marriott Says No Official Dinner Planned on Bombing Day," *Daily Times* (Lahore), September 23, 2008.

[11] See, for example, "Admit It: This is Pakistan's War" (editorial), *News* (Karachi), September 22, 2008.

[12] See Secretary of State Clinton's confirmation hearing statements at *http://www.foreignpolicy.com/files/KerryClintonQFRs.pdf.*

[13] John Kerry, "Pakistan Needs Our Support" (op-ed), *Washington Times*, January 23, 2009.

[14] See the December 7, 2008, "Meet the Press" transcript at http://www.msnbc.msn.com/id

[15] See, for example, Robert Dreyfuss, "Obama's Afghan Dilemma" (essay), *Nation*, December 3, 2008.

[16] Asif Ali Zardari, "Partnering With Pakistan" (op-ed), *Washington Post*, January 28, 2009.

[17] See http://www.foreignpolicy.com/files/KerryClintonQFRs.pdf.

[18] "Special Representative Holbrooke's Role in Afghanistan and Pakistan" at http://www.state.gov/secretary/rm/2009a/02/116314.htm.

[19] See http://www.state.gov/secretary/rm/2009a/01/115297.htm. In 2008, Holbrooke penned a *Foreign Affairs* article in which he declared that Afghanistan and Pakistan "now constitute a single theater of war." Among the major problem areas identified with regard to U.S. efforts in Afghanistan, he called pacifying the "insurgent sanctuaries" in Pakistan's tribal areas as being the toughest, noting that "Pakistan can destabilize Afghanistan at will—and has" ("Mastering a Daunting Agenda," *Foreign Affairs*, September/October 2008).

[20] See http://www.state.gov/r/pa/prs/dpb/2009/jan/115448.htm.

[21] "New Envoy Unnerves South Asia," *Los Angeles Times*, February 2, 2009; "South Asian Chasm of Mistrust Awaits Obama's Envoy," Reuters, February 8, 2009.

[22] "For Holbrooke, Situation in Pakistan, Afghanistan is 'Dim and Dismal'" (interview with Bruce Riedel), Council on Foreign Relations, January 28, 2009; Daniel Markey, "So You Want to Be a Special Envoy," *Foreign Policy* (online), January 2009; Lisa Curtis, *U.S. South Asia Regional—Not Kashmir—Envoy Needed*, Heritage Foundation WebMemo No. 2158, December 5, 2008.

[23] See also CRS Report RS22983, *Pakistan's Capital Crisis: Implications for U.S. Policy*.

[24] "Moody's Cuts Pakistan's Bond Outlook to Negative," *Reuters*, September 23, 2008; "Electricity Outages Anger, Frustrate Pakistanis," *Associated Press*, June 4, 2008. See also "Troubled Pakistan Economy Compounds Leaders' Woes," *Wall Street Journal*, September 19, 2008.

[25] In October, the lead U.S. diplomat for the region told an Islamabad audience that the purpose of the Friends of Pakistan effort was not to "throw money on the table" or to provide "a cash advance," but rather to forward a "systematic process" in which foreign aid to Pakistan is optimally targeted (see http://www.state.gov/p/sca/rls/rm/2008/ 111084.htm).

[26] "Pakistan Needs $10-15 Bln Fast, Says PM's Adviser," *Reuters*, October 21, 2008.

[27] See http://www.imf.org/external/pubs/ft/survey/so/2008/car111508a.htm and *http://www.imf.org/external/np/vc/*2008/121108.htm; "Pakistan Gets $500 Mln From China, Officials Say," Reuters, January 26, 2009.

[28] "Pakistan Predicts Growth of Up to 4%," *Financial Times* (London), January 28, 2009.

[29] DNI Statement before the House Committee on Intelligence, February 7, 2008; http://wits.nctc.gov/reports/ crot2007nctcannexfinal.pdf ; "Asif Ali Zardari, "The Terrorists Want to Destroy Pakistan, Too" (op-ed), *New York Times*, December 9, 2008.

[30] See http://www.satp.org/satporgtp/countries/pakistan/database ; "Suicide Attacks a Growing Threat in Pakistan," *Christian Science Monitor*," October 10, 2008; "Neither Safe Nor Sorry," *Herald* (Karachi), December 2008; "Pakistan Losing Fight Against Militants," Associated Press, December 5, 2008.

[31] "Jihadist Groups Bond on Battle Over Afghanistan," *Chicago Tribune*, July 14, 2008; "Pakistani Militants Teaming Up, Officials Say," *Washington Post*, February 9, 2008.

[32] "Like the Wild, Wild West, Plus Al Qaeda," *Washington Post*, March 30, 2008; "Analysts Fear Pakistan Could Fall to Extremists," *Los Angeles Times*, September 23, 2008; "The Long Road to Chaos in Pakistan," *New York Times*, September 28, 2008; "Islamist Insurgency Threatens Pakistan's Fledgling Democracy," Agence France Presse, December 7, 2008.

[33] "Taliban Bring Vigilante Law to Pakistan's Peshawar," *Reuters*, June 27, 2008; "Taleban Bring New Fear to Peshawar," BBC News, November 13, 2008. Paramilitary commanders reported having secured most areas surrounding the city during offensive operations in November. Yet, that same month, gunmen shot and killed an American aid worker and his driver as they drove to work in Peshawar. Days later, an Iranian diplomat in Peshawar was kidnaped by suspected Sunni militants, and a Japanese journalist and his Afghan colleague were shot and wounded. Then, in December, a massive truck bombing left at least 22 people dead in central Peshawar.

[34] "Pakistan's Deal With the Devil," *Salon*, July 8, 2008; "In City of Tolerance, Shadow of the Taliban," *New York Times*, November 3, 2008.

[35] Ziauddin Sardar, "Pakistan Must Cure Itself of the Taliban" (op-ed), *New Statesman* (London), July 24, 2008; "NWFP May Be Lost, Coalition Leaders Warn," *News* (Karachi), July 25, 2008.

[36] See http://www.terrorfreetomorrow.org/upimagestft/PakistanPollReportJune08.pdf and http://www.iri.org/mena/ pakistan/2008-07-16-Pakistan.asp.

[37] "Terrorist Attacks in Pakistan Stir Anger at U.S.," *Christian Science Monitor*, October 1, 2008.

[38] See http://www.dni.gov/testimonies/20080227_testimony

[39] Joshua White, "Pakistan's Islamist Frontier," Center on Faith and International Affairs, Religion and Security Monograph Series No. 1, November 12, 2008. See also "Is Pakistan Failing in the FATA?," *Jane's Islamic Affairs Analyst*, December 18, 2008.

[40] See http://www.dni.gov/testimonies/20080227_testimony and http://www.cfr.org/content/ publications/attachments/PakistanPolicyWorkingGroupReport.pdf. One mid-2008 Pakistani newspaper editorial estimated that only 30% of the country or less was under the effective writ of the state, down from about half in the late 1990s. Another lamented that "it is quite obvious that the militants call the shots" in much of western Pakistan. According to the Human Rights Commission of Pakistan, "Militancy is spreading and recruitment is in full swing." The group cites what it calls credible reports that "militants are being handled with kid gloves while security forces are regularly using excessive force against noncombatants" ("Is There Peace Deal with the Terrorists or Not?" (editorial), *Daily Times* (Lahore), June 11, 2008; "Militant Menace" (editorial), *News* (Karachi), June 25, 2008; "HRCP Urges Holistic Approach to Combating Militants," Press Release, June 3, 2008).

[41] See also "Al Qaeda's Resurgence in Pakistan" section below.

[42] "News Briefing with Secretary Gates and Gen. Cartwright From the Pentagon," December 21, 2007.

[43] See http://www.whitehouse.gov/agenda/foreign_policy.

[44] "Foreign Fighters of Harsher Bent Bolster Taliban," *New York Times*, October 30, 2007; "In Pakistan, Tentacles of Al Qaeda," *Associated Press*, October 26, 2008; Transcript: House Select Committee on Intelligence Holds Hearing on Al Qaeda, April 9, 2008.

[45] "Pakistan Admits Al Qaeda Moves Freely," *McClatchy News*, September 2, 2008.

[46] "Pakistan Claims Win in Crucial NW Valley," *Washington Post*, December 15, 2007; "Forces Launch New Offensive in Swat," *Dawn* (Karachi), January 6, 2008; "Army Vows to Clear Swat of Militants," *News* (Karachi), February 26, 2008.

[47] Pakistan Clashes Take Heavy Toll," *BBC News*, August 4, 2008; "Pakistan Army Kills Swat Rebels," *BBC News*, August 23, 2008.

[48] "Desperate Moves On to Secure Swat – The Lost Valley," *Dawn* (Karachi), January 15, 2008; "In Pakistan, Radio Amplifies Terror of Taliban," *New York Times*, January 25, 2009; Kamila Hyat, "Debacle in Swat" (op-ed), *News* (Karachi), January 22, 2009; "In Pakistan, Swat Valley Cops Give Up Fight," *Christian Science Monitor*, February 5, 2009.

[49] See http://www.ispr.gov.pk/front/main.asp?o=t-press

[50] "Pakistan Lifts Veil on Not-So-Secret Waziristan War," *Reuters*, May 20, 2008.

[51] "Mehsud Spending Up to 3bn on Militancy Annually: Ghani," *Daily Times* (Lahore), May 30, 2008; "Pakistan Marble Helps Taliban Stay in Business," *New York Times*, July 14, 2008; "Taliban Leader Flaunts Power Inside Pakistan," *New York Times*, June 2, 2008.

[52] "Tehrik-e-Taliban Pakistan (TTP)," *Jane's World Insurgency and Terrorism*, October 28, 2008; Hassan Abbas, "A Profile of the Tehrik-i-Taliban Pakistan," *CTC Sentinel*, January 2008; "Pakistan Government Bans Taliban," *BBC News*, August 25, 2008.

[53] "Tribal Tribulations – The Pakistani Taliban in Waziristan," *Jane's Intelligence Review*, January 13, 2009.

[54] See also CRS Report RL30588, *Afghanistan: Post-War Governance, Security, and U.S. Policy.*

[55] See, for example, statements made at a January 23, 2008, House Armed Services Committee hearing on U.S. strategy and operations in Afghanistan.

[56] Statement before the House Armed Services Committee, September 10, 2008.

[57] See the December 7, 2008, "Meet the Press" transcript at http://www.msnbc.msn.com/id

[58] "Petraeus: Afghan, Pakistan Problems Are Really One," Associated Press, January 9, 2009. See also "National Security Advisor Say Pakistan is Top U.S. Challenge," *Wall Street Journal*, January 7, 2009.

[59] "Defense Chiefs Call for Wider War on Militants," *Los Angeles Times*, September 11, 2008; "Obama to Explore New Approach in Afghanistan War," *Washington Post*, November 11, 2008. A brief primer on the cross-border aspects of the insurgency is at http://news.bbc.co.uk/2/hi/south_asia/7601748.stm.

[60] U.S. Department of Defense, "Report on Progress Toward Security and Stability in Afghanistan," June 2008; NATO commander quoted in "Ragtag Taliban Show Tenacity in Afghanistan," *New York Times*, August 4, 2008; "Gates is Pessimistic on Pakistani Support," *Washington Post*, September 24, 2008.

[61] See http://www.mofa.gov.pk/Press_Releases/2008/June/PR_156_08.htm. Some nongovernmental commentators in Pakistan openly insist that Pakistan's domestic security is the primary goal and helping Afghanistan is a secondary objective, only (see, for example, Khalid Aziz, "Has Waziristan Stabilized?" (op-ed), *News* (Karachi), June 7, 2008).

[62] "Karzai Threatens to Send Soldiers Into Pakistan," *New York Times*, June 15, 2008; http://www.mofa.gov.pk/ Press _Releases/2008/June/PR _176 _08 .htm.

[63] "Right at the Edge," *New York Times*, September 7, 2008; "Pakistan's Dangerous Double Game," *Newsweek*, September 15, 2008.

[64] See, for example, "U.S. Pays Pakistan to Fight Terror, But Patrols Ebb," *New York Times*, May 20, 2007; "Killing Ourselves in Afghanistan," *Salon.com*, March 10, 2008. One U.S. military officer claimed that Pakistani military forces flew multiple helicopter missions to resupply Taliban fighters inside Afghanistan's Nangarhar province in 2007. The Islamabad government angrily denied the claims and a former top U.S. military commander in Afghanistan cast doubt on their veracity. In another example, an October 2008 press report claimed that British officials covered up evidence that a Taliban commander killed in Afghanistan in 2007 was in fact a Pakistani military officer ("Pakistani Forces Helped

Taliban in 2007: U.S. Lt. Col.," *Defense News*, September 22, 2008; "Taliban Leader Killed by SAS Was Pakistan Officer," *London Sunday Times*, October 12, 2008).

[65] "Border Complicates War in Afghanistan," *Washington Post*, April 4, 2008; "Democrat Questions US Aid to Pakistan," *Associated Press*, May 27, 2008.

[66] See, for example, "As ISAF Command Changes, Time for a Reality Check on the Conflict in Afghanistan and Pakistan," *Defense & Foreign Affairs Special Analysis*, June 4, 2008; "American Failure in Afghanistan & Need for a New Social Contract in the FATA," Center for Research and Security Studies, Islamabad, July 2008.

[67] See http://www.mofa.gov.pk/Press_Releases/2008/July/PR_208_08.htm; "Stopping Terrorists" (editorial), *News* (Karachi), June 10, 2008.

[68] "Pakistan Launches Assault in Northwest," *Washington Post*, December 31, 2008; "Taliban Hits NATO Supply Line," *New York Times*, February 4, 2009.

[69] "Pentagon Seeks New Afghan Supply Routes," *Financial Times* (London), September 23, 2008.

[70] "10,000 Urge Pakistan to Cut US-NATO Supply Line," Associated Press, December 18, 2008.

[71] "Taliban is Seizing, Destroying More NATO Supplies," *Wall Street Journal*, August 12, 2008; "Taliban Ambushes Threaten Nato's Vital Logistics Route Into Afghanistan," *Sunday Telegraph* (London), August 31, 2008; "US Plays Down Impact of Convoy Attacks in Pakistan," Reuters, December 8, 2008; "Pakistan: 10 Trucks Torched Along US Supply Line," Associated Press, February 4, 2009.

[72] "U.S. to Widen Supply Routes in Afghan War," *New York Times*, December 31, 2008; "U.S. Secures New Supply Routes to Afghanistan," *New York Times*, January 21, 2009; "Seeking Safe Supply Routes," *Chicago Tribune*, February 2, 2009.

[73] "Kidnapings and Suicide Attacks Shake Morale of Pakistan's Armed Force," *Times of London*, September 20, 2007.

[74] "Pakistan May Step Up Action Against Insurgents," *Los Angeles Times*, August 3, 2008.

[75] "Taliban Opens New Front in Pakistan," *Daily Telegraph* (London), September 19, 2008.

[76] "Six Killed in Orakzai Agency Suicide Blast," *Daily Times* (Lahore), December 6, 2008; "Orakzai Becomes New Haven for Taliban," *Daily Times* (Lahore), February 4, 2009.

[77] "46 Die in Taliban Attack on Pakistani Troops," *New York Times*, January 12, 2009.

[78] "Troops Take Control in Pakistan's North," *Washington Post*, June 29, 2008; "Swat Taliban Reject Peace Negotiations," *Daily Times* (Lahore), June 30, 2008; "Pakistan Says Peace Deal Reached in Khyber Region," *Associated Press*, July 9, 2008.

[79] See, for example, "The Bara Operation is a Lie, Plain and Simple" (editorial), *News* (Karachi), July 1, 2008.

[80] "Battle of Bajaur: A Critical Test for Pakistan's Daunted Military," *New York Times*, September 23, 2008; "Pakistan's Fresh Resolve in Latest Battle Against Taliban," *Christian Science Monitor*, October 6, 2008; "Gates Lauds Pakistan Push in Tribal Areas," *Los Angeles Times*, September 24, 2008.

[81] "'Stability in Bajaur Within Two Months,'" *Daily Times* (Lahore), September 27, 2008; "Pakistan and Taliban Battle for Key Tunnel," *London Sunday Times*, October 19, 2008.

[82] "Pakistani Troops Destroy Taliban Stronghold," *Financial Times* (London), September 30, 2008; "8,000 Pakistani Soldiers Take on Al Qaeda in Volatile Tribal Region," *London Times*, September 27, 2008.

[83] "Pakistanis Mired in Brutal Battle to Oust Taliban," *New York Times*, November 11, 2008; "Pakistan Tribal Agency Suffers Intensifying Clashes," *Jane's Country Risk Daily Report*, January 21, 2009; commander quoted in "In Afghan South, Taliban Fills NATO's Big Gaps," *New York Times*, January 22, 2009.

[84] "Tribesmen Demand Peace Talks in Pakistan Tribal Area," Agence France Presse, January 27, 2009.

[85] "Pakistanis Displaced by Fighting in 'Dire Need,'" *Reuters*, August 25, 2008; http://islamabad.usembassy.gov/pr08082003.html; "Pakistanis Flee Into Afghanistan," *BBC*

News, September 29, 2008; "War on Taliban Sparks Refugee Crisis," *Sunday Times* (London), November 16, 2008.

86 "U.S. Hopes to Arm Pakistani Tribes Against Al Qaeda," *New York Times*, November 19, 2007; Peter Brookes, "The Tribal Option" (op-ed), *New York Post*, November 20, 2007; "Will Iraq Playbook Work in Pakistan?," *Christian Science Monitor*, January 15, 2008.

87 "Taliban Rift With Pakistan Tribes May Help U.S., Official Says," *Bloomberg News*, October 30, 2008.

88 "Pakistani Tribesmen Organize to Fight Taliban Insurgents," *McClatchy News*, September 27, 2008; "Pakistan Turns to Tribal Militias," *Wall Street Journal*, September 30, 2008; "More Tribesmen Take Up Arms Against Taliban," *Daily Times* (Lahore), October 7, 2008; "Pakistan Will Give Arms to Tribal Militias," *Washington Post*, October 23, 2008.

89 "Pakistan Uses Tribal Militias in Taliban War," *New York Times*, October 24, 2008; "Pakistan's Risky Military Strategy," *BBC News*, October 15, 2008. See also "As Taliban Overwhelm Police, Pakistanis Hit Back With Posses," *New York Times*, November 2, 2008; "Pakistan's Support of Militias Against Taliban Could Backfire," *Washington Times*, November 10, 2008.

90 Ayesha Siddiqa, "Outsourcing Security" (op-ed), *Dawn* (Karachi), January 30, 2009.

91 "When Spies Don't Play Well with Their Allies," *New York Times*, July 20, 2008.

92 See, for example, "The ISI and Terrorism: Beyond the Accusations," Council on Foreign Relations Backgrounder, July 9, 2008.

93 "Spy Agency Confusion in Pakistan," *BBC News*, July 27, 2008; "Pakistan Puts Move to Rein in Spies on Ice," *Reuters*, August 5, 2008; "Pakistan's 'Rogue' Spy Agency Attacked," *Financial Times* (London), August 19, 2008.

94 "Pakistan 'Behind Afghan Attacks,'" *BBC News*, July 14, 2008; "India Blames Pakistan in Embassy Bombing," *Associated Press*, July 21, 2008; http://www.mofa.gov.pk/Spokesperson/2008/Aug/Spokes_13_08_08.html.

95 Seth Jones, "Counterinsurgency in Afghanistan," RAND Counterinsurgency Study 4, 2008, at http://www.rand.org/ pubs/monographs/MG595/index.html, p. xiv. A spokesman for Pakistan's Inter-Services Public Relations rejected the report's findings as "misleading, factually incorrect, and based on propaganda," saying it was part of a "smear campaign" aimed at disrupting Pakistan's relations with its partners in fighting terrorism (http://www.ispr.gov.pk/ Archive&Press/CurrentMonth/10-Jun-2008.htm).

96 "C.I.A. Outlines Pakistan Links With Militants," *New York Times*, July 30, 2008; "Pakistanis Aided Attack in Kabul, U.S. Officials Say," *New York Times*, August 1, 2008; "Pakistan's Dangerous Double Game," *Newsweek*, September 22, 2008.

97 "Pakistan Denies 'Malicious' Report on CIA Confrontation," *Agence France Presse*, July 30, 2008; "Pakistan Concedes Some ISI Spies Sympathetic to Taliban," *Los Angeles Times*, August 2, 2008.

98 "Bush Voices Concern Over ISI Role," *News* (Karachi), July 31, 2008.

99 "A Conversation With Yousaf Raza Gillani," Council on Foreign Relations transcript, July 29, 2008; "U.S. Presses Pakistani Government to Place Its Spy Agency Under Civilian Control," *New York Times*, August 2, 2008.

100 "Leader Emerging in Pakistan," *Wall Street Journal*, September 2, 2008; "Zardari's ISI Honeymoon," *Jane's Intelligence Digest*, October , 2008.

101 "The Mystery Spymaster," *Newsweek*, October 13, 2008; "Pakistan Picks New Chief for Intelligence Agency," *Washington Post*, September 29, 2008.

102 "Pakistan Disbands Political Wing of Spy Agency," Reuters, November 23, 2008.

103 "'Terror is Our Enemy, Not India'" (interview with Lt. Gen. Ahmed Shuja Pasha), *Spiegel* (Hamburg), January 6, 2009.

104 "US Weighs Tougher Forays Into Pakistan," *Associated Press*, August 9, 2008; "U.S. Debates Going After Militants in Pakistan," *Los Angeles Times*, August 23, 2008.

105 "Secret Order Lets U.S. Raid Al Qaeda in Many Countries, *New York Times*, November 10, 2008.

[106] "Sen. Carl Levin and Sen. Bob Casey Hold a News Conference on Their Trip to Pakistan and Afghanistan," *CQ Transcriptions*, June 3, 2008.

[107] "Mullen Counsels Caution in Working With Pakistanis," *Associated Press*, September 26, 2008.

[108] See, for example, Lisa Curtis, "U.S. Strategy Must Address Afghan-Pakistan Tension," Heritage Foundation WebMemo No. 2087, September 26, 2008.

[109] "Special Ops Chief See Opportunities to Assist Pakistani Military," *Inside the Pentagon*, February 7, 2008; "Pakistan's Musharraf Says No to US Troops," *Associated Press*, January 24, 2008; http://www.pid.gov.pk/ Final%20Speech%20of%20President.doc; "Zardari to U.S.: Let Pakistan Go After Terrorists" (interview), *MSNBC.com*, September 22, 2008.

[110] See, for example, Marvin Weinbaum, "Wrong Way in Pakistan" (op-ed), *Washington Post*, October 27, 2008.

[111] "Sen. Carl Levin and Sen. Bob Casey Hold a News Conference on Their Trip to Pakistan and Afghanistan," *CQ Transcriptions*, June 3, 2008.

[112] Beneath US-Pakistani Tension, A New Cooperation," *Christian Science Monitor*, October 29, 2008; "U.S., Pakistan Work Together in Afghan Border Operation," *Wall Street Journal*, November 14, 2008; "Pakistan and U.S. Rebuild Strained Military Ties," *Wall Street Journal*, January 5, 2009.

[113] "Vice President Joseph R. Biden Jr. on CBS's 'Face the Nation,'" CQ Transcripts, January 25, 2009; "Transcript: General David McKiernan Speaks at Council's Commander Series," Federal News Service, November 18, 2008. See also an ISAF press releases at http://www.nato.int/isaf/docu/pressreleases/2008/1 1-november/pr08 11 17-622.html and http://www.nato.int/isaf/docu/pressreleases/2008/1 1-november/pr08 1 120-630.html.

[114] "U.S.-Funded Intelligence Center Struggles in Khyber Region," *Washington Post*, January 12, 2009.

[115] "US Raid Complicating Pakistani's Presidential Bid," *Associated Press*, September 4, 2008; "US Air Attack Could Shake Zardari Regime," *Financial Times* (London), September 8, 2008; "Playing With Firepower," *London Sunday Times*, September 14, 2008; Hasan-Askari Rizvi, "Double-Speak" (op-ed), *Daily Times* (Lahore), September 21, 2008.

[116] Rodney Jones, "American Boot, Pakistani Soil: Solution?," (op-ed), *Friday Times* (Lahore), September 12, 2008; "Pakistan Could End Cooperation in War on Terror," *Associated Press*, September 12, 2008; Robert Baer, "Washington is Risking War With Pakistan" (op-ed), *Time*, September 17, 2008; Tariq Ali, "The American War Moves to Pakistan" (op-ed), *Outlook* (Delhi), September 17, 2008.

[117] "U.S. Raids Hurt Cause By Angering Pakistanis - Envoy," *Reuters*, September 5, 2008; "Enough, Uncle Sam" (editorial), *News* (Karachi), September 12, 2008. See also "Unwise US Policy" (editorial), *Dawn* (Karachi), September 12, 2008, and "US Strategy: Excessive and Unnecessary" (editorial), *Daily Times* (Lahore), September 13, 2008.

[118] See the statement of Daniel Markey before the House Government Reform and Oversight Subcommittee on National Security and Foreign Affairs, September 24, 2008.

[119] See http://www.state.gov/s/d/2008/109857.htm.

[120] "U.S. Commanders Seeking to Widen Pakistan Attacks," *New York Times*, April 20, 2008. U.S. military forces operating in the FATA would likely face significant resistance from well-armed tribesmen with a proud martial history. The military strength of the FATA tribes is unclear, but one estimate counts some 200,000 young, unemployed males who could be considered potential fighters, especially against what was perceived to be a foreign invasion. Also among the radical Islamist militants operating in the FATA are an estimated 2,000 battle-hardened Uzbeks (Brian Cloughley, "Insurrection in Pakistan's Tribal Areas," Pakistan Security Research Unit Brief 29, January 24, 2008; "Open Borders and the Militant Uzbeks of Pakistan," *Jane's Intelligence Digest*, January 25, 2008).

[121] "Bush Said to Give Orders Allowing Raids in Pakistan," *New York Times*, September 10, 2008; "Pakistan Did Not Agree to New Rules, Officials Say," *Washington Post*, September 12, 2008; http://www.state.gov/r/pa/prs/ps/2008/ sept/110444.htm.

[122] "US Troops Poised to Cross Afghan Border for Raid on Bases," *Times* (London), July 16, 2008; "Afghan NATO Force Hits Targets Inside Pakistan," *Reuters*, July 16, 2008.

[123] "Pakistan Fears Over US Air Raids," *BBC News*, July 14, 2008. See also "Unilateral Action by U.S. a Growing Fear in Pakistan," *New York Times*, July 22, 2008.

[124] See, for example, "Ringed by Foes, Pakistanis Fear the U.S., Too," *New York Times*, November 23, 2008.

[125] See http://www.mofa.gov.pk/Press_Releases/2008/June/PR_164_08.htm; "Pakistan Says U.S. Airstrike Killed 11 of Its Soldiers," *New York Times*, June 10, 2008; http://www.mofa.gov.pk/Press_Releases/2008/June/PR_173_08.htm.

[126] "Pakistan Post Was Not in U.S. Records," *New York Times*, July 16, 2008; "Pakistan Disputes U.S. Air Strike Due to Database Gap," *Reuters*, July 17, 2008.

[127] "US Strikes Undercut Efforts on Pakistan-Afghan Border," *Associated Press*, June 11, 2008; "Air Strike Damages Trust in Pakistan-US Alliance," *Reuters*, June 12, 2008.

[128] See http://www.ispr.gov.pk/Archive&Press/Sep2008/3-sep-2008.htm; http://www.mofa.gov.pk/Press_Releases/ Printer_Friendly/Sep/PR_Print_264_08.htm.

[129] See http://www.ispr.gov.pk/Archive&Press/Sep2008/10-Sep-2008.htm; "'No Predators, Please'" (interview with Mahmood Durrani), *Newsweek*, November 17, 2008.

[130] "U.S. Stops Spec Ops Raids Into Pakistani Tribal Areas," *Army Times*, October 6, 2008; "United States Takes to Air to Hit Militants Inside Pakistan," *New York Times*, October 27, 2008.

[131] "Unilateral Strike Called a Model for U.S. Operations in Pakistan," *Washington Post*, February 19, 2008. In mid- 2008, the Predator drones operating in the Pakistan-Afghanistan border region reportedly were fitted with sophisticated new surveillance systems that were employed successfully in Iraq. These systems allow for much better tracking of human targets, even those inside buildings ("Higher-Tech Predators Targeting Pakistan," *Los Angeles Times*, September 12, 2008).

[132] "Suspected U.S. Missile Strike Kills 18 in Pakistan," Associated Press, January 23, 2009.

[133] "Petraeus: Afghan Tribes Needed to Fight Militants," *Associated Press*, November 6, 2008.

[134] "US Launches Waziristan UAV Strike With Tacit Pakistani Approval," *Jane's Defense Weekly*, March 19, 2008.

[135] David Ignatius, "A Quiet Deal With Pakistan" (op-ed), *New York Times*, November 4, 2008; "Pakistan and U.S. Have Tacit Deal on Airstrikes," *Washington Post*, November 16, 2008; "No Understanding With US on Drone Attacks: FM," *Daily Times* (Lahore), November 18, 2008; Gates statement in "Senate Armed Services Committee Holds Hearing on Challenges Facing the Defense Department" (transcript), January 27, 2009. In October 2008, Pakistan's Ambassador to the United States acknowledged that there is "definitely" bilateral cooperation "in using strategic equipment that is used against specific targets," but that U.S. military aircraft do not overfly or launch strikes on Pakistani territory (see http://www.cfr.org/publication/17567).

[136] "Pakistan Condemns US Strikes in Border Regions," *Associated Press*, October 10, 2008; http://www.mofa.gov.pk/ Press _Releases/2008/Oct/PR _33 1_08.htm; "U.S. Airstrikes Creating Tension, Pakistan Warns," *Washington Post*, November 3, 2008.

[137] "Al Qaeda Vs Predator," *Jane's Terrorism and Security Monitor*, December 19, 2008; "Predators on the Hunt in Pakistan," *Newsweek*, February 9, 2009; "Pakistan Tested by Battles with Al Qaeda, Taliban," *Christian Science Monitor*, January 13, 2009.

[138] "Taliban Kills 6 'US Spies' in North Waziristan," *Daily Times* (Lahore), January 21, 2009.

[139] "American craft Kills 5 Militants in Pakistan," *New York Times*, November 20, 2008; http://www.mofa.gov.pk/ Press Releases/2008/Nov/PR 349_08.htm; "Pakistani General Calls for Halt to Missile Strikes," Reuters, November 20, 2608.

[140] "Pakistan Can Stop Drone Raids: Air Force chief," Reuters, November 25, 2008.

[141] "Two Qaeda Leaders Killed in U.S. Strike in Pakistan," *New York Times*, January 8, 2009.

[142] "Pakistani Leader Seeks New US Policy," *Associated Press*, November 10, 2008; "President Orders Air Strikes on Villages in Tribal Area," *Guardian* (London), January 24, 2009; "U.S. Missiles 'Don't Help' Pakistan War Effort," Reuters, January 25, 2009.

[143] See also CRS Report R40087, *Terrorist Attacks in Mumbai, India, and Implications for U.S. Interests*.

[144] "India to Protest to Pakistan Over Border Shooting," *Reuters*, May 19, 2008; "Skirmishes Can Hurt India-Pakistan Peace Process," *Reuters*, July 30, 2008; "Despite Warning, Pak Violates Ceasefire Again," *Times of India* (Delhi), August 14, 2008.

[145] "Pakistan 'Behind Afghan Attacks,'" *BBC News*, July 14, 2008; "India Blames Pakistan in Embassy Bombing," *Associated Press*, July 21, 2008; "Pakistanis Aided Attack in Kabul, U.S. Officials Say," *New York Times*, August 1, 2008.

[146] "Briefing by Foreign Secretary After India-Pakistan Foreign Secretary-Level Talks," Indian Ministry of External Affairs, July 21, 2008; "India Official Sees Sinking Relations With Pakistan," *New York Times*, August 1, 2008.

[147] "India Says Peace Talks With Pakistan Under Threat," *Associated Press*, August 15, 2008; "India Suggests Pakistani Hand in New Delhi Blasts," *Associated Press*, September 15, 2008; "Pakistan Warns of New Nuclear Arms Race With India," *Associated Press*, July 23, 2008.

[148] Indian Ministry of External Affairs Press Briefing, August 7, 2008; "India Reacts 'Strongly' to Pakistan Comments on Kashmir Violence," *BBC Monitoring South Asia*, August 12, 2008; Pakistan Ministry of Foreign Affairs statement at *http://www.mofa.gov.pk/Press_Releases/2008/Aug/PR_247_08.htm.*

[149] "Q&A With Indian National Security Advisor MK Narayanan," *Straits Times* (Singapore), August 12, 2008.

[150] "India, Pakistan Leaders Agree to Kickstart Peace Talks," Agence France Presse, September 24, 2008.

[151] See http://www.mofa.gov.pk/Press_Releases/2008/Oct/PR_312_08.htm; "India Says Pakistan Violating Truce, 5 Rebels Dead," *Reuters*, October 28, 2008; *http://www.mofa.gov.pk/Spokesperson/2008/Oct/Spokes_31_10_08.html.*

[152] Indian Ministry of External Affairs, "Opening Statement by Minster of External Affairs," November 26, 2008; "Signs of Thaw in Bitter South Asian Dispute," *Christian Science Monitor*, November 26, 2008.

[153] See also CRS Report R40087, *Terrorist Attacks in Mumbai, India, and Implications for U.S. Interests*.

[154] H.Res. 1532.

[155] "Mumbai Attack is Test of Pakistan's Ability to Curb Militants," *New York Times*, December 4, 2008; "Time for Truth" (editorial), *Washington Post*, December 22, 2008.

[156] See, for example, "Pakistan's President Zardari Attempts the Impossible," *Spiegel* (Hamburg), December 17, 2008.

[157] "UK Demands Quicker Mumbai Probe," BBC News, January 16, 2009; "Pakistan Must Cooperate With India on Mumbai – UN," Reuters, February 4, 2009.

[158] "Pakistan's Probe Finds Local Links to Attacks on Mumbai," *Wall Street Journal*, December 31, 2008; "Pakistan Arrests Top Leaders of Lashkar-e-Taiba," *Wall Street Journal*, January 15, 2009; "Pakistan Takes Over Main Center of Suspect Charity," Associated Press, January 25, 2009.

[159] "Promising Start By Pakistan, But Need More: US," Reuters, January 8, 2009.

[160] "India Says Pakistan's Spy Agency Linked to Mumbai Raid Planners," Reuters, February 4, 2009; http://www.mofa.gov.pk/Press_Releases/2009/Feb/PR_54_09.htm.

[161] "India, Pakistan Draw Different Conclusions in Investigations on Nov Attacks on Mumbai," *Wall Street Journal*, February 5, 2009; "Pakistan Takes First Step to Mumbai Prosecution," Reuters, February 9, 2009.

[162] "India, Pakistan Tread Lightly After Mumbai Attack," Associated Press, December 2, 2008; "Public Anger Strains India-Pakistan Cooperation," *Christian Science Monitor*, December

5, 2008. In one example of heightened public emotion, tens of thousands of demonstrators gathered in southern Mumbai a week after the attacks began to express their anger, at times chanting "death to Pakistan" ("As Rice Presses Pakistan, Tens of Thousands Take to Streets in Mumbai," *New York Times*, December 4, 2008).

[163] "Pakistani Jets Scramble as India Hardens Tone," *Wall Street Journal*, December 23, 2008: "Pakistan Cancels Army Leave, India Tensions Rise," Reuters, December 26, 2008.

[164] "India's Singh Plays Down Possibility of War With Pakistan," *Washington Post*, December 23, 2008; "No Easy Indian Response to Pakistan's Troop Shift," *New York Times*, December 29, 2008; "Pakistan May Outsmart India in Diplomatic Poker," Reuters, January 6, 2009.

[165] "'Terror is Our Enemy, Not India'" (interview with Lt. Gen. Ahmed Shuja Pasha), *Spiegel* (Hamburg), January 6, 2009.

[166] Indian Ministry of External Affairs, "Briefing by Foreign Secretary on Mumbai Terror Attacks," January 5, 2009; "India PM Says Pakistan 'Agencies' Linked to Attack," Reuters, January 6, 2009. The dossier's contents may be viewed at *http://www.hinduonnet.com/nic/dossier.htm.*

[167] See http://www.mofa.gov.pk/Press_Releases/2009/Jan/PR_12_09.htm; "Pakistan Dismisses Indian Data as 'Not Evidence,'" Associated Press, January 14, 2009.

[168] "US, UK Not Doing Enough to Rein in Pak: Pranab," *Times of India* (Delhi), December 23, 2008.

[169] "India Says Pakistan Attitude Unchanged on Militants," Reuters, January 2, 2009. Many independent Indian analysts concur and see in Islamabad's response to the Mumbai attacks evidence that the government there lacks both the will and the resources to reverse the perceived spread of a jihadist agenda (Praveen Swami, "Understanding Pakistan's Response to Mumbai" (op-ed), *Hindu* (Chennai), January 26, 2009).

[170] Quoted in "Pakistan is in a State of Denial: Pranab," *Times of India* (Delhi), January 17, 2009.

[171] Indian Ministry of External Affairs, "Address by Prime Minister at CM's Conference," January 6, 2009. In mid- January, ten former Indian ambassadors, including four former foreign secretaries, signed a letter urging the New Delhi government to downgrade its diplomatic ties with Islamabad due to Pakistan's allegedly inability to take meaningful action against suspected orchestrators of the Mumbai attack. At about the same time, India's newly seated home minister stated that business, transport, and tourism links with Pakistan will become weaker and "one day snap" if Islamabad does not cooperate in bringing the perpetrators to justice ("'Downgrade Diplomatic Ties With Pakistan,'" Hindu (Chennai), January 9, 2009; "Ties May Snap: Chidambaram," *Hindu* (Chennai), January 14, 2009).

[172] "Attacks Stir Another India-Pakistan Border Dispute," *Wall Street Journal*, January 13, 2009.

[173] See http://www.mofa.gov.pk/Spokesperson/2009/Jan/Spokes_15_01_09.htm.

[174] "'Mumbai Attacks Planned Outside Pakistan,'" *Daily Times* (Lahore), January 29, 2009.

[175] See http://www.csis.org/media

[176] See http://www.cfr.org/content/publications/attachments/PakistanPolicyWorkingGroupReport.pdf.

[177] See http://www.foreignaffairs.org/20081001faessay87603/barnett-r-rubin-ahmed-rashid/from-great-game-to-grandbargain.html.

[178] See http://www.carnegieendowment.org/files/pb64_tellis_pakistan_final.pdf.

[179] See http://www.americanprogress.org/issues/2008/11/pdf/pakistan.pdf.

[180] See http://www.csis.org/media

[181] "President's Address at Royal United Services Institute, London," January 25, 2008.

[182] Asif Ali Zardari, "Partnering With Pakistan" (op-ed), *Washington Post*, January 28, 2009.

[183] See http://usembassy.state.gov/pakistan/h06030404.html.

[184] See the December 7, 2008, "Meet the Press" transcript at http://www.msnbc.msn.com/id

[185] See also "Democracy and Governance" section below.

[186] See also CRS Report RL32615, *Pakistan's Domestic Political Developments*.

[187] "In Musharraf' s Shadow, a New Hope for Pakistan Arises," *New York Times*, January 7, 2008.

[188] See http://www.whitehouse.gov/news/releases/2006/02/20060222-2.html and *http:// www.whitehouse.gov/news/* releases/2006/03/20060304-2.html; Rice interview with the New York Post editorial board, October 1, 2007; "Biden Warns Musharraf of Consequences for Poor Elections," *Associated Press*, December 17, 2007.

[189] "Sidelined Musharraf Still Exerts Influence," *Washington Post*, May 18, 2008.

[190] Declaration text available at http://thenews.jang.com.pk/updates.asp?id

[191] Musharraf's opponents say the court was established as a means of intimidating and coercing politicians to join the PML-Q, which Gillani had refused to do ("Profile: Yusuf Raza Gillani," *BBC News*, March 23, 2008).

[192] "Decades of Enmity Threaten Pakistani Coalition, Say Analysts," *Agence France -Presse*, February 22, 2008.

[193] "Judges Not Being Restored Due to American Pressure: APDM," *News* (Karachi), June 19, 2008; "Hold Your Horses, Zardari Tells Lawyers," *News* (Karachi), May 24, 2008; "Pakistan TV Show Discusses Judges' Restoration Issue," *BBC Monitoring South Asia*, March 18, 2008.

[194] See, for example, "Reforming the Judiciary in Pakistan," International Crisis Group Asia Report 160, October 16, 2008.

[195] "Nov 3 Actions Cannot Be Undone: Naek," *News* (Karachi), August 28, 2008; "Aitzaz Deplores Oath By Eight SHC Judges," *Daily Times* (Lahore), August 28, 2008; "Resignations of PML-N Ministers Will Be Accepted Soon: PM," *Daily Times* (Lahore), August 30, 2008; Asif Edzi, "In Musharraf' s Footsteps" (op-ed), *News* (Karachi), October 30, 2008.

[196] See "The Lawyers' Crusade," *New York Times*, June 1, 2008.

[197] "Civil Rights Activist Criticizes U.S. as 'Oblivious'" (interview), *Washington Times*, July 3, 2008. See also, Aitzaz Ahsan, "Pakistan's Tyranny Continues" (op-ed), *New York Times*, December 23, 2007. When asked during a Senate hearing about the status of judges dismissed under Musharraf' s emergency proclamation, Deputy Secretary of State John Negroponte conceded that the U.S. government had "been silent on the subject" ("Sen. Joseph R. Biden Jr. Holds a Hearing on U.S. Policy Options in Post-Election Pakistan," *CQ Transcripts*, February 28, 2008).

[198] "Coalition Partner Leaves Pakistan's Cabinet in Dispute Over Reinstating Judges," *New York Times*, May 13, 2008.

[199] See http://www.state.gov/p/sca/rls/2008/106495.htm; "Leave Musharraf Alone, Boucher Tells Nawaz," *Daily Times* (Lahore), July 2, 2008.

[200] "Allies Call on Beleaguered Musharraf to Quit," *Reuters*, August 10, 2008; "Pakistan Army Won't Support Musharraf - Government," *Reuters*, August 12, 2008.

[201] See, for example, "M.B. Naqvi, "While Rome Burns, Plain Words" (op-ed), *News* (Karachi), August 6, 2008; S. Sathananthan, "Retrieving Democracy?" (op-ed), *Outlook* (Delhi), August 12, 2008; "The Zardari Card" (editorial), *News* (Karachi), August 22, 2008.

[202] "Milna' ry Cuts Power From Under Musharraf," *Financial Times* (London), August 13, 2008; "Musharraf Expected to Resign Within Days," *New York Times*, August 15, 2008.

[203] "Going, Going, Gone!," *Daily Times*, (Lahore), August 19, 2008. Speech text at http://www.cfr.org/publication/16999/president_musharrafs_resignation_speech.html?breadcrumb=%2Fregion%2F279%2Fsouth_asia.

[204] "Interview With Nawaz Sharif," *Wall Street Journal*, August 21, 2008.

[205] "Fractious Coalition in Pakistan Breaks Apart," *New York Times*, August 25, 2008; "Pakistani Stability Hope Fades With Coalition Split," *Reuters*, August 26, 2008; Moeed Yusuf, "Back to the Past" (op-ed), *Friday Times* (Lahore), August 29, 2008.

[206] "Numbers Game Tilts in Favor of People's Party," *Daily Times* (Lahore), August 22, 2008; "Zardari on the Hot Seat," *Newsweek* (online), August 20, 2008; "Battle Scars On Show as Zardari in Spotlight," *Financial Times* (London), August 25, 2008.

[207] "Pakistan's Next President is a Category 5 Disaster" (op-ed), *Wall Street Journal*; "Bhutto's Homeland Has Little Love for Zardari," Agence France Presse, both September 2, 2008; "bhutto Widower With Clouded Past is Poised to Lead Pakistan," *New York Times*, September 5, 2008.

[208] See, for example, "Establishment Determined to Stop Zardari to Become President," *Business Recorder* (Karachi), August 30, 2008.

[209] Asif Ali Zardari, "Democracy Within Our Reach" (op-ed), *Washington Post*, September 4, 2008.

[210] See http://www.pid.gov.pk/Final%20Speech%20of%20President.doc; "Government to Revoke Article 58(2)b: Gillani," *News* (Karachi), September 7, 2008.

[211] "Pakistan Agencies 'Recommended' Mumbai Gunman News," Reuters, January 8, 2009.

[212] See, for example, Hasan Askari Rizvi, "A Year of Hope and Disappointment" (op-ed), *Friday Times* (Lahore), January 2, 2009; Asif Ezdi, "Heading for a Fall" (op-ed), *News* (Karachi), February 3, 2009; Maleeha Lodhi, "Rule Without Governance" (op-ed), *News* (Karachi), February 5, 2009.

[213] See http://www.iri.org/newsreleases/2008-12-18-Pakistan

[214] "Pakistan's Top General Reins in Own Army," *Christian Science Monitor*, December 12, 2008.

[215] "Pakistan Military Retreats From Musharraf' s Influence," *McClatchy Newspapers*, January 18, 2008; "Army Chief Urges Harmony Among Pakistan's Leaders," *Reuters*, March 6, 2008; "Quiet General Tries to Keep Army Out of Politics," *Wall Street Journal*, August 22, 2008.

[216] Remarks by Ambassador Husain Haqqani at the Center for Strategic and International Studies, Washington, D.C., August 20, 2008.

[217] Federal Register 73, 69, p. 19276-19277, April 9, 2008.

[218] See http://www.state.gov/g/drl/rls/afdr/2008/104862.htm and http://www.whitehouse.gov/news/releases/2008/03/ 20080325-3.html.

[219] See http://islamabad.usembassy.gov/pr_03272008.html.

[220] See, for example, "Pressure on Asif, Nawaz to Work With President," *Dawn* (Karachi), February 23, 2008; M.B. Naqvi, "Untangling the Web of Intrigues" (op-ed), *News* (Karachi), April 16, 2008; "Pakistan TV Show Discusses Continuing US, Army Support for Musharraf;" *BBC Monitoring South Asia*, June 1, 2008; "Pakistan TV Show Discusses US Government's Continuing Support to Musharraf," *BBC Monitoring South Asia*, June 6, 2008.

[221] "Press Statement - Deputy Secretary John Negroponte," U.S. Embassy Press Release, March 27, 2008; "US Cautious Amid Musharraf Resignation Reports," *Agence France Presse*, August 15, 2008.

[222] "US Wants 'Honorable' Stay for President of Pakistan," *Dawn* (Karachi), August 11, 2008; "As Musharraf Faltered, U.S. Stayed at a Distance," *Washington Post*, August 19, 2008; "How Bush Was Persuaded to Let Musharraf Go," *Dawn* (Karachi), August 19, 2008; "McCain, Obama Welcome Musharraf Resignation," *Agence France Presse*, August 18, 2008.

[223] While levels of violence in Kashmir declined significantly in 2007 as compared to the previous year, some Indian analysts see signs that Islamist militants will seek to reverse this trend, perhaps with the urging and even support of Pakistani government elements (see, for example, "Negotiating War," *Outlook* (Delhi), May 28, 2008).

[224] See, for example, Bruce Riedel, "Pakistan and Terror: The Eye of the Storm," *Annals of the American Academy of Political and Social Science,* 618, 31 July 2008.

[225] See, for example, Praful Bidwai, "Changing Pakistan," *Frontline* (Chennai), July 4, 2008.

[226] http://www.indianembassy.org/press

[227] See Pakistan Foreign Ministry Press Release No. 8 1/2007 at http://www.mofa.gov.pk/Press_Releases/2007/March/ PR _81 _07.htm.

[228] See http://www.mofa.gov.pk/Spokesperson/2007/Sep/Spokes_17_09_07.htm.

[229] "As Pakistan Boils, India Watches," *Chicago Tribune*, December 30, 2007; "Pakistan Turmoil Draws Muted Concern in India," *Washington Post*, January 19, 2008; Indian Ministry of External Affairs Press Statement, February 20, 2008.

[230] "Benazir Bhutto's Widower Wants Improved Relations With India," Associated Press, February 29, 2008; "India PM Wants to Meet Pakistan's Leaders Halfway," Reuters, March 5, 2008.

[231] See http://www.mofa.gov.pk/Press_Releases/2008/May/PR_134_08.html.

[232] See also CRS Report RS20871, *The Iran Sanctions Act (ISA)*.

[233] "IPI Project: Iran Backs Out of Gas Deal," *News* (Karachi), November 13, 2008; Khaled Ahmed, "A Requiem for the IPI Project" (op-ed), *Friday Times* (Lahore), January 2, 2009.

[234] See http://www.cfr.org/content/publications/attachments/PakistanPolicyWorkingGroupReport.pdf.

[235] Documentary evidence indicates that Islamabad provided military and economic support, perhaps including the combat troops, to the Afghan Taliban during the latter half of the 1990s (see "Pakistan: 'The Taliban's Godfather'?," National Security Archive Briefing Book 227, August 14, 2007).

[236] Pakistan is home to some 28 million Pashto-speaking people, most of them living near the border with Afghanistan, which is home to another 13.5 million ethnic Pashtuns (also known as Pakhtuns or Pathans). A hardy people with a proud martial history (they are disproportionately represented in the Pakistani military), Pashtuns played an important role in the anti-Soviet resistance of the 1980s.

[237] Polly Nayak, "The Impact of Pakistan's and Bangladesh's National Strategies on U.S. Interests," *Strategic Asia 2008-2009*, National Bureau of Asian Research, September 2008.

[238] "Pakistan Leader Snubs Afghan Meeting," Reuters, August 8, 2007; "Afghan Rebels Find Haven in Pakistan, Musharraf Says," *New York Times*, August 12, 2007. Declaration text at http://www.dailytimes.com.pk/ print.asp?page=2007\08\13\story_13-8-2007_pg7_48.

[239] "Pakistan 'Behind Afghan Attacks,'" *BBC News*, July 14, 2008; "Kabul Pulls Out of Talks With Pakistan," *Daily Times* (Lahore), July 14, 2008.

[240] "Afghanistan, Pakistan to Fight Al Qaeda Together," Associated Press, December 5, 2008; Joint Declaration at http://www.mofa.gov.pk/Press_Releases/2009/Jan/PR_14_09.htm.

[241] Husain Haqqani and Said Jawad, "Pakistan and Afghanistan Unite Against Terrorism" (op-ed), *Wall Street Journal*, September 26, 2008.

[242] See CRS Report RL3 1555, *China and Proliferation of Weapons of Mass Destruction and Missiles: Policy Issues*.

[243] "Pakistan Secures China's Help to Build 2 Nuclear Reactors," *Wall Street Journal*, October 20, 2008.

[244] See http://markey.house.gov/index.php?option=com_content&task=view&id

[245] See http://www.ispr.gov.pk/front/main.asp?o=t-press and *http://www.ispr.gov.pk/front/main.asp?o=t-press_release&date=2008/12/20.*

[246] See, for example, "Pakistan Key Partner in War on Terror, Defense Department Says," U.S. Department of State *Washington File*, March 6, 2006; "Pakistan 'Indispensable' in Global Anti-Terrorism Fight," U.S. Department of State *Washington File*, July 25, 2007.

[247] "Musharraf: Bhutto Knew of Risks" (interview), *CBS News*, January 6, 2008.

[248] Some more critical observers—many of them Indian—identify a Pakistani connection to nearly all major jihadi terrorist attacks worldwide; a few even seek to link elements of Pakistan's military-intelligence establishment to most jihadi terrorist attacks in the South Asia region (see, for example, Wilson John, "Pakistan's Drift Into Extremism and Its Impact," Observer Research Foundation (Delhi), January 8, 2008; K.P.S. Gill, "The ISI Mark," *Outlook* (Delhi), June 11, 2008).

[249] "In Pakistan's Mountains, Jihadis Train for War," *Wall Street Journal*, July 28, 2008. One report claims that more than 100 "terror camps" are operating in western Pakistan, nearly a third of these in the Waziristan agencies ("'More Than 100 Terror Camps' in Operation in Northwestern Pakistan," *Long War Journal*, July 11, 2008).

[250] Statement before the Senate Armed Services Committee, February 27, 2007. A July 2007 National Intelligence Estimate on the terrorist threat included the assessment that Al Qaeda has "protected or regenerated" its capability to attack the United States, in part due to its enjoying "safehaven" in Pakistan's tribal areas (see http://www.dni.gov/press_releases/20070717_release.pdf).

[251] See http://www.state.gov/p/us/rm/2007/89418.htm.

[252] "Pakistani President Reviews Political, Economic, Anti-Terrorism Measures," *BBC Monitoring South Asia*, June 4, 2007.

[253] See http://www.state.gov/s/ct/rls/crt/2007/103709.htm.

[254] See http://www.gao.gov/new.items/d08622.pdf; http://internationalrelations.house.gov/ press

[255] "Terrorism Fears and Economic Trouble Shake Pakistan's Faith in New Leader," *New York Times*, September 27, 2008; "Is Pakistan's New Leader Up to the Job?," *Los Angles Times*, September 29, 2008; Asif Ali Zardari, "Pakistan Will Prevail Against Terrorism" (op-ed), *Boston Globe*, September 25, 2008.

[256] See http://islamabad.usembassy.gov/pr-08120303.html.

[257] "Cheney Warns Pakistan to Act on Terrorism," *New York Times*, February 25, 2007; "US May Be 'Undermining' Pakistan," *BBC News*, March 1, 2007; "UK's War 'Failure Sparked Pakistan Violence,'" *Telegraph* (London), March 26, 2008; author interviews with Pakistani government officials.

[258] See, for example, Ali Abbas Rizvi, "American Connection to the Waziristan Problem" (op-ed), *News* (Karachi), January 29, 2008. Author discussions with Pakistani nationals commonly touch upon this historical narrative.

[259] See http://www.dni.gov/press

[260] See http://www.dni.gov/testimonies/20080227_testimony

[261] "Bush Would Send Troops Inside Pakistan to Catch bin Laden," *CNN*, September 20, 2006.

[262] See, for example, Bruce Riedel, "Al Qaeda Strikes Back," *Foreign Affairs*, May 2007; "Influx of Al Qaeda, Money Into Pakistan Is Seen," *Los Angeles Times*, May 20, 2007.

[263] "U.S. Cites Big Gains Against Al Qaeda," *Washington Post*, May 30, 2008; Peter Bergen, "Al Qaeda at 20 Dead or Alive?" (op-ed), *Washington Post*, August 17, 2008.

[264] Statement of Henry Crumpton before the Senate Foreign Relations Committee, June 13, 2006. After conducting interviews with numerous active and retired Pakistan army and intelligence officials, one American reporter concluded in 2007 that "many officers of Pakistan's covert security agencies remain emotionally committed to jihad and hostile to the U.S. role in the region" ("Role of Pakistan's 'Captain' Shows Enduring Taliban Ties," *Newsday*, October 14, 2007).

[265] Statement of Gen. James Jones before the Senate Foreign Relations Committee, September 21, 2006. See also "In the Land of the Taliban," *New York Times*, October 22, 2006; "Next-Gen Taliban," *New York Times*, January 6, 2008. The Pakistani Taliban differ from their Afghan brethren in several respects, perhaps most significantly in a lack of organization and cohesion, and they possess no unified leadership council. Moreover, the Pakistani Taliban appear to have more limited objectives, in contrast with the Afghan Taliban who are struggling to regain national power in Kabul. At the same time, however, both groups pledge fealty to a single leader—Mullah Omar—and both share fundamental policy objectives with regard to U.S. and other Western government roles in the region (see "The Emergence of the Pakistani Taliban," *Jane's Islamic Affairs Analyst*, January 1, 2008).

[266] U.S. forces have no official authorization to cross the border into Pakistan. One U.S. press report claimed that Pentagon documents from 2004 gave U.S. special forces in Afghanistan authority to enter Pakistani territory—even without prior notice to Islamabad—while in "hot pursuit" of Al Qaeda and Taliban fighters or to take direct action against "the Big 3": Osama bin Laden, Ayman al Zawahri, or Mullah Omar. A Pakistani military spokesman called the report "nonsense" and denied there was any such arrangement ("U.S. OK'd Troop Terror Hunts in Pakistan," Associated Press, August 23, 2007).

[267]Author interview with senior Pakistani official, Islamabad, September 2006; "President General Pervez Musharraf' s Address to the Nation," July 20, 2006; "White House Backing New Plan to Defuse Insurrection in Pakistan," *McClatchy* , August 16, 2006.

[268] A translated version of the pact is at http://www.pbs.org/wgbh/pages/frontline/taliban/etc/nwdeal.html.

[269] Statement before the Senate Select Committee on Intelligence, January 11, 2007.

[270] See, for example, Evangoras Leventis, "The Waziristan Accord," *Middle East Review of International Affairs* 11,4, December 2007.

[271] "Tougher Stance on Pakistan Took Months," *Washington Post*, August 5, 2007.

[272] "U. S . Boosts Pressure on Musharraf Over Al Qaeda," Reuters, July 18, 2007.

[273] "We Have Credible Evidence: Manmohan," *Hindu* (Madras), October 25, 2006; Pakistan Ministry of Foreign Affairs Media Briefing, October 2, 2006.

[274] According to India's national security advisor, most terrorist activity in India has been "generated from outside"("MK Narayanan" (interview), *India Abroad*, September 21, 2007).

[275] Data reported by the U.S. Department of Defense. See also CRS Report RS22757, *U.S. Arms Sales to Pakistan*.

[276] "US Sanctions Frigate Transfer to Pakistan," *Jane's Naval International*, October 22, 2008.

[277] Pakistani pilots are slated to receive U.S. training in precision nighttime ground attack beginning in early 2009 ("Pakistani Pilots Will Get U.S. Training in F-16 Ground Attack," *Bloomberg News*, September 16, 2008).

[278] See http://www.state.gov/p/sca/rls/rm/2007/97946.htm.

[279] See, for example, Selig Harrison, "Support to Pakistan Distorts Asia's Balance of Power" (op-ed), *Boston Globe*, September 27, 2008.

[280] "Urgent Plea: Send More Gear," *Newsweek*, December 22, 2008; "Taking on the Taliban," ABC News (online), January 14, 2009.

[281] "Pentagon Wants $2.6 Bn for Pakistan," Bloomberg News, December 17, 2008.

[282] "U.S. Aid to Pakistan Misses Al Qaeda Target," *Los Angeles Times*, November 5, 2007.

[283] "Assessments of the Impact of 1206-Funded Projects in Selected Countries," CNA Corporation, July 2008.

[284] "Pentagon Draws Up Plans to Train, Expand Pakistani Frontier Corps," *Agence France - Presse*, November 19, 2007; "U.S. to Step Up Training of Pakistanis," *Washington Post*, January 24, 2008; "Joint Chiefs Chairman and Musharraf Discuss Terror Threat," *New York Times*, February 10, 2008. One Harvard University-based analyst and former Pakistani police official opines that, without fundamental structural reforms, the prospects for meaningfully improving Frontier Corps capabilities are dim. Among his recommended changes are the appointment of more local tribesmen into command positions and a restoration of the authority of local political agents (Hassan Abbas, "Transforming Pakistan's Frontier Corps," *Terrorism Monitor*, March 29, 2007).

[285] See, for example, Seth Jones, et al., "Securing Tyrants or Fostering Reform?," RAND Corporation Monograph, January 7, 2007.

[286] "Reforming Pakistan's Police," International Crisis Group Asia Report No. 157, July 14, 2008.

[287] See also CRS Report RL33515, *Combat Aircraft Sales to South Asia: Potential Implications*.

[288] See http://www.dsca.osd.mil/PressReleases/36-b/2006/Pakistan *http://www.dsca.osd.mil /PressReleases/*36-b/2006/Pakistan_06-34.pdf;and *http://www.dsca.osd.mil/PressReleases/36-b/2006/Pakistan_06-10.pdf.*

[289] "Plans Would Use Antiterror Aid on Pakistani Jets," *New York Times*, July 24, 2008; http://www.state.gov/r/pa/prs/ dpb/2008/july/107436.htm; the July 27, 2008, Lowey-Berman statement is at *http://www.internationalrelations.house.gov/ press*

[290] "House Foreign Affairs Subcommittee on the Middle East and South Asia Holds Hearing on Pakistan's F-16 Program," *CQ Transcripts*, September 16, 2008.

[291] See also CRS Report RL32115, *Missile Proliferation and the Strategic Balance in South Asia*, and CRS Report RL34248, *Pakistan's Nuclear Weapons: Proliferation and Security Issues*.

[292] "Pakistan Jets Said to be Nuclear-Capable," Associated Press, July 25, 1989.

[293] Statement of J. Michael McConnell before the Senate Select Committee on Intelligence, February 5, 2008, at http://intelligence

[294] "Pakistan President Says Supports No-First-Use Nuclear Policy," Agence France Presse, November 23, 2008.

[295] See also CRS Report RL32745, *Pakistan's Nuclear Proliferation Activities and the Recommendations of the 9/11 Commission: U.S. Policy Constraints and Options*.

[296] " Smugglers Had Design for Advanced Warhead," *Washington Post*, June 15, 2008; "Nuclear Ring Was More Advanced Than thought, U.N. Says," *Washington Post*, September 12, 2008.

[297] Pakistan's Ambassador to the United States later reportedly said that if Khan had not been a national hero, "we would have strung him from the highest tree" ("A 'Worrisome' Time in Pakistan" [interview], *USA Today*, May 23, 2007).

[298] See, for example, Adrian Levy and Catherine Scott-Clark, *Deception: Pakistan, the United States, and the Secret Trade in Nuclear Weapons* (Walker & Company, 2007).

[299] "Pakistani Says Army Knew Atomic Parts Were Shipped," *Associated Press*, July 5, 2008.

[300] Douglas Frantz and Catherine Collins, "Pakistan's Dr. Doom" (op-ed), *Los Angeles Times*, December 2, 2007.

[301] See http://www.iiss.org/publications/strategic-dossiers/nbm; "A.Q. Khan's Nuclear Wal-Mart: Out of Business or Under New Management?," Joint Hearing of the House Foreign Affairs Subcommittee on the Middle East and South Asia and the Subcommittee on Terrorism, Nonproliferation, and Trade, June 27, 2007.

[302] "Atom Expert Restrictions 'Eased.'" *BBC News*, May 22, 2008; "Khan: Pakistan Claims 'Are False,'" *BBC News*, May 29, 2008; "US Fears Over A.Q. Khan Nuclear Ring," *Financial Times* (London), June 15, 2008; "Court Silences Pakistan Nuclear Scientist," *Associated Press*, July 21, 2008.

[303] Khan's release spurred House Foreign Affairs Committee Chairman Rep. Howard Berman to express "deep concern" and to take the matter into account when legislating future U.S. assistance to Pakistan ("US Lawmaker Says Aid to Pakistan Could Be Reviewed," Associated Press, February 6, 2009).

[304] See http://www.dni.gov/speeches/20080529_speech

[305] See http://www.isis-online and http://www.isis-online.org/ publications/southasia/ chashma.pdf; "U.S. Says It Knew Of Pakistani Reactor Plan," *Washington Post*, July 25, 2006.

[306] See also CRS Report RL34248, *Pakistan's Nuclear Weapons: Proliferation and Security Issues*.

[307] Speech at the Carnegie Endowment for International Peace, Washington, DC, October 24, 2006.

[308] Statement of Michael Krepon before the Senate Committee on Homeland Security and Governmental Affairs, June 12, 2008.

[309] See, for example, "Political Fallout: The Threat to Pakistan's Nuclear Stability," *Jane's Intelligence Review*, January 1, 2008.

[310] See http://www.preventwmd.gov.

[311] Farhan Bokhari, "Pakistan's Nuclear Assets—Myths Vs Reality" (op-ed), *Tehran Times*, December 11, 2007; "Pakistan Nukes Safely Guarded: Narayanan," *Hindu* (Chennai), December 18, 2007.

[312] "Pakistan Rejects IAEA Chief's Concerns, *United Press International*, January 9, 2008; "Why is the World Scared of Pakistan?" (editorial), *Daily Times*, January 10, 2008.

[313] "U.S. Secretly Aids Pakistan in Guarding Nuclear Arms," *New York Times*, November 18, 2007; Pakistani statements at http://www.mofa.gov.pk/Spokesperson/2007/

Nov/Spokes_12_11_07.htm and http://www.mofa.gov.pk/ Press _Releases/2007/Nov/PR _281 _07.htm.

314 "Inside Pakistan's Drive to Guard It's A-Bombs," *Wall Street Journal*, November 29, 2007; "Pakistan Says Its Nuclear Assets Are Safe From Militants," *Associated Press*, January 26, 2008; "Calculating the Risks in Pakistan," *Washington Post*, December 2, 2007.

315 "The Worst Pakistan Nightmare for Obama," *New York Times*, January 11, 2009. Pakistan's Foreign Ministry called the information in this story "unfortunate and contrary to the facts" (see http://www.mofa.gov.pk/Press_Releases/2009/Jan/PR_21_09.htm).

316 These include continuation of a nuclear testing moratorium; commitments not to deploy nuclear weapons; commitments not to deploy ballistic missiles that can carry nuclear weapons and to restrain the ranges and types of missiles developed or deployed; agreement by both governments to bring their export controls in accord with the guidelines and requirements of the Nuclear Suppliers Group and other international guidelines; establishment of a modern, effective systems to control the export of sensitive dual-use items related to WMD; and the conduct of bilateral meetings between senior Pakistani and Indian officials to discuss security issues and establish confidence- building measures with respect to nuclear policies and programs. The act also makes it the policy if the United States to encourage and work with the Pakistani and Indian governments to establish "effective systems to protect and secure their nuclear devices and materiel from unauthorized use, accidental employment, or theft" (without recognizing those countries as nuclear weapon states as defined in the NPT).

317 Text at http://www.presidentofpakistan.gov.pk/FilesSpeeches/Addresses/1020200475758 AMword%20file.pdf.

318 See Polly Nayak and Michael Krepon, "US Crisis Management in South Asia's Twin Peaks Crisis" at http://www.stimson.org/southasia/pdf/USCrisisManagement.pdf.

319 http://www.indianembassy.org/press

320 "Pakistani Says Concessions Could Produce Kashmir Pact," *New York Times*, December 6, 2006.

321 See "Simmering Balochistan," *Jane's Islamic Affairs Analyst*, March 1, 2008.

322 "Bugti's Killing Is the Biggest Blunder Since Bhutto's Execution" (editorial), *Daily Times* (Lahore), August 28, 2006.

323 See also "Pakistan: The Forgotten Conflict in Balochistan," International Crisis Group Asia Briefing No. 69, October 22, 2007.

324 "Musharraf Sees Foreign Hand in Baluchistan Insurgency," *Dawn* (Karachi), August 5, 2008; Frederic Grare, "Pakistan: The Resurgence of Baluch Nationalism," Carnegie Paper No. 65, January 2006.

325 "Pakistani Court Frees Musharraf Opponent," *Agence France -Presse*, May 9, 2008; "No Country for Peace," *Herald* (Karachi), October 2008.

326 See also CRS Report RL32686, *Afghanistan: Narcotics and U.S. Policy*.

327 See http://www.state.gov/p/inl/rls/prsrl/ps/109777.htm.

328 See http://www.state.gov/p/inl/rls/nrcrpt/2008/vol1/html/100779.htm.

329 United Nations, *World Drug Report 2007*. See also "Is Afghanistan a Narco-State?," *New York Times*, July 27, 2008.

330 Statement of Amb. Wendy Chamberlain before the House International Relations Subcommittee on Asia and the Pacific, March 20, 2003.

331 See http://www.state.gov/p/inl/rls/nrcrpt/2008/vol1/html/100779.htm.

332 "Security: Pakistan," *Jane's Sentinel Security Assessments*, March 5, 2008; "Taliban Reaping Opium Profits," Associated Press, April 11, 2007.

333 In a late 2007 public opinion survey, 48% of Pakistani respondents completely agreed that "religion and government should be separate," up from only 33% in 2002 (see http://pewglobal.org/reports/pdf/258.pdf).

334 See http://www.iri.org/newsreleases/2008-12-18-Pakistan

[335] See, for example, "Pakistan: Do School Texts Fuel Bias?," *Christian Science Monitor*, January 21, 2009.

[336] Author interviews in Islamabad, September 2006.

[337] Statement of Stephen Cohen before the Senate Foreign Relations Committee, July 14, 2004. More than three years later, country expert Lisa Curtis warned a House panel about "the increasingly shrill anti-Americanism that is gripping Pakistani civil society" (statement before the House Armed Services Committee, October 10, 2007).

[338] "10 Questions for Pervez Musharraf," *Time*, October 3, 2005; "A Conversation With Yousaf Raza Gillani," Council on Foreign Relations transcript, July 29, 2008.

[339] See http://www.iri.org/newsreleases/2008-12-18-Pakistan

[340] See http://www.gallup.com/poll/110926/Few-Pakistanis-Perceive-Benefits-From-Alliance-US.aspx and http://www.iri.org/newsreleases/2008-12-18-Pakistan. and *http://www.gallup.com/poll/113455/Pakistanis-SupportTougher-Stance-Terrorism.aspx.*

[341] See also CRS Report RS22009, *Education Reform in Pakistan*, and CRS Report RS21654, *Islamic Religious Schools, Madrasas: Background.*

[342] Statement before the House Appropriations Committee, March 10, 2004.

[343] Marc Sageman, *Understanding Terror Networks* (University of Pennsylvania Press, 2004). See also Mariam Abou Zahab and Olivier Roy, *Islamist Networks* (Columbia University Press, 2004); Peter Bergen and Swati Pandney, "The Madrassa Myth," *New York Times*, June 14, 2005.

[344] "Pak Madrassas Breeding Ground for Militants: Pak Leader," *Press Trust of India*, June 1, 2008.

[345] P.W. Singer, "Pakistan's Madrassahs: Ensuring a System of Education Not Jihad," Brookings Institution Analysis Paper 14, November 2001; Ali Riaz, "Global Jihad, Sectarianism, and the Madrassahs in Pakistan," Institute of Defence and Strategic Studies, Singapore, August 2005.

[346] See http://www.state.gov/g/drl/rls/irf/2007/90233.htm; "Some Madrassas Bad: Musharraf," *Daily Times* (Lahore), September 8, 2004.

[347] See "Pakistan: Reforming the Education Sector," International Crisis Group Report 84, October 7, 2004; "Radical Teachings in Pakistan Schools," *Boston Globe*, September 29, 2006. Author interviews with Pakistani government officials and scholars tend to confirm that movement on madrassa reform is slow, at best.

[348] "At an Islamic School, Hints of Extremist Ties," *Washington Post*, June 13, 2004; Vali Nasr, "Military Rule, Islamism, and Democracy in Pakistan," *Middle East Journal* 58, 2, Spring 2004.

[349] "Full Transcript Musharraf Interview," *ABC News* (online), November 30, 2007. As of January 2008, more than 14,600 madrassas were reportedly registered with the government, leaving up to 1,500 yet to register ("Madressah Reforms Put on Hold for Next Government," *Dawn* (Karachi), January 12, 2008).

[350] See http://www.usaid.gov/pk/education/index.htm.

[351] See also CRS Report RL34240, *Pakistan's Political Crises*, and CRS Report RL34449, *Pakistan's 2008 Elections: Results and Implications for U.S. Policy.*

[352] "Pakistan's Musharraf Wins Landslide, Fraud Alleged," Reuters, May 1, 2002.

[353] Hasan-Askari Rizvi, "Towards a Solution of the Present Crisis" (op-ed), *Daily Times* (Lahore), June 17, 2007.

[354] See, for example, Peter Beinart, "How to Deal with Dictators" (op-ed), *Time*, July 26, 2007.

[355] Ayesha Siddiqa, *Military Inc: Inside Pakistan's Military Economy* (Pluto Press, 2007).

[356] See, for example, Jonathan Power, "In Defense of Pakistan's Military Dictator" (op-ed), *Toronto Star*, January 6, 2008.

[357] Author interview with Benazir Bhutto, Washington, DC, February 2006, and with numerous other PPP officials.

[358] Benazir Bhutto, "Why the World Needs Democracy in Pakistan," *Christian Science Monitor*, December 10, 2007.

[359] See http://www.state.gov/p/sca/rls/rm/2007/96566.htm.

[360] For example, two former senior Clinton Administration officials criticized President Bush for choosing to "back the dictator" rather than offer clear support for democracy and rule of law in Pakistan. They contended that such a policy has damaged U.S. interests in South Asia and in the Muslim world. In late 2007 Senate testimony, one former U.S. diplomat offered that, "Overall U.S. policy toward Pakistan until very recently gave no serious attention to encouraging democracy in Pakistan." Numerous other former U.S. officials have opined that the Bush Administration's relatively meager attention to Pakistani democratization has been rooted in an aversion to any moves that could alienate Musharraf and so reduce his cooperation on counterterrorism (Sandy Berger and Bruce Riedel, "America's Stark Choice" (op-ed), *International Herald Tribune*, October 9, 2007; Statement of Amb. Teresita Schaffer before the Senate Foreign Relations Committee, December 6, 2007; "Democracy Gets Small Portion of U.S. Aid," *Washington Post*, January 6, 2008).

[361] See http://www.state.gov/secretary/rm/2008/05/104634.htm.

[362] Statement of Husain Haqqani before the House Armed Services Committee, October 10, 2007.

[363] See http://www.state.gov/g/drl/rls/hrrpt/2006/78874.htm.

[364] "US Warned Over Backing for Musharraf," *Financial Times* (London), June 12, 2007; Lisa Curtis, Statement before the House Committee on Foreign Affairs Subcommittee on the Middle East and South Asia, January 16, 2008; Ashley Tellis, "Pakistan: Conflicted Ally in the War on Terror," *Carnegie Endowment Policy Brief* 56, December 2007.

[365] See http://www.state.gov/g/drl/rls/hrrpt/2007/100619.htm.

[366] See http://www.state.gov/documents/organization/105501.pdf.

[367] See http://www.unelections.org/files/PakistaniNGOs_LettertoFM_5May08_0.pdf.

[368] See http://www.amnesty.org/en/for-media http://hrw.org/english/docs/2008/07/02/pakist19238.htm.

[369] See http://www.state.gov/g/drl/rls/hrrpt/2007/100619.htm; "Violence Against Pakistani Women," *BBC News*, April 15, 2008.

[370] See http://www.state.gov/g/drl/rls/irf/2008/108505.htm.

[371] See http://www.uscirf.gov. See also "Tough Times for Pakistan's Religious Minorities," Associated Press, January 23, 2008.

[372] See http://www.rsf.org/article.php3?id

[373] See http://cpj.org/backsliders/index.html.

[374] See http://hrw.org/english/docs/2007/06/06/pakist16084.htm.

[375] See http://usembassy.state.gov/pakistan/h07092101.html.

[376] See http://www.state.gov/g/drl/rls/hrrpt/2007/100619.htm.

[377] "Pakistan: A Land of Systematic Disappearances," Asian Center for Human Rights, March 28, 2007; "Pakistani Wife Embodies Cause Of 'Disappeared,'" *New York Times*, July 19, 2007.

[378] "Picture of Secret Detentions Emerges in Pakistan," *New York Times*, December 19, 2007.

[379] See http://www.mofa.gov.pk/Spokesperson/2008/Mar/Spokes_12_03_08.htm.

[380] See also CRS Report RS22983, *Pakistan's Capital Crisis: Implications for U.S. Policy*.

[381] "Pakistan Stocks Tumble Amid Violence," Associated Press, December 31, 2007; "Fear Stalks Pakistani Business After Bhutto's Murder," Reuters, January 2, 2008; "As Pakistan Churns, Economy Takes Hit," *Wall Street Journal*, February 4, 2008; "Price of Pakistan's Economic Woes," *BBC News*, April 14, 2008.

[382] "Pakistan Orders Public Spending Cuts," *Financial Times* (London), May 8, 2008; "Pakistan Battles Power Shortages," *BBC News*, May 15, 2008.

[383] See http://hdr.undp.org/en/reports/global/hdr2007-2008.

[384] "Modern and Muslim: In Turbulent Pakistan, Start-Ups Drive a Boom," *Wall Street Journal*, September 5, 2007.

[385] Ali Cheema, "The Political Economy of Crises" (op-ed), *Friday Times* (Lahore), October 24, 2008.

[386] See http://siteresources.worldbank.org/SOUTHASIAEXT/Resources/Publications/448813-1188777211460/ pakceasummary.pdf.

[387] See http://www.adb.org/Documents/Books/ADO/2008/PAK.pdf.

[388] "Hungry for More Than Change," *Los Angeles Times*, November 28, 2007; "Pakistan Likely to Miss Most Economic Targets - Minister," Reuters, April 9, 2008.

[389] See http://www.csis.org/media

[390] See http://www.census.gov/foreign-trade

[391] The International Intellectual Property Alliance, a coalition of U.S. copyright-based industries, estimated U.S. losses of $156 million due to copyright piracy in Pakistan in 2007 (see http://www.iipa.com/rbc/2008/ 2008SPEC301PAKISTAN.pdf).

[392] See http://www.ustr.gov/assets asset_upload_file961_14674.pdf.

[393] See http://www.ustr.gov/assets asset_upload_file553_14869.pdf.

[394] "Pakistan Investors Wary of Political Instability," Reuters, August 27, 2007. Pakistan's Finance Ministry reports that foreign investment rates were down by nearly half for the nine-month period ending March 2008.

[395] According to the U.S. Trade Representative, "a small but significant number of differences have persisted on issues of considerable importance to the United States and [BIT] negotiations are currently suspended" (USTR, *2008 Trade Policy Agenda and 2007 Annual Report*, March 2008).

[396] See http://www.heritage.org/Index/Country/Pakistan

[397] See http://www.transparency.

[398] U.S. Department of State FY2008 Congressional Budget Justification for Foreign Operations (Revised), May 2, 2007.

[399] "US Aid 'Failing to Reach Target,'" *BBC News*, May 16, 2008.

[400] The Foreign Operations FY2005 Appropriations bill (P.L. 108-447) established a new "base program" of $300 million for military assistance for Pakistan.

[401] "Premier Says Pakistan Needs More U. S. Aid," *Wall Street Journal*, May 29, 2008.

[402] "Sen. Joseph R. Biden Jr. and Sen. Richard G. Lugar Hold a News Conference on Pakistan," *CQ Transcriptions*, July 15, 2008.

[403] See http://www.usaid.gov/pk/mission/news/fata.htm.

[404] Statement of Acting Deputy USAID Administrator James Kunder before the Senate Foreign Relations Committee, December 6, 2007.

[405] "Doubts Engulf an American Aid Plan for Pakistan," *New York Times*, December 25, 2007; "US Aid 'Failing to Reach Target,'" *BBC News*, May 16, 2008.

[406] "U.S. Aims to Turn Hostile Pakistani Tribes Friendly," Reuters, January 30, 2008.

[407] Statement of Amb. Teresita Schaffer before the Senate Foreign Relations Committee, December 6, 2007; Hamid Waleed, "Establishment of Reconstruction Opportunity Zones Almost Impossible" (op-ed), *Daily Times* (Lahore), January 13, 2007.

[408] Daniel Markey, "Securing Pakistan's Tribal Belt," Council on Foreign Relations Special Report No. 36, July 2008.

[409] See http://www.state.gov/p/sca/rls/rm/2007/96566.htm.

[410] Statement before the Senate Armed Services Committee, February 6, 2008.

[411] See http://www.state.gov/p/sca/rls/rm/2007/96566.htm; "U.S. Payments to Pakistan Face New Scrutiny," *Washington Post*, February 21, 2008; "Pakistani Military 'Misspent Up to 70% of American Aid,'" *Guardian* (London), February 28, 2008; "Democrats Question $6 Billion in Pakistan Aid," *Associated Press*, May 6, 2008; "Revamping Aid to Pakistan is Expected in Bush Report," *New York Times*, December 7, 2008.

[412] See http://www.gao.gov/new.items/d08806.pdf. See also "Pentagon Puts Brakes on Funds to Pakistan," *Los Angeles Times*, May 7, 2008.

[413] Quoted in "Where's the Money?," *Sunday Times* (London), August 10, 2008.

[414] Craig Cohen, "A Perilous Course: U.S. Strategy and Assistance to Pakistan," Center for Strategic and International Studies, August 2007.

[415] See, for example, Daniel Markey, "Securing Pakistan's Tribal Belt," Council on Foreign Relations Special Report No. 36, July 2008.

[416] See, for example, Lisa Curtis, "Denying Terrorists Safe Haven in Pakistan," Heritage Foundation Backgrounder No. 1981, October 26, 2006.

[417] "New Priorities in South Asia: U.S. Policy Toward India, Pakistan, and Afghanistan," Chairmen's Report of an Independent Task Force Cosponsored by the Council on Foreign Relations and the Asia Society, October 2003.

[418] See, for example, Frederic Grare, "Rethinking Western Strategies Toward Pakistan," Carnegie Endowment for International Peace, 2007.

[419] See, for example, "Senate Leader Wants Bush to Pressure Pakistan," Reuters, January 10, 2008; "Democrat Questions US Aid to Pakistan," Associated Press, May 27, 2008.

[420] See, for example, Daniel Markey, "A False Choice in Pakistan," *Foreign Affairs*, July 2007.

[421] Ashley Tellis, "Pakistan: Conflicted Ally in the War on Terror," *Carnegie Endowment Policy Brief 56*, December 2007.

[422] See http://www.mofa.gov.pk/Press_Releases/2007/july/PR_199_07.htm.

[423] "Pakistan Rejects Call for Conditions on U.S. Aid," Reuters, January 11, 2008; State Department claim at http://www.state.gov/p/sca/rls/rm/2007/97946.htm.

[424] "Pakistan Unrest Raises Fresh Calls for U.S. Aid," *Reuters*, September 23, 2008; Anatol Lieven, "Urgent Aid for Pakistan" (op-ed), *International Herald Tribune*, September 7, 2008.

[425] See http://www.whitehouse.gov/news/releases/2008/03/20080325-2.html; Federal Register 73, 69, p. 19276-19277, April 9, 2008.

[426] The Agricultural Export Relief Act of 1998 (P.L. 105-194) allowed U.S. wheat sales to Pakistan after July 1998. The India-Pakistan Relief Act of 1998 (in P.L. 105-277) authorized a one-year sanctions waiver exercised by President Clinton in November 1998. The Department of Defense Appropriations Act, 2000 (P.L. 106-79) gave the President permanent authority to waive nuclear-test-related sanctions applied against Pakistan and India after October 1999, when President Clinton waived economic sanctions on India (Pakistan remained under sanctions as a result of the October 1999 coup). (See CRS Report RS20995, *India and Pakistan: U.S. Economic Sanctions*.)

Chapter Sources

The following chapters have been previously published:

Chapter 1 – This is an edited, reformatted and augmented version of a United States Congressional Research Service publication, Report Order Code R40361, dated February 25, 2009.

Chapter 2 – This is an edited, reformatted and augmented version of a United States Congressional Research Service publication, Report Order Code RL33498, dated February 6, 2009.

INDEX

A

D

E

F

G

H

I

J

K

L

M

N

O

P

Q

R

S

T

U

V

W

X